Honda GL1200 Gold Wing Owners Workshop Manual

Clay County Public Library
116 Guffey Street
Celina, TN 38551
(931) 243-3442

**by Alan Ahlstrand
and John H Haynes**
Member of the Guild of Motoring Writers

Models covered:
Honda GL1200 Gold Wing carbureted models. 1182 cc.
1984 through 1987

(10M1 - 2199)   ABCDE
                 FGHIJ
                 KLM

Haynes Publishing
Sparkford Nr Yeovil
Somerset BA22 7JJ England

Haynes North America, Inc
861 Lawrence Drive
Newbury Park
California 91320 USA

Acknowledgments

Special thanks to Honda of Milpitas, Milpitas, California, for locating the motorcycle used in these photographs and to Pete Sirett, service manager, for arranging the facilities and fitting the mechanical work into his shop's busy schedule. Ron Pennel lent us his well-maintained 1986 Aspencade for the disassembly photographs. Bruce Farley, a leading authority on Gold Wings, gave us the benefit of his extensive experience with these motorcycles while doing the mechanical work.

© Haynes North America, Inc. 1997
With permission from J.H. Haynes & Co. Ltd.

A book in the Haynes Owners Workshop Manual Series

Printed in the U.S.A.

All rights reserved. No part of this book may be reproduced or transmitted in any form or by any means, electronic or mechanical, including photocopying, recording or by any information storage or retrieval system, without permission in writing from the copyright holder.

ISBN 1 56392 199 5

Library of Congress Catalog Card Number 97-80262

British Library Cataloguing in Publication Data
A catalogue record for this book is available from the British Library

We take great pride in the accuracy of information given in this manual, but motorcycle manufacturers make alterations and design changes during the production run of a particular motorcycle of which they do not inform us. No liability can be accepted by the authors or publishers for loss, damage or injury caused by any errors in, or omissions from, the information given.

Contents

Introductory pages

About this manual	0-5
Introduction to the Honda GL1200	0-5
Identification numbers	0-6
Buying parts	0-7
General specifications	0-7
Maintenance techniques, tools and working facilities	0-8
Safety first!	0-14
Motorcycle chemicals and lubricants	0-16
Troubleshooting	0-17

Chapter 1
Tune-up and routine maintenance 1-1

Chapter 2
Engine, clutch and transmission 2-1

Chapter 3
Cooling system 3-1

Chapter 4
Fuel and exhaust systems 4-1

Chapter 5
Ignition system 5-1

Chapter 6
Steering, suspension and final drive 6-1

Chapter 7
Brakes, wheels and tires 7-1

Chapter 8
Fairing, bodywork and frame 8-1

Chapter 9
Electrical system 9-1

Wiring diagrams 9-19

Conversion factors

Index IND-1

1986 Honda GL1200 Gold Wing

About this manual

Its purpose

The purpose of this manual is to help you get the best value from your motorcycle. It can do so in several ways. It can help you decide what work must be done, even if you choose to have it done by a dealer service department or a repair shop; it provides information and procedures for routine maintenance and servicing; and it offers diagnostic and repair procedures to follow when trouble occurs.

We hope you use the manual to tackle the work yourself. For many simpler jobs, doing it yourself may be quicker than arranging an appointment to get the vehicle into a shop and making the trips to leave it and pick it up. More importantly, a lot of money can be saved by avoiding the expense the shop must pass on to you to cover its labor and overhead costs. An added benefit is the sense of satisfaction and accomplishment that you feel after doing the job yourself.

Using the manual

The manual is divided into Chapters. Each Chapter is divided into numbered Sections, which are headed in bold type between horizontal lines. Each Section consists of consecutively numbered paragraphs or steps.

At the beginning of each numbered Section you will be referred to any illustrations which apply to the procedures in that Section. The reference numbers used in illustration captions pinpoint the pertinent Section and the Step within that Section. That is, illustration 3.2 means the illustration refers to Section 3 and Step (or paragraph) 2 within that Section.

Procedures, once described in the text, are not normally repeated. When it's necessary to refer to another Chapter, the reference will be given as Chapter and Section number. Cross references given without use of the word 'Chapter' apply to Sections and/or paragraphs in the same Chapter. For example, 'see Section 8' means in the same Chapter.

References to the left or right side of the vehicle assume you are sitting on the seat, facing forward.

Motorcycle manufacturers continually make changes to specifications and recommendations, and these, when notified, are incorporated into our manuals at the earliest opportunity.

Even though we have prepared this manual with extreme care, neither the publisher nor the authors can accept responsibility for any errors in, or omissions from, the information given.

NOTE

A **Note** provides information necessary to properly complete a procedure or information which will make the procedure easier to understand.

CAUTION

A **Caution** provides a special procedure or special steps which must be taken while completing the procedure where the Caution is found. Not heeding a Caution can result in damage to the assembly being worked on.

WARNING

A **Warning** provides a special procedure or special steps which must be taken while completing the procedure where the Warning is found. Not heeding a Warning can result in personal injury.

Introduction to the Honda GL1200 Gold Wing

The GL1200 Gold Wing was Honda's top-of-the-line touring bike during its model run.

The engine on all models is a liquid-cooled, horizontally opposed four with single overhead camshafts and hydraulically operated lifters.

Fuel is delivered to four side-draft CV carburetors by an electric fuel pump.

The front suspension uses a pair of conventional damper rod forks with an anti-dive device built in.

The rear suspension uses a pair of air-adjustable shock absorbers and a swingarm, with an optional on-board compressor system to adjust air pressure in the shocks. Final drive is by a shaft.

The front brake uses dual discs and the rear brake uses a single disc. The front and rear brakes interlinked; the brake pedal operates the left front brake as well as the rear brake. The right front brake is operated by the lever on the right handlebar independently of the rear and left front brakes.

Identification numbers

The frame number is stamped in the steering head . . .

. . . and is also displayed on a plate

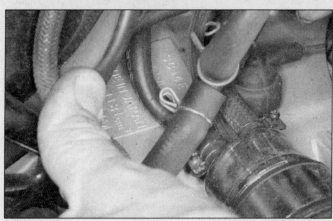

The engine number is stamped in the right side of the crankcase

The frame serial number is stamped into the steering head and printed on a label affixed to the frame. The engine number is stamped into the right side of the crankcase. Both of these numbers should be recorded and kept in a safe place so they can be furnished to law enforcement officials in the event of a theft.

The frame serial number, engine serial number and carburetor identification number should also be kept in a handy place (such as with your driver's license) so they are always available when purchasing or ordering parts for your machine.

The models covered by this manual are as follows:
Honda GL1200 Gold Wing, 1984 through 1987 carbureted models.

Identifying model years

The procedures in this manual identify the bikes by model year. To determine which model year a given machine is, look for the following identification codes in the engine and frame numbers.

Year	Engine numbers	Frame numbers
1984 Standard		
Except California	SC14E 2400107 to 2416951	SC140 FA000101 to 022728
California	SC14E 2400107 to 2416951	SC143 FA010373 to FA022588
1984 Interstate		
Except California	SC14E 2400107-on	SC141 FA000118 to FA034654
California	SC14E 2400107 to 2435135	SC144 FA010761 to FA032091
1984 Aspencade		
Except California	SC14E 2436841 to 2435673	SC142 FA0022273 to FA034452
California	SC14E 2436841 to 2435673	SC145 FA010863 to FA033387
1985 Interstate		
Except California	SC14E 2500006 to 2525763	SC141 FA101553 to FA126181
California	SC14E 2500025 to 2514675	SC144 FA101976 to FA126016
1985 Aspencade		
Except California	SC14E 2500008 to 2527164	SC142 FA102502 to FA126301
California	SC14E 2500207 to 2514364	SC145 FA100116 to FA114611
1986 Interstate		
Except California	SC14E 2610010 to 2628680	SC141 GA200106 to GA223917
California	SC14E 2610001 to 2627607	SC144 GA200101 to 218115
1986 Aspencade		
Except California	SC14E 2610002 to 2628642	SC142 GA200536 to GA223978
California	SC14E 2610020 to 2627502	SC145 GA200116 to GA216300
1987 Interstate		
Except California	SC14E 2710011 to 2721396	SC141 HA300106 to HA310085
California	SC14E 2716254 to 2721397	SC144 HA308407 to HA310325
1987 Aspencade		
Except California	SC14E 2710009 to 2721399	SC142 HA300101 to HA309605
California	SC14E 2710003 to 2721400	SC145 HA300105 to HA310080

Buying parts

Once you have found all the identification numbers, record them for reference when buying parts. Since the manufacturers change specifications, parts and vendors (companies that manufacture various components on the machine), providing the ID numbers is the only way to be reasonably sure that you are buying the correct parts.

Whenever possible, take the worn part to the dealer so direct comparison with the new component can be made. Along the trail from the manufacturer to the parts shelf, there are numerous places that the part can end up with the wrong number or be listed incorrectly.

The two places to purchase new parts for your motorcycle - the accessory store and the franchised dealer - differ in the type of parts they carry. While dealers can obtain virtually every part for your motorcycle, the accessory dealer is usually limited to normal high wear items such as shock absorbers, tune-up parts, various engine gaskets, cables, chains, brake parts, etc. Rarely will an accessory outlet have major suspension components, cylinders, transmission gears, or cases.

Used parts can be obtained for roughly half the price of new ones, but you can't always be sure of what you're getting. Once again, take your worn part to the wrecking yard (breaker) for direct comparison.

Whether buying new, used or rebuilt parts, the best course is to deal directly with someone who specializes in parts for your particular make.

General specifications

Wheelbase	1610 mm (63.4 inches)
Overall length	
Standard	2355 mm (92.7 inches)
Interstate and Aspencade	2505 mm (98.6 inches)
Overall width	
Standard	920 mm (36.2 inches)
Interstate and Aspencade	970 mm (38.2 inches)
Overall height	
Standard	1170 mm (46.1 inches)
Interstate and Aspencade	1510 mm (59.4 inches)
Seat height	790 mm (30.7 inches)
Ground clearance	140 mm (5.5 inches)
Weight (with oil and full fuel tank)	
Standard	296 kg (652 lbs)
Interstate	
US except California	341 kg (752 lbs)
California	342 kg (754 lbs)
Aspencade	
1984 and 1985	353 kg (778 lbs)
1986	
US except California	355 kg (783 lbs)
California	356 kg (785 lbs)
1987	
US except California	363 kg (800 lbs)
California	364 kg (802 lbs)

Maintenance techniques, tools and working facilities

Basic maintenance techniques

There are a number of techniques involved in maintenance and repair that will be referred to throughout this manual. Application of these techniques will enable the amateur mechanic to be more efficient, better organized and capable of performing the various tasks properly, which will ensure that the repair job is thorough and complete.

Fastening systems

Fasteners, basically, are nuts, bolts and screws used to hold two or more parts together. There are a few things to keep in mind when working with fasteners. Almost all of them use a locking device of some type (either a lockwasher, locknut, locking tab or thread adhesive). All threaded fasteners should be clean, straight, have undamaged threads and undamaged corners on the hex head where the wrench fits. Develop the habit of replacing all damaged nuts and bolts with new ones.

Rusted nuts and bolts should be treated with a penetrating oil to ease removal and prevent breakage. Some mechanics use turpentine in a spout type oil can, which works quite well. After applying the rust penetrant, let it work for a few minutes before trying to loosen the nut or bolt. Badly rusted fasteners may have to be chiseled off or removed with a special nut breaker, available at tool stores.

If a bolt or stud breaks off in an assembly, it can be drilled out and removed with a special tool called an E-Z out (or screw extractor). Most dealer service departments and motorcycle repair shops can perform this task, as well as others (such as the repair of threaded holes that have been stripped out).

Flat washers and lock washers, when removed from an assembly, should always be replaced exactly as removed. Replace any damaged washers with new ones. Always use a flatwasher between a lockwasher and any soft metal surface (such as aluminum), thin sheet metal or plastic. Special locknuts can only be used once or twice before they lose their locking ability and must be replaced.

Tightening sequences and procedures

When threaded fasteners are tightened, they are often tightened to a specific torque value (torque is basically a twisting force). Overtightening the fastener can weaken it and cause it to break, while under-tightening can cause it to eventually come loose. Each bolt, depending on the material it's made of, the diameter of its shank and the material it is threaded into, has a specific torque value, which is noted in the Specifications. Be sure to follow the torque recommendations closely.

Fasteners laid out in a pattern (i.e. cylinder head bolts, engine case bolts, etc.) must be loosened or tightened in a sequence to avoid warping the component. Initially, the bolts/nuts should go on finger tight only. Next, they should be tightened one full turn each, in a crisscross or diagonal pattern. After each one has been tightened one full turn, return to the first one tightened and tighten them all one half turn, following the same pattern. Finally, tighten each of them one quarter turn at a time until each fastener has been tightened to the proper torque. To loosen and remove the fasteners the procedure would be reversed.

Disassembly sequence

Component disassembly should be done with care and purpose to help ensure that the parts go back together properly during reassembly. Always keep track of the sequence in which parts are removed. Take note of special characteristics or marks on parts that can be installed more than one way (such as a grooved thrust washer on a shaft). It's a good idea to lay the disassembled parts out on a clean surface in the order that they were removed. It may also be helpful to make sketches or take instant photos of components before removal.

When removing fasteners from a component, keep track of their locations. Sometimes threading a bolt back in a part, or putting the washers and nut back on a stud, can prevent mix-ups later. If nuts and bolts can't be returned to their original locations, they should be kept in a compartmented box or a series of small boxes. A cupcake or muffin tin is ideal for this purpose, since each cavity can hold the bolts and nuts from a particular area (i.e. engine case bolts, valve cover bolts, engine mount bolts, etc.). A pan of this type is especially helpful when working on assemblies with very small parts (such as the carburetors and the valve train). The cavities can be marked with paint or tape to identify the contents.

Whenever wiring looms, harnesses or connectors are separated, it's a good idea to identify the two halves with numbered pieces of masking tape so they can be easily reconnected.

Gasket sealing surfaces

Throughout any motorcycle, gaskets are used to seal the mating surfaces between components and keep lubricants, fluids, vacuum or pressure contained in an assembly.

Many times these gaskets are coated with a liquid or paste type gasket sealing compound before assembly. Age, heat and pressure can sometimes cause the two parts to stick together so tightly that they are very difficult to separate. In most cases, the part can be loosened by striking it with a soft-faced hammer near the mating surfaces. A regular hammer can be used if a block of wood is placed between the hammer and the part. Do not hammer on cast parts or parts that could be easily damaged. With any particularly stubborn part, always recheck to make sure that every fastener has been removed.

Avoid using a screwdriver or bar to pry apart components, as they can easily mar the gasket sealing surfaces of the parts (which must remain smooth). If prying is absolutely necessary, use a piece of wood, but keep in mind that extra clean-up will be necessary if the wood splinters.

After the parts are separated, the old gasket must be carefully scraped off and the gasket surfaces cleaned. Stubborn gasket material can be soaked with a gasket remover (available in aerosol cans) to soften it so it can be easily scraped off. A scraper can be fashioned from a piece of copper tubing by flattening and sharpening one end. Copper is recommended because it is usually softer than the surfaces to be scraped, which reduces the chance of gouging the part. Some gaskets can be removed with a wire brush, but regardless of the method used, the mating surfaces must be left clean and smooth. If for some reason the gasket surface is gouged, then a gasket sealer thick enough to fill scratches will have to be used during reassembly of the components. For most applications, a non-drying (or semi-drying) gasket sealer is best.

Hose removal tips

Hose removal precautions closely parallel gasket removal precautions. Avoid scratching or gouging the surface that the hose mates against or the connection may leak. Because of various chemical reactions, the rubber in hoses can bond itself to the metal spigot that the hose fits over. To remove a hose, first loosen the hose clamps that secure it to the spigot. Then, with slip joint pliers, grab the hose at the clamp and rotate it around the spigot. Work it back and forth until it is completely free, then pull it off (silicone or other lubricants will ease removal if they can be applied between the hose and the outside of the spigot). Apply the same lubricant to the inside of the hose and the outside of the spigot to simplify installation.

If a hose clamp is broken or damaged, do not reuse it. Also, do not reuse hoses that are cracked, split or torn.

Maintenance techniques, tools and working facilities

Spark plug gap adjusting tool

Feeler gauge set

Control cable pressure luber

Hand impact screwdriver and bits

Tools

A selection of good tools is a basic requirement for anyone who plans to maintain and repair a motorcycle. For the owner who has few tools, if any, the initial investment might seem high, but when compared to the spiraling costs of routine maintenance and repair, it is a wise one.

To help the owner decide which tools are needed to perform the tasks detailed in this manual, the following tool lists are offered: *Maintenance and minor repair*, *Repair and overhaul* and *Special*. The newcomer to practical mechanics should start off with the *Maintenance and minor repair* tool kit, which is adequate for the simpler jobs. Then, as confidence and experience grow, the owner can tackle more difficult tasks, buying additional tools as they are needed. Eventually the basic kit will be built into the *Repair and overhaul* tool set. Over a period of time, the experienced do-it-yourselfer will assemble a tool set complete enough for most repair and overhaul procedures and will add tools from the *Special* category when it is felt that the expense is justified by the frequency of use.

Maintenance and minor repair tool kit

The tools in this list should be considered the minimum required for performance of routine maintenance, servicing and minor repair work. We recommend the purchase of combination wrenches (box end and open end combined in one wrench); while more expensive than

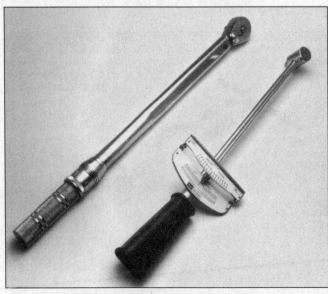

Torque wrenches (left - click; right - beam type)

Maintenance techniques, tools and working facilities

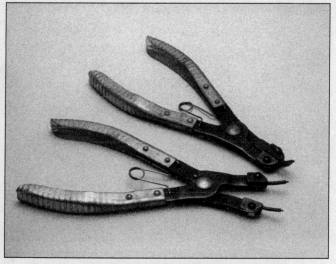
Snap-ring pliers (top - external; bottom - internal)

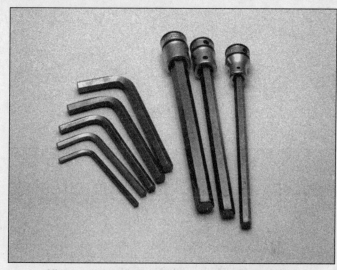
Allen wrenches (left), and Allen head sockets (right)

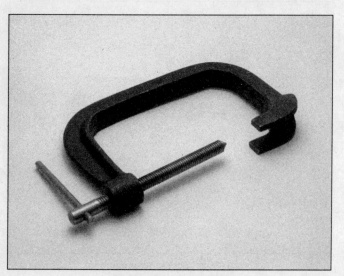
Valve spring compressor

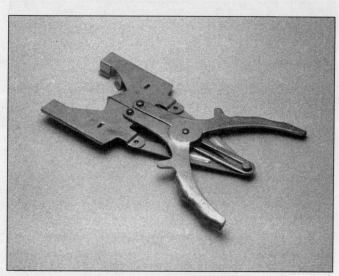
Piston ring removal/installation tool

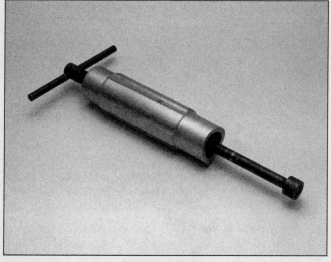
Piston pin puller

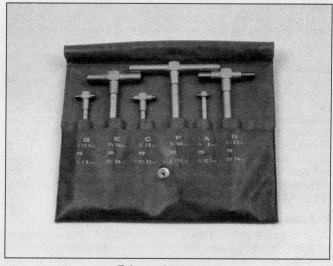
Telescoping gauges

Maintenance techniques, tools and working facilities 0-11

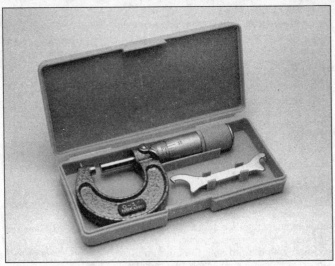
0-to-1 inch micrometer

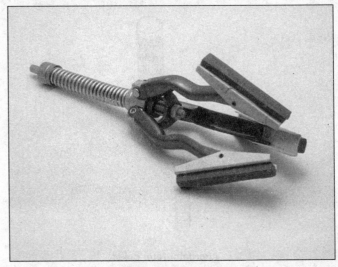
Cylinder surfacing hone

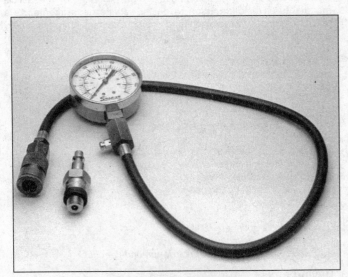
Cylinder compression gauge

Dial indicator set

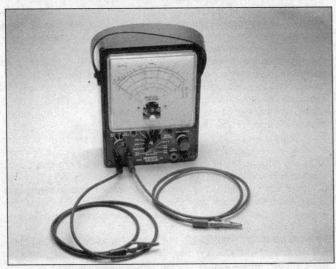
Multimeter (volt/ohm/ammeter)

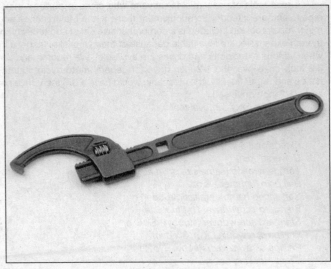
Adjustable spanner

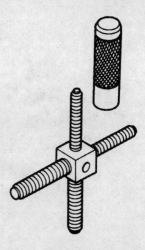

Alternator rotor puller

open-ended ones, they offer the advantages of both types of wrench.

Combination wrench set (6 mm to 22 mm)
Adjustable wrench - 8 in
Spark plug socket (with rubber insert)
Spark plug gap adjusting tool
Feeler gauge set
Standard screwdriver (5/16 in x 6 in)
Phillips screwdriver (No. 2 x 6 in)
Allen (hex) wrench set (4 mm to 12 mm)
Combination (slip-joint) pliers - 6 in
Hacksaw and assortment of blades
Tire pressure gauge
Control cable pressure luber
Grease gun
Oil can
Fine emery cloth
Wire brush
Hand impact screwdriver and bits
Funnel (medium size)
Safety goggles
Drain pan
Work light with extension cord

Repair and overhaul tool set

These tools are essential for anyone who plans to perform major repairs and are intended to supplement those in the Maintenance and minor repair tool kit. Included is a comprehensive set of sockets which, though expensive, are invaluable because of their versatility (especially when various extensions and drives are available). We recommend the 3/8 inch drive over the 1/2 inch drive for general motorcycle maintenance and repair (ideally, the mechanic would have a 3/8 inch drive set and a 1/2 inch drive set).

Alternator rotor removal tool
Socket set(s)
Reversible ratchet
Extension - 6 in
Universal joint
Torque wrench (same size drive as sockets)
Ball pein hammer - 8 oz
Soft-faced hammer (plastic/rubber)
Standard screwdriver (1/4 in x 6 in)
Standard screwdriver (stubby - 5/16 in)
Phillips screwdriver (No. 3 x 8 in)
Phillips screwdriver (stubby - No. 2)
Pliers - locking
Pliers - lineman's
Pliers - needle nose
Pliers - snap-ring (internal and external)
Cold chisel - 1/2 in
Scriber
Scraper (made from flattened copper tubing)
Center punch
Pin punches (1/16, 1/8, 3/16 in)
Steel rule/straightedge - 12 in
Pin-type spanner wrench
A selection of files
Wire brush (large)

Note: *Another tool which is often useful is an electric drill with a chuck capacity of 3/8 inch (and a set of good quality drill bits).*

Special tools

The tools in this list include those which are not used regularly, are expensive to buy, or which need to be used in accordance with their manufacturer's instructions. Unless these tools will be used frequently, it is not very economical to purchase many of them. A consideration would be to split the cost and use between yourself and a friend or friends (i.e. members of a motorcycle club).

This list primarily contains tools and instruments widely available to the public, as well as some special tools produced by the vehicle manufacturer for distribution to dealer service departments. As a result, references to the manufacturer's special tools are occasionally included in the text of this manual. Generally, an alternative method of doing the job without the special tool is offered. However, sometimes there is no alternative to their use. Where this is the case, and the tool can't be purchased or borrowed, the work should be turned over to the dealer service department or a motorcycle repair shop.

Paddock stand (for models not fitted with a centerstand)
Valve spring compressor
Piston ring removal and installation tool
Piston pin puller
Telescoping gauges
Micrometer(s) and/or dial/Vernier calipers
Cylinder surfacing hone
Cylinder compression gauge
Dial indicator set
Multimeter
Adjustable spanner
Manometer or vacuum gauge set
Small air compressor with blow gun and tire chuck

Buying tools

For the do-it-yourselfer who is just starting to get involved in motorcycle maintenance and repair, there are a number of options available when purchasing tools. If maintenance and minor repair is the extent of the work to be done, the purchase of individual tools is satisfactory. If, on the other hand, extensive work is planned, it would be a good idea to purchase a modest tool set from one of the large retail chain stores. A set can usually be bought at a substantial savings over the individual tool prices (and they often come with a tool box). As additional tools are needed, add-on sets, individual tools and a larger tool box can be purchased to expand the tool selection. Building a tool set gradually allows the cost of the tools to be spread over a longer period of time and gives the mechanic the freedom to choose only those tools that will actually be used.

Tool stores and motorcycle dealers will often be the only source of some of the special tools that are needed, but regardless of where tools are bought, try to avoid cheap ones (especially when buying screwdrivers and sockets) because they won't last very long. There are plenty of tools around at reasonable prices, but always aim to purchase items which meet the relevant national safety standards. The expense involved in replacing cheap tools will eventually be greater than the initial cost of quality tools.

It is obviously not possible to cover the subject of tools fully here. For those who wish to learn more about tools and their use, there is a book entitled *Motorcycle Workshop Practice Manual* (Book no. 1454) available from the publishers of this manual. It also provides an intro-

Maintenance techniques, tools and working facilities

duction to basic workshop practice which will be of interest to a home mechanic working on any type of motorcycle.

Care and maintenance of tools

Good tools are expensive, so it makes sense to treat them with respect. Keep them clean and in usable condition and store them properly when not in use. Always wipe off any dirt, grease or metal chips before putting them away. Never leave tools lying around in the work area.

Some tools, such as screwdrivers, pliers, wrenches and sockets, can be hung on a panel mounted on the garage or workshop wall, while others should be kept in a tool box or tray. Measuring instruments, gauges, meters, etc. must be carefully stored where they can't be damaged by weather or impact from other tools.

When tools are used with care and stored properly, they will last a very long time. Even with the best of care, tools will wear out if used frequently. When a tool is damaged or worn out, replace it; subsequent jobs will be safer and more enjoyable if you do.

Working facilities

Not to be overlooked when discussing tools is the workshop. If anything more than routine maintenance is to be carried out, some sort of suitable work area is essential.

It is understood, and appreciated, that many home mechanics do not have a good workshop or garage available and end up removing an engine or doing major repairs outside (it is recommended, however, that the overhaul or repair be completed under the cover of a roof).

A clean, flat workbench or table of comfortable working height is an absolute necessity. The workbench should be equipped with a vise that has a jaw opening of at least four inches.

As mentioned previously, some clean, dry storage space is also required for tools, as well as the lubricants, fluids, cleaning solvents, etc. which soon become necessary.

Sometimes waste oil and fluids, drained from the engine or cooling system during normal maintenance or repairs, present a disposal problem. To avoid pouring them on the ground or into a sewage system, simply pour the used fluids into large containers, seal them with caps and take them to an authorized disposal site or service station. Plastic jugs (such as old antifreeze containers) are ideal for this purpose.

Always keep a supply of old newspapers and clean rags available. Old towels are excellent for mopping up spills. Many mechanics use rolls of paper towels for most work because they are readily available and disposable. To help keep the area under the motorcycle clean, a large cardboard box can be cut open and flattened to protect the garage or shop floor.

Whenever working over a painted surface (such as the fuel tank) cover it with an old blanket or bedspread to protect the finish.

Safety first!

Professional mechanics are trained in safe working procedures. However enthusiastic you may be about getting on with the job at hand, take the time to ensure that your safety is not put at risk. A moment's lack of attention can result in an accident, as can failure to observe simple precautions.

There will always be new ways of having accidents, and the following is not a comprehensive list of all dangers; it is intended rather to make you aware of the risks and to encourage a safe approach to all work you carry out on your bike.

Essential DOs and DON'Ts

DON'T start the engine without first ascertaining that the transmission is in neutral.

DON'T suddenly remove the pressure cap from a hot cooling system - cover it with a cloth and release the pressure gradually first, or you may get scalded by escaping coolant.

DON'T attempt to drain oil until you are sure it has cooled sufficiently to avoid scalding you.

DON'T grasp any part of the engine or exhaust system without first ascertaining that it is cool enough not to burn you.

DON'T allow brake fluid or antifreeze to contact the machine's paint work or plastic components.

DON'T siphon toxic liquids such as fuel, hydraulic fluid or antifreeze by mouth, or allow them to remain on your skin.

DON'T inhale dust - it may be injurious to health (see *Asbestos* heading).

DON'T allow any spilled oil or grease to remain on the floor - wipe it up right away, before someone slips on it.

DON'T use ill fitting wrenches or other tools which may slip and cause injury.

DON'T attempt to lift a heavy component which may be beyond your capability - get assistance.

DON'T rush to finish a job or take unverified short cuts.

DON'T allow children or animals in or around an unattended vehicle.

DON'T inflate a tire to a pressure above the recommended maximum. Apart from over stressing the carcase and wheel rim, in extreme cases the tire may blow off forcibly.

DO ensure that the machine is supported securely at all times. This is especially important when the machine is blocked up to aid wheel or fork removal.

DO take care when attempting to loosen a stubborn nut or bolt. It is generally better to pull on a wrench, rather than push, so that if you slip, you fall away from the machine rather than onto it.

DO wear eye protection when using power tools such as drill, sander, bench grinder etc.

DO use a barrier cream on your hands prior to undertaking dirty jobs - it will protect your skin from infection as well as making the dirt easier to remove afterwards; but make sure your hands aren't left slippery. Note that long-term contact with used engine oil can be a health hazard.

DO keep loose clothing (cuffs, ties etc. and long hair) well out of the way of moving mechanical parts.

DO remove rings, wristwatch etc., before working on the vehicle - especially the electrical system.

DO keep your work area tidy - it is only too easy to fall over articles left lying around.

DO exercise caution when compressing springs for removal or installation. Ensure that the tension is applied and released in a controlled manner, using suitable tools which preclude the possibility of the spring escaping violently.

DO ensure that any lifting tackle used has a safe working load rating adequate for the job.

DO get someone to check periodically that all is well, when working alone on the vehicle.

DO carry out work in a logical sequence and check that everything is correctly assembled and tightened afterwards.

DO remember that your vehicle's safety affects that of yourself and others. If in doubt on any point, get professional advice.

IF, in spite of following these precautions, you are unfortunate enough to injure yourself, seek medical attention as soon as possible.

Asbestos

Certain friction, insulating, sealing and other products - such as brake pads, clutch linings, gaskets, etc. - contain asbestos. *Extreme care must be taken to avoid inhalation of dust from such products since it is hazardous to health.* If in doubt, assume that they *do* contain asbestos.

Fire

Remember at all times that gasoline (petrol) is highly flammable. Never smoke or have any kind of naked flame around, when working on the vehicle. But the risk does not end there - a spark caused by an electrical short-circuit, by two metal surfaces contacting each other, by careless use of tools, or even by static electricity built up in your body under certain conditions, can ignite gasoline (petrol) vapor, which in a confined space is highly explosive. Never use gasoline (petrol) as a cleaning solvent. Use an approved safety solvent.

Always disconnect the battery ground (earth) terminal before working on any part of the fuel or electrical system, and never risk spilling fuel on to a hot engine or exhaust.

It is recommended that a fire extinguisher of a type suitable for fuel and electrical fires is kept handy in the garage or workplace at all times. Never try to extinguish a fuel or electrical fire with water.

Fumes

Certain fumes are highly toxic and can quickly cause unconsciousness and even death if inhaled to any extent. Gasoline (petrol) vapor comes into this category, as do the vapors from certain solvents such as trichloroethylene. Any draining or pouring of such volatile flu-

Safety first! 0-15

ids should be done in a well ventilated area.

When using cleaning fluids and solvents, read the instructions carefully. Never use materials from unmarked containers - they may give off poisonous vapors.

Never run the engine of a motor vehicle in an enclosed space such as a garage. Exhaust fumes contain carbon monoxide which is extremely poisonous; if you need to run the engine, always do so in the open air or at least have the rear of the vehicle outside the workplace.

The battery

Never cause a spark, or allow a naked light near the vehicle's battery. It will normally be giving off a certain amount of hydrogen gas, which is highly explosive.

Always disconnect the battery ground (earth) terminal before working on the fuel or electrical systems (except where noted).

If possible, loosen the filler plugs or cover when charging the battery from an external source. Do not charge at an excessive rate or the battery may burst.

Take care when topping up, cleaning or carrying the battery. The acid electrolyte, even when diluted, is very corrosive and should not be allowed to contact the eyes or skin. Always wear rubber gloves and goggles or a face shield. If you ever need to prepare electrolyte yourself, always add the acid slowly to the water; never add the water to the acid.

Electricity

When using an electric power tool, inspection light etc., always ensure that the appliance is correctly connected to its plug and that, where necessary, it is properly grounded (earthed). Do not use such appliances in damp conditions and, again, beware of creating a spark or applying excessive heat in the vicinity of fuel or fuel vapor. Also ensure that the appliances meet national safety standards.

A severe electric shock can result from touching certain parts of the electrical system, such as the spark plug wires (HT leads), when the engine is running or being cranked, particularly if components are damp or the insulation is defective. Where an electronic ignition system is used, the secondary (HT) voltage is much higher and could prove fatal.

Motorcycle chemicals and lubricants

A number of chemicals and lubricants are available for use in motorcycle maintenance and repair. They include a wide variety of products ranging from cleaning solvents and degreasers to lubricants and protective sprays for rubber, plastic and vinyl.

Contact point/spark plug cleaner is a solvent used to clean oily film and dirt from points, grime from electrical connectors and oil deposits from spark plugs. It is oil free and leaves no residue. It can also be used to remove gum and varnish from carburetor jets and other orifices.

Carburetor cleaner is similar to contact point/spark plug cleaner but it usually has a stronger solvent and may leave a slight oily reside. It is not recommended for cleaning electrical components or connections.

Brake system cleaner is used to remove grease or brake fluid from brake system components (where clean surfaces are absolutely necessary and petroleum-based solvents cannot be used); it also leaves no residue.

Silicone-based lubricants are used to protect rubber parts such as hoses and grommets, and are used as lubricants for hinges and locks.

Multi-purpose grease is an all purpose lubricant used wherever grease is more practical than a liquid lubricant such as oil. Some multi-purpose grease is colored white and specially formulated to be more resistant to water than ordinary grease.

Gear oil (sometimes called gear lube) is a specially designed oil used in transmissions and final drive units, a s well as other areas where high friction, high temperature lubrication is required. It is available in a number of viscosities (weights) for various applications.

Motor oil, of course, is the lubricant specially formulated for use in the engine. It normally contains a wide variety of additives to prevent corrosion and reduce foaming and wear. Motor oil comes in various weights (viscosity ratings) of from 0 to 60. The recommended weight of the oil depends on the seasonal temperature and the demands on the engine. Light oil is used in cold climates and under light load conditions; heavy oil is used in hot climates and where high loads are encountered. Multi-viscosity oils are designed to have characteristics of both light and heavy oils and are available in a number of weights from 5W-20 to 20W-50.

Gas (petrol) additives perform several functions, depending on their chemical makeup. They usually contain solvents that help dissolve gum and varnish that build up on carburetor and intake parts. They also serve to break down carbon deposits that form on the inside surfaces of the combustion chambers. Some additives contain upper cylinder lubricants for valves and piston rings.

Brake fluid is a specially formulated hydraulic fluid that can withstand the heat and pressure encountered in brake systems. Care must be taken that this fluid does not come in contact with painted surfaces or plastics. An opened container should always be resealed to prevent contamination by water or dirt.

Chain lubricants are formulated especially for use on motorcycle final drive chains. A good chain lube should adhere well and have good penetrating qualities to be effective as a lubricant inside the chain and on the side plates, pins and rollers. Most chain lubes are either the foaming type or quick drying type and are usually marketed as sprays.

Degreasers are heavy duty solvents used to remove grease and grime that may accumulate on engine and frame components. They can be sprayed or brushed on and, depending on the type, are rinsed with either water or solvent.

Solvents are used alone or in combination with degreasers to clean parts and assemblies during repair and overhaul. The home mechanic should use only solvents that are non-flammable and that do not produce irritating fumes.

Gasket sealing compounds may be used in conjunction with gaskets, to improve their sealing capabilities, or alone, to seal metal-to-metal joints. Many gasket sealers can withstand extreme heat, some are impervious to gasoline and lubricants, while others are capable of filling and sealing large cavities. Depending on the intended use, gasket sealers either dry hard or stay relatively soft and pliable. They are usually applied by hand, with a brush, or are sprayed on the gasket sealing surfaces.

Thread cement is an adhesive locking compound that prevents threaded fasteners from loosening because of vibration. It is available in a variety of types for different applications.

Moisture dispersants are usually sprays that can be used to dry out electrical components such as the fuse block and wiring connectors. Some types can also be used as treatment for rubber and as a lubricant for hinges, cables and locks.

Waxes and polishes are used to help protect painted and plated surfaces from the weather. Different types of paint may require the use of different types of wax polish. Some polishes utilize a chemical or abrasive cleaner to help remove the top layer of oxidized (dull) paint on older vehicles. In recent years, many non-wax polishes (that contain a wide variety of chemicals such as polymers and silicones) have been introduced. These non-wax polishes are usually easier to apply and last longer than conventional waxes and polishes.

Troubleshooting

Contents

Symptom	Section
Engine doesn't start or is difficult to start	
Starter motor doesn't rotate	1
Starter motor rotates but engine does not turn over	2
Starter works but engine won't turn over (seized)	3
No fuel flow	4
Engine flooded	5
No spark or weak spark	6
Compression low	7
Stalls after starting	8
Rough idle	9
Poor running at low speed	
Spark weak	10
Fuel/air mixture incorrect	11
Compression low	12
Poor acceleration	13
Poor running or no power at high speed	
Firing incorrect	14
Fuel/air mixture incorrect	15
Compression low	16
Knocking or pinging	17
Miscellaneous causes	18
Overheating	
Engine overheats	19
Firing incorrect	20
Fuel/air mixture incorrect	21
Compression too high	22
Engine load excessive	23
Lubrication inadequate	24
Miscellaneous causes	25
Clutch problems	
Clutch slipping	26
Clutch not disengaging completely	27
Gear shifting problems	
Doesn't go into gear, or lever doesn't return	28
Jumps out of gear	29
Overshifts	30

Symptom	Section
Abnormal engine noise	
Knocking or pinging	31
Piston slap or rattling	32
Valve noise	33
Other noise	34
Abnormal driveline noise	
Clutch noise	35
Transmission noise	36
Final drive noise	37
Abnormal frame and suspension noise	
Front end noise	38
Shock absorber noise	39
Brake noise	40
Oil pressure light comes on	
Engine lubrication system	41
Electrical system	42
Excessive exhaust smoke	
White smoke	43
Black smoke	44
Brown smoke	45
Poor handling or stability	
Handlebar hard to turn	46
Handlebar shakes or vibrates excessively	47
Handlebar pulls to one side	48
Poor shock absorbing qualities	49
Braking problems	
Brakes are spongy, don't hold	50
Brake lever or pedal pulsates	51
Brakes drag	52
Electrical problems	
Battery dead or weak	53
Battery overcharged	54

Engine doesn't start or is difficult to start

1 Starter motor does not rotate

1 Engine kill switch Off.
2 Fuse blown. Check fuse block (Chapter 9).
3 Battery voltage low. Check and recharge battery (Chapter 9).
4 Starter motor defective. Make sure the wiring to the starter is secure. Make sure the starter relay clicks when the start button is pushed. If the relay clicks, then the fault is in the wiring or motor.
5 Starter relay faulty. Check it according to the procedure in Chapter 9.
6 Starter button not contacting. The contacts could be wet, corroded or dirty. Disassemble and clean the switch (Chapter 9).
7 Wiring open or shorted. Check all wiring connections and harnesses to make sure that they are dry, tight and not corroded. Also check for broken or frayed wires that can cause a short to ground (see wiring diagram, Chapter 9).
8 Ignition switch defective. Check the switch according to the procedure in Chapter 9. Replace the switch with a new one if it is defective.
9 Engine kill switch defective. Check for wet, dirty or corroded contacts. Clean or replace the switch as necessary (Chapter 9).
10 Faulty starter lockout circuit. Check the wiring and the switch itself according to the procedures in Chapter 9.

2 Starter motor rotates but engine does not turn over

1   Starter clutch defective. Inspect and repair or replace (Chapter 2).
2   Damaged idler or starter gears. Inspect and replace the damaged parts (Chapter 2).

3 Starter works but engine won't turn over (seized)

Seized engine caused by one or more internally damaged components. Failure due to wear, abuse or lack of lubrication. Damage can include seized valves, valve lifters, camshaft, pistons, crankshaft, connecting rod bearings, or transmission gears or bearings. Refer to Chapter 2 for engine disassembly.

4 No fuel flow

1   No fuel in tank.
2   Fuel tap in off position.
3   Tank cap air vent obstructed. Usually caused by dirt or water. Remove it and clean the cap vent hole.
4   Inline fuel filter clogged. Replace the filter (Chapter 1).
5   Electric fuel pump not working. Test it according to the procedures in Chapter 4.
6   Fuel line clogged. Pull the fuel line loose and carefully blow through it.
7   Inlet needle valve clogged. For all of the valves to be clogged, either a very bad batch of fuel with an unusual additive has been used, or some other foreign material has entered the tank. Many times after a machine has been stored for many months without running, the fuel turns to a varnish-like liquid and forms deposits on the inlet needle valves and jets. The carburetors should be removed and overhauled if draining the float bowls doesn't solve the problem.

5 Engine flooded

1   Float level too high. Check and adjust as described in Chapter 4.
2   Inlet needle valve worn or stuck open. A piece of dirt, rust or other debris can cause the inlet needle to seat improperly, causing excess fuel to be admitted to the float bowl. In this case, the float chamber should be cleaned and the needle and seat inspected. If the needle and seat are worn, then the leaking will persist and the parts should be replaced with new ones (Chapter 4).
3   Starting technique incorrect. Under normal circumstances (i.e., if all the carburetor functions are sound) the machine should start with little or no throttle. When the engine is cold, the choke should be operated and the engine started without opening the throttle. When the engine is at operating temperature, only a very slight amount of throttle should be necessary. If the engine is flooded, turn the fuel tap off and hold the throttle open while cranking the engine. This will allow additional air to reach the cylinders. Remember to turn the fuel tap back on after the engine starts.

6 No spark or weak spark

1   Ignition switch Off.
2   Engine kill switch turned to the Off position.
3   Battery voltage low. Check and recharge battery as necessary (Chapter 9).
4   Spark plug dirty, defective or worn out. Locate reason for fouled plug(s) using spark plug condition chart and follow the plug maintenance procedures in Chapter 1.
5   Spark plug cap or secondary wiring faulty. Check condition. Replace either or both components if cracks or deterioration are evident (Chapter 5).
6   Spark plug cap not making good contact. Make sure that the plug cap fits snugly over the plug end.
7   ECM defective. Check the unit, referring to Chapter 5 for details.
8   Pulse generator(s) defective. Check the unit, referring to Chapter 5 for details.
9   Ignition coil(s) defective. Check the coils, referring to Chapter 5.
10 Ignition or kill switch shorted. This is usually caused by water, corrosion, damage or excessive wear. The switches can be disassembled and cleaned with electrical contact cleaner. If cleaning does not help, replace the switches (Chapter 9).
11 Wiring shorted or broken between:
   a) *Ignition switch and engine kill switch (or blown fuse)*
   b) *ECM and engine kill switch*
   c) *ECM and ignition coil*
   d) *Ignition coil and plug*
   e) *ECM and pulse generator*

Make sure that all wiring connections are clean, dry and tight. Look for chafed and broken wires (Chapters 5 and 9).

7 Compression low

1   Spark plug loose. Remove the plug and inspect the threads. Reinstall and tighten to the specified torque (Chapter 1).
2   Cylinder head not sufficiently tightened down. If the cylinder head is suspected of being loose, then there's a chance that the gasket or head is damaged if the problem has persisted for any length of time. The head bolts should be tightened to the proper torque in the correct sequence (Chapter 2).
3   Improper valve clearance. This means that the valve is not closing completely and compression pressure is leaking past the valve. Inspect the hydraulic valve lifters and rocker assemblies (Chapter 1).
4   Cylinder and/or piston worn. Excessive wear will cause compression pressure to leak past the rings. This is usually accompanied by worn rings as well. A top end overhaul is necessary (Chapter 2).
5   Piston rings worn, weak, broken, or sticking. Broken or sticking piston rings usually indicate a lubrication or carburetion problem that causes excess carbon deposits or seizures to form on the pistons and rings. Top end overhaul is necessary (Chapter 2).
6   Piston ring-to-groove clearance excessive. This is caused by excessive wear of the piston ring lands. Piston replacement is necessary (Chapter 2).
7   Cylinder head gasket damaged. If the head is allowed to become loose, or if excessive carbon build-up on the piston crown and combustion chamber causes extremely high compression, the head gasket may leak. Retorquing the head is not always sufficient to restore the seal, so gasket replacement is necessary (Chapter 2).
8   Cylinder head warped. This is caused by overheating or improperly tightened head bolts. Machine shop resurfacing or head replacement is necessary (Chapter 2).
9   Valve spring broken or weak. Caused by component failure or wear; the spring(s) must be replaced (Chapter 2).
10 Valve not seating properly. This is caused by a bent valve (from over-revving or improper valve adjustment), burned valve or seat (improper carburetion) or an accumulation of carbon deposits on the seat (from carburetion or lubrication problems). The valves must be cleaned and/or replaced and the seats serviced if possible (Chapter 2).

8 Stalls after starting

1   Improper choke action. Make sure the choke rod is getting a full stroke and staying in the out position.
2   Ignition malfunction (Chapter 5).
3   Carburetor malfunction (Chapter 6).
4   Fuel contaminated. The fuel can be contaminated with either dirt or water, or can change chemically if the machine is allowed to sit for

Troubleshooting 0-19

several months or more. Drain the tank and float bowls (Chapter 4).
5   Intake air leak. Check for loose carburetor-to-intake manifold connections, loose or missing vacuum gauge access port cap or hose, or loose carburetor top (Chapter 4).
6   Engine idle speed incorrect. Turn throttle stop screw until the engine idles at the specified rpm (Chapter 1).

9 Rough idle

1   Ignition malfunction (Chapter 5).
2   Idle speed incorrect (Chapter 1).
3   Carburetors not synchronized. Adjust carburetors with vacuum gauge or manometer set as described in Chapter 1.
4   Carburetor malfunction (Chapter 4).
5   Fuel contaminated. The fuel can be contaminated with either dirt or water, or can change chemically if the machine is allowed to sit for several months or more. Drain the tank and float bowls (Chapter 5).
6   Intake air leak. Check for loose carburetor-to-intake manifold connections, loose or missing vacuum gauge access port cap or hose, or loose carburetor top (Chapter 4).
7   Air cleaner clogged. Service or replace air filter element (Chapter 1).

Poor running at low speed

10 Spark weak

1   Battery voltage low. Check and recharge battery (Chapter 9).
2   Spark plug fouled, defective or worn out. Refer to Chapter 1 for spark plug maintenance.
3   Spark plug cap or high tension wiring defective. Refer to Chapters 1 and 5 for details on the ignition system.
4   Spark plug cap not making contact.
5   Incorrect spark plug. Wrong type, heat range or cap configuration. Check and install correct plugs listed in Chapter 1. A cold plug or one with a recessed firing electrode will not operate at low speeds without fouling.
6   ECM defective (Chapter 5).
7   Pulse generator defective (Chapter 5).
8   Ignition coil(s) defective (Chapter 5).

11 Fuel/air mixture incorrect

1   Pilot screw(s) out of adjustment (Chapters 1 and 4).
2   Pilot jet or air passage clogged. Remove and overhaul the carburetors (Chapter 4).
3   Air bleed holes clogged. Remove carburetor and blow out all passages (Chapter 4).
4   Air cleaner clogged, poorly sealed or missing.
5   Air cleaner-to-carburetor boot poorly sealed. Look for cracks, holes or loose clamps and replace or repair defective parts.
6   Fuel level too high or too low. Adjust the floats (Chapter 4).
7   Fuel tank air vent obstructed. Make sure that the air vent passage in the filler cap is open.
8   Carburetor intake manifolds loose. Check for cracks, breaks, tears or loose clamps or bolts. Repair or replace the rubber boots.

12 Compression low

1   Spark plug loose. Remove the plug and inspect the threads. Reinstall and tighten to the specified torque (Chapter 1).
2   Cylinder head not sufficiently tightened down. If the cylinder head is suspected of being loose, then there's a chance that the gasket and head are damaged if the problem has persisted for any length of time. The head bolts should be tightened to the proper torque in the correct sequence (Chapter 2).
3   Improper valve clearance. This means that the valve is not closing completely and compression pressure is leaking past the valve. Inspect the hydraulic lifters and rocker assemblies (Chapter 1).
4   Cylinder and/or piston worn. Excessive wear will cause compression pressure to leak past the rings. This is usually accompanied by worn rings as well. A top end overhaul is necessary (Chapter 2).
5   Piston rings worn, weak, broken, or sticking. Broken or sticking piston rings usually indicate a lubrication or carburetion problem that causes excess carbon deposits or seizures to form on the pistons and rings. Top end overhaul is necessary (Chapter 2).
6   Piston ring-to-groove clearance excessive. This is caused by excessive wear of the piston ring lands. Piston replacement is necessary (Chapter 2).
7   Cylinder head gasket damaged. If the head is allowed to become loose, or if excessive carbon build-up on the piston crown and combustion chamber causes extremely high compression, the head gasket may leak. Retorquing the head is not always sufficient to restore the seal, so gasket replacement is necessary (Chapter 2).
8   Cylinder head warped. This is caused by overheating or improperly tightened head bolts. Machine shop resurfacing or head replacement is necessary (Chapter 2).
9   Valve spring broken or weak. Caused by component failure or wear; the spring(s) must be replaced (Chapter 2).
10 Valve not seating properly. This is caused by a bent valve (from over-revving or improper valve adjustment), burned valve or seat (improper carburetion) or an accumulation of carbon deposits on the seat (from carburetion, lubrication problems). The valves must be cleaned and/or replaced and the seats serviced if possible (Chapter 2).

13 Poor acceleration

1   Carburetors leaking or dirty. Overhaul the carburetors (Chapter 4).
2   Timing not advancing. The pulse generator(s) or the ECM may be defective. If so, they must be replaced with new ones, as they can't be repaired.
3   Carburetors not synchronized. Adjust them with a vacuum gauge set or manometer (Chapter 1).
4   Engine oil viscosity too high. Using a heavier oil than that recommended in Chapter 1 can damage the oil pumps or lubrication system and cause drag on the engine.
5   Brakes dragging. Usually caused by debris which has entered the brake piston sealing boot, or from a warped disc or bent axle. Repair as necessary (Chapter 7).

Poor running or no power at high speed

14 Firing incorrect

1   Air filter restricted. Clean or replace filter (Chapter 1).
2   Spark plug fouled, defective or worn out. See Chapter 1 for spark plug maintenance.
3   Spark plug cap or secondary (HT) wiring defective. See Chapters 1 and 5 for details of the ignition system.
4   Spark plug cap not in good contact (Chapter 5).
5   Incorrect spark plug. Wrong type, heat range or cap configuration. Check and install correct plugs listed in Chapter 1.
6   ECM defective (Chapter 5).
7   Ignition coil(s) defective (Chapter 5).

Troubleshooting

15 Fuel/air mixture incorrect

1 Main jet clogged. Dirt, water or other contaminants can clog the main jets. Replace the fuel filter and clean the float bowl area, and the jets and carburetor orifices (Chapter 4).
2 Main jet wrong size. The standard jetting is for sea level atmospheric pressure and oxygen content.
3 Throttle shaft-to-carburetor body clearance excessive. Refer to Chapter 4 for inspection and part replacement procedures.
4 Air bleed holes clogged. Remove and overhaul carburetors (Chapter 4).
5 Air filter clogged, poorly sealed, or missing.
6 Air filter-to-carburetor boot poorly sealed. Look for cracks, holes or loose clamps, and replace or repair defective parts.
7 Fuel level too high or too low. Adjust the float(s) (Chapter 4).
8 Fuel tank air vent obstructed. Make sure the air vent passage in the filler cap is open.
9 Carburetor intake manifolds loose. Check for cracks, breaks, tears or loose clamps or bolts. Repair or replace the rubber boots (Chapter 4).
10 Fuel tap clogged. Remove the tap and clean it (Chapter 4).
11 Fuel line clogged. Pull the fuel line loose and carefully blow through it.
12 Fuel filter clogged. Replace it.

16 Compression low

1 Spark plug loose. Remove the plug and inspect the threads. Reinstall and tighten to the specified torque (Chapter 1).
2 Cylinder head not sufficiently tightened down. If the cylinder head is suspected of being loose, then there's a chance that the gasket and head are damaged if the problem has persisted for any length of time. The head bolts should be tightened to the proper torque in the correct sequence (Chapter 2).
3 Improper valve clearance. This means that the valve is not closing completely and compression pressure is leaking past the valve. Inspect the hydraulic valve lifters and rocker assemblies (Chapter 2).
4 Cylinder and/or piston worn. Excessive wear will cause compression pressure to leak past the rings. This is usually accompanied by worn rings as well. A top end overhaul is necessary (Chapter 2).
5 Piston rings worn, weak, broken, or sticking. Broken or sticking piston rings usually indicate a lubrication or carburetion problem that causes excess carbon deposits or seizures to form on the pistons and rings. Top end overhaul is necessary (Chapter 2).
6 Piston ring-to-groove clearance excessive. This is caused by excessive wear of the piston ring lands. Piston replacement is necessary (Chapter 2).
7 Cylinder head gasket damaged. If the head is allowed to become loose, or if excessive carbon build-up on the piston crown and combustion chamber causes extremely high compression, the head gasket may leak. Retorquing the head is not always sufficient to restore the seal, so gasket replacement is necessary (Chapter 2).
8 Cylinder head warped. This is caused by overheating or improperly tightened head bolts. Machine shop resurfacing or head replacement is necessary (Chapter 2).
9 Valve spring broken or weak. Caused by component failure or wear; the spring(s) must be replaced (Chapter 2).
10 Valve not seating properly. This is caused by a bent valve (from over-revving or improper valve adjustment), burned valve or seat (improper carburetion) or an accumulation of carbon deposits on the seat (from carburetion or lubrication problems). The valves must be cleaned and/or replaced and the seats serviced if possible (Chapter 2).

17 Knocking or pinging

1 Carbon build-up in combustion chamber. Use of a fuel additive that will dissolve the adhesive bonding the carbon particles to the crown and chamber is the easiest way to remove the build-up. Otherwise, the cylinder head will have to be removed and decarbonized (Chapter 2).
2 Incorrect or poor quality fuel. Old or improper grades of fuel can cause detonation. This causes the piston to rattle, thus the knocking or pinging sound. Drain old fuel and always use the recommended fuel grade (Chapter 9).
3 Spark plug heat range incorrect. Uncontrolled detonation indicates the plug heat range is too hot. The plug in effect becomes a glow plug, raising cylinder temperatures. Install the proper heat range plug (Chapter 1).
4 Improper air/fuel mixture. This will cause the cylinder to run hot, which leads to detonation. Clogged jets or an air leak can cause this imbalance (Chapter 4).

18 Miscellaneous causes

1 Throttle valve doesn't open fully. Adjust the cable slack (Chapter 1).
2 Clutch slipping. May be caused by loose or worn clutch components. Refer to Chapter 2 for clutch component replacement.
3 Timing not advancing.
4 Engine oil viscosity too high. Using a heavier oil than the one recommended in Chapter 1 can damage the oil pump or lubrication system and cause drag on the engine.
5 Brakes dragging. Usually caused by debris which has entered the brake piston sealing boot, or from a warped disc or bent axle. Repair as necessary.

Overheating

19 Engine overheats

1 Coolant level low. Check coolant level as described in Chapter 1. If coolant level is low, the engine will overheat.
2 Leak in cooling system. Check cooling system hoses and radiator for leaks and other damage. Repair or replace parts as necessary (Chapter 3).
3 Thermostat stuck closed. Check and replace as described in Chapter 3.
4 Faulty radiator cap. Remove the cap and have it pressure checked.
5 Coolant passages clogged. Drain and flush the entire system, then refill with new coolant.
6 Water pump defective. Remove the pump and check the components.
7 Clogged radiator fins. Clean them by blowing compressed air through the fins from the back side.
8 Engine oil level low. Check and add oil (Chapter 1).
9 Wrong type of oil. If you're not sure what type of oil is in the engine, drain it and fill with the correct type (Chapter 1).
10 Air leak at carburetor intake manifold. Check and tighten or replace as necessary (Chapter 4).
11 Float level low. Check and adjust if necessary (Chapter 4).
12 Worn oil pump or clogged oil passages. Check oil pressure (Chapter 2). Replace pump or clean passages as necessary.
13 Clogged oil lines. Remove and check for foreign material (Chapter 2).
14 Carbon build-up in combustion chambers. Use of a fuel additive that will dissolve the adhesive bonding the carbon particles to the piston crowns and chambers is the easiest way to remove the build-up. Otherwise, the cylinder head will have to be removed and decarbonized (Chapter 2).

Troubleshooting 0-21

20 Firing incorrect

1   Spark plug fouled, defective or worn out. See Chapter 1 for spark plug maintenance.
2   Incorrect spark plug (see Chapter 1).
3   Faulty ignition coil(s) (Chapter 5).

21 Fuel/air mixture incorrect

1   Main jet clogged. Dirt, water and other contaminants can clog the main jets. Clean the fuel tap filter, the float bowl area and the jets and carburetor orifices (Chapter 4).
2   Main jet wrong size. The standard jetting is for sea level atmospheric pressure and oxygen content.
3   Air filter poorly sealed or missing.
4   Air filter-to-carburetor boot poorly sealed. Look for cracks, holes or loose clamps and replace or repair.
5   Fuel level too low. Adjust the float(s) (Chapter 4).
6   Fuel tank air vent obstructed. Make sure that the air vent passage in the filler cap is open.
7   Carburetor intake manifold loose. Check for cracks, breaks, tears or loose fasteners. Replace the gaskets (Chapter 4).

22 Compression too high

1   Carbon build-up in combustion chamber. Use of a fuel additive that will dissolve the adhesive bonding the carbon particles to the piston crown and chamber is the easiest way to remove the build-up. Otherwise, the cylinder head will have to be removed and decarbonized (Chapter 2).
2   Improperly machined head surface or installation of incorrect gasket during engine assembly.

23 Engine load excessive

1   Clutch slipping. Can be caused by damaged, loose or worn clutch components. Refer to Chapter 2 for overhaul procedures.
2   Engine oil level too high. The addition of too much oil will cause pressurization of the crankcase and inefficient engine operation. Check Specifications and drain to proper level (Chapter 1).
3   Engine oil viscosity too high. Using a heavier oil than the one recommended in Chapter 1 can damage the oil pump or lubrication system as well as cause drag on the engine.
4   Brakes dragging. Usually caused by debris which has entered the brake piston sealing boot, or from a warped disc or bent axle. Repair as necessary.

24 Lubrication inadequate

1   Engine oil level too low. Friction caused by intermittent lack of lubrication or from oil that is overworked can cause overheating. The oil provides a definite cooling function in the engine. Check the oil level (Chapter 1).
2   Poor quality engine oil or incorrect viscosity or type. Oil is rated not only according to viscosity but also according to type. Some oils are not rated high enough for use in this engine. Check the Specifications section and change to the correct oil (Chapter 1).
3   Camshaft or journals worn. Excessive wear causing drop in oil pressure. Replace cam and/or cylinder head. Abnormal wear could be caused by oil starvation at high rpm from low oil level or improper weight or type of oil (Chapter 1).
4   Crankshaft and/or bearings worn. Same problems as paragraph 3. Check and replace crankshaft and/or bearings (Chapter 2).

25 Miscellaneous causes

Modification to exhaust system. Most aftermarket exhaust systems cause the engine to run leaner, which makes it run hotter. When installing an accessory exhaust system, always rejet the carburetors.

Clutch problems

26 Clutch slipping

1   Friction plates worn or warped. Overhaul the clutch assembly (Chapter 2).
2   Metal plates worn or warped (Chapter 2).
3   Clutch springs broken or weak. Old or heat-damaged springs (from slipping clutch) should be replaced with new ones (Chapter 2).
4   Worn or warped clutch plates. Replace (Chapter 2).
5   Clutch release mechanism defective. Replace any defective parts (Chapter 2).
6   Clutch boss or housing unevenly worn. This causes improper engagement of the plates. Replace the damaged or worn parts (Chapter 2).

27 Clutch not disengaging completely

1   Clutch lever play excessive (see Chapter 1). Air in clutch line or hydraulic system components worn. Bleed clutch or repair hydraulic components (Chapter 2).
2   Clutch plates warped or damaged. This will cause clutch drag, which in turn will cause the machine to creep. Overhaul the clutch assembly (Chapter 2).
3   Clutch spring tension uneven. Usually caused by a sagged or broken spring. Check and replace the springs (Chapter 2).
4   Engine oil deteriorated. Old, thin, worn out oil will not provide proper lubrication for the plates, causing the clutch to drag. Replace the oil and filter (Chapter 1).
5   Engine oil viscosity too high. Using a heavier oil than recommended in Chapter 1 can cause the plates to stick together, putting a drag on the engine. Change to the correct weight oil (Chapter 1).
6   Clutch housing seized on shaft. Lack of lubrication, severe wear or damage can cause the housing to seize on the shaft. Overhaul of the clutch, and perhaps transmission, may be necessary to repair the damage (Chapter 2).
7   Clutch release mechanism defective. Worn or damaged release mechanism parts can stick and fail to apply force to the pressure plate. Overhaul the release mechanism (Chapter 2).
8   Loose clutch hub nut. Causes housing and boss misalignment putting a drag on the engine. Engagement adjustment continually varies. Overhaul the clutch assembly (Chapter 2).

Gear shifting problems

28 Doesn't go into gear or lever doesn't return

1   Clutch not disengaging. See Section 27.
2   Shift fork(s) bent or seized. Often caused by dropping the machine or from lack of lubrication. Overhaul the transmission (Chapter 2).
3   Gear(s) stuck on shaft. Most often caused by a lack of lubrication or excessive wear in transmission bearings and bushings. Overhaul the transmission (Chapter 2).
4   Shift drum binding. Caused by lubrication failure or excessive

wear. Replace the drum and bearing (Chapter 2).
5   Shift lever return spring weak or broken (Chapter 2).
6   Shift lever broken. Splines stripped out of lever or shaft, caused by allowing the lever to get loose or from dropping the machine. Replace necessary parts (Chapter 2).
7   Shift mechanism pawl broken or worn. Full engagement and rotary movement of shift drum results. Replace shaft assembly (Chapter 2).
8   Pawl spring broken. Allows pawl to float, causing sporadic shift operation. Replace spring (Chapter 2).

29 Jumps out of gear

1   Shift fork(s) worn. Overhaul the transmission (Chapter 2).
2   Gear groove(s) worn. Overhaul the transmission (Chapter 2).
3   Gear dogs or dog slots worn or damaged. The gears should be inspected and replaced. No attempt should be made to service the worn parts.

30 Overshifts

1   Pawl spring weak or broken (Chapter 2).
2   Shift drum stopper lever not functioning (Chapter 2).
3   Overshift limiter broken or distorted (Chapter 2).

Abnormal engine noise

31 Knocking or pinging

1   Carbon build-up in combustion chamber. Use of a fuel additive that will dissolve the adhesive bonding the carbon particles to the piston crown and chamber is the easiest way to remove the build-up. Otherwise, the cylinder head will have to be removed and decarbonized (Chapter 2).
2   Incorrect or poor quality fuel. Old or improper fuel can cause detonation. This causes the pistons to rattle, thus the knocking or pinging sound. Drain the old fuel and always use the recommended grade fuel (Chapter 4).
3   Spark plug heat range incorrect. Uncontrolled detonation indicates that the plug heat range is too hot. The plug in effect becomes a glow plug, raising cylinder temperatures. Install the proper heat range plug (Chapter 1).
4   Improper air/fuel mixture. This will cause the cylinders to run hot and lead to detonation. Clogged jets or an air leak can cause this imbalance (Chapter 4).

32 Piston slap or rattling

1   Cylinder-to-piston clearance excessive. Caused by improper assembly. Inspect and overhaul top end parts (Chapter 2).
2   Connecting rod bent. Caused by over-revving, trying to start a badly flooded engine or from ingesting a foreign object into the combustion chamber. Replace the damaged parts (Chapter 2).
3   Piston pin or piston pin bore worn or seized from wear or lack of lubrication. Replace damaged parts (Chapter 2).
4   Piston ring(s) worn, broken or sticking. Overhaul the top end (Chapter 2).
5   Piston seizure damage. Usually from lack of lubrication or overheating. Replace the pistons and bore the cylinders, as necessary (Chapter 2).
6   Connecting rod upper or lower end clearance excessive. Caused by excessive wear or lack of lubrication. Replace worn parts.

33 Valve noise

1   Incorrect valve clearances. Adjust the clearances by referring to Chapter 1.
2   Valve spring broken or weak. Check and replace weak valve springs (Chapter 2).
3   Camshaft or cylinder head worn or damaged. Lack of lubrication at high rpm is usually the cause of damage. Insufficient oil or failure to change the oil at the recommended intervals are the chief causes. Since there are no replaceable bearings in the head, the head itself will have to be replaced if there is excessive wear or damage (Chapter 2).

34 Other noise

1   Cylinder head gasket leaking.
2   Exhaust pipe leaking at cylinder head connection. Caused by improper fit of pipe(s) or loose exhaust flange. All exhaust fasteners should be tightened evenly and carefully. Failure to do this will lead to a leak.
3   Crankshaft runout excessive. Caused by a bent crankshaft (from over-revving) or damage from an upper cylinder component failure.
4   Engine mounting bolts loose. Tighten all engine mount bolts to the specified torque (Chapter 2).
5   Crankshaft bearings worn (Chapter 2 or Chapter 3).
6   Camshaft chain tensioner defective. Replace according to the procedure in Chapter 2.
7   Camshaft chain, sprockets or guides worn (Chapter 2).

Abnormal driveline noise

35 Clutch noise

1   Clutch housing/friction plate clearance excessive (Chapter 2).
2   Loose or damaged clutch pressure plate and/or bolts (Chapter 2).

36 Transmission noise

1   Bearings worn. Also includes the possibility that the shafts are worn. Overhaul the transmission (Chapter 2).
2   Gears worn or chipped (Chapter 2).
3   Metal chips jammed in gear teeth. Probably pieces from a broken clutch, gear or shift mechanism that were picked up by the gears. This will cause early bearing failure (Chapter 2).
4   Engine oil level too low. Causes a howl from transmission. Also affects engine power and clutch operation (Chapter 1).

37 Final drive noise

1   Final drive oil level too low (Chapter 1).
2   Final drive gear lash out of adjustment.
3   Final drive gear(s) damaged or worn.

Abnormal frame and suspension noise

38 Front end noise

1   Low fluid level or improper viscosity oil in forks. This can sound

Troubleshooting 0-23

like spurting and is usually accompanied by irregular fork action (Chapter 6).
2   Spring weak or broken. Makes a clicking or scraping sound. Fork oil, when drained, will have a lot of metal particles in it (Chapter 6).
3   Steering head bearings loose or damaged. Clicks when braking. Check and adjust or replace as necessary (Chapter 6).
4   Fork clamps loose. Make sure all fork clamp pinch bolts are tight (Chapter 6).
5   Fork tube bent. Good possibility if machine has been dropped. Replace tube with a new one (Chapter 6).
6   Front axle loose. Tighten to the specified torque (Chapter 7).

39 Shock absorber noise

1   Fluid level incorrect. Indicates a leak caused by defective seal. Shock will be covered with oil. Replace shock (Chapter 6).
2   Defective shock absorber with internal damage. This is in the body of the shock and can't be remedied. The shock must be replaced with a new one (Chapter 6).
3   Bent or damaged shock body. Replace the shock with a new one (Chapter 6).

40 Brake noise

1   Squeal caused by pad shim not installed or positioned correctly (Chapter 7).
2   Squeal caused by dust on brake pads. Usually found in combination with glazed pads. Clean using brake cleaning solvent (Chapter 7).
3   Contamination of brake pads. Oil, brake fluid or dirt causing brake to chatter or squeal. Clean or replace pads (Chapter 7).
4   Pads glazed. Caused by excessive heat from prolonged use or from contamination. Do not use sandpaper, emery cloth, carborundum cloth or any other abrasive to roughen the pad surfaces as abrasives will stay in the pad material and damage the disc. A very fine flat file can be used, but pad replacement is suggested as a cure (Chapter 7).
5   Disc warped. Can cause a chattering, clicking or intermittent squeal. Usually accompanied by a pulsating lever and uneven braking. Replace the disc (Chapter 7).
6   Loose or worn wheel bearings. Check and replace as needed (Chapter 7).

Oil pressure light comes on

41 Engine lubrication system

1   Engine oil pump(s) defective (see Chapter 2).
2   Engine oil level low. Inspect for leak or other problem causing low oil level and add recommended oil (Chapters 1 and 2).
3   Engine oil viscosity too low. Very old, thin oil or an improper viscosity of oil used in the engine. Change to correct oil (Chapter 1).
4   Camshafts or journals worn. Excessive wear causing drop in oil pressure. Replace cams and/or heads. Abnormal wear could be caused by oil starvation at high rpm from low oil level or improper oil viscosity or type (see Chapter 1).

42 Electrical system

1   Oil pressure switch defective. Check the switch according to the procedure in Chapter 9. Replace it if it's defective.
2   Oil pressure indicator light circuit defective. Check for pinched, shorted, disconnected or damaged wiring (Chapter 9).

Excessive exhaust smoke

43 White smoke

1   Piston oil ring worn. The ring may be broken or damaged, causing oil from the crankcase to be pulled past the piston into the combustion chamber. Replace the rings with new ones (Chapter 2).
2   Cylinders worn, cracked, or scored. Caused by overheating or oil starvation. If worn or scored, the cylinders will have to be rebored and new pistons installed. If cracked, the cylinder block will have to be replaced (Chapter 2).
3   Valve oil seal damaged or worn. Replace oil seals with new ones (Chapter 2).
4   Valve guide worn. Perform a complete valve job (Chapter 2).
5   Engine oil level too high, which causes the oil to be forced past the rings. Drain oil to the proper level (Chapter 1).
6   Head gasket broken between oil return and cylinder. Causes oil to be pulled into the combustion chamber. Replace the head gasket and check the head for warpage (Chapter 2).
7   Abnormal crankcase pressurization, which forces oil past the rings. Clogged breather or hoses usually the cause (Chapter 2).

44 Black smoke

1   Air filter clogged. Clean or replace the element (Chapter 1).
2   Main jet too large or loose. Compare the jet size to the Specifications (Chapter 4).
3   Choke stuck, causing fuel to be pulled through choke circuit (Chapter 4).
4   Fuel level too high. Check and adjust the float level as necessary (Chapter 4).
5   Inlet needle held off needle seat. Clean the float bowls and fuel line and replace the needles and seats if necessary (Chapter 4).

45 Brown smoke

1   Main jet too small or clogged. Lean condition caused by wrong size main jet or by a restricted orifice. Clean float bowl and jets and compare jet size to Specifications (Chapter 4).
2   Fuel flow insufficient. Fuel inlet needle valve stuck closed due to chemical reaction with old fuel. Float level incorrect. Restricted fuel line. Clean line and float bowl and adjust floats if necessary.
3   Carburetor intake manifolds loose (Chapter 4).
4   Air filter poorly sealed or not installed (Chapter 1).

Poor handling or stability

46 Handlebar hard to turn

1   Steering stem locknut too tight (Chapter 6).
2   Bearings damaged. Roughness can be felt as the bars are turned from side-to-side. Replace bearings and races (Chapter 6).
3   Races dented or worn. Denting results from wear in only one position (e.g., straight ahead), from a collision or hitting a pothole or from dropping the machine. Replace races and bearings (Chapter 6).
4   Steering stem lubrication inadequate. Causes are grease getting hard from age or being washed out by high pressure car washes. Disassemble steering head and repack bearings (Chapter 6).
5   Steering stem bent. Caused by a collision, hitting a pothole or by dropping the machine. Replace damaged part. Don't try to straighten the steering stem (Chapter 6).
6   Front tire air pressure too low (Chapter 1).

47 Handlebar shakes or vibrates excessively

1 Tires worn or out of balance (Chapter 7).
2 Swingarm bearings worn. Replace worn bearings by referring to Chapter 6.
3 Rim(s) warped or damaged. Inspect wheels for runout (Chapter 7).
4 Wheel bearings worn. Worn front or rear wheel bearings can cause poor tracking. Worn front bearings will cause wobble (Chapter 6).
5 Handlebar clamp bolts loose (Chapter 6).
6 Steering stem or fork clamps loose. Tighten them to the specified torque (Chapter 6).
7 Engine mount bolts loose. Will cause excessive vibration with increased engine rpm (Chapter 2).

48 Handlebar pulls to one side

1 Frame bent. Definitely suspect this if the machine has been dropped. May or may not be accompanied by cracking near the bend. Replace the frame (Chapter 6).
2 Wheel out of alignment. Caused by improper location of axle spacers or from bent steering stem or frame (Chapter 6).
3 Swingarm bent or twisted. Caused by age (metal fatigue) or impact damage. Replace the arm (Chapter 6).
4 Steering stem bent. Caused by impact damage or by dropping the motorcycle. Replace the steering stem (Chapter 6).
5 Fork leg bent. Disassemble the forks and replace the damaged parts (Chapter 6).
6 Fork oil level uneven. Check and add or drain as necessary (Chapter 6).

49 Poor shock absorbing qualities

1 Too hard:
   a) Fork oil level excessive (Chapter 6).
   b) Fork oil viscosity too high. Use a lighter oil (see the Specifications in Chapter 1).
   c) Fork tube bent. Causes a harsh, sticking feeling (Chapter 6).
   d) Shock shaft or body bent or damaged (Chapter 6).
   e) Fork internal damage (Chapter 6).
   f) Anti-dive O-ring swollen (Chapter 6).
   g) Shock internal damage.
   h) Tire pressure too high (Chapter 1).
2 Too soft:
   a) Fork or shock oil insufficient and/or leaking (Chapter 6).
   b) Fork oil level too low (Chapter 6).
   c) Fork oil viscosity too light (Chapter 6).
   d) Fork springs weak or broken (Chapter 6).

Braking problems

50 Brakes are spongy, don't hold

1 Air in brake line. Caused by inattention to master cylinder fluid level or by leakage. Locate problem and bleed brakes (Chapter 7).
2 Pad or disc worn (Chapters 1 and 7).
3 Brake fluid leak. See paragraph 1.
4 Contaminated pads. Caused by contamination with oil, grease, brake fluid, etc. Clean or replace pads. Clean disc thoroughly with brake cleaner (Chapter 7).
5 Brake fluid deteriorated. Fluid is old or contaminated. Drain system, replenish with new fluid and bleed the system (Chapter 7).
6 Master cylinder internal parts worn or damaged causing fluid to bypass (Chapter 7).
7 Master cylinder bore scratched by foreign material or broken spring. Repair or replace master cylinder (Chapter 7).
8 Disc warped. Replace disc (Chapter 7).

51 Brake lever or pedal pulsates

1 Disc warped. Replace disc (Chapter 7).
2 Axle bent. Replace axle (Chapter 7).
3 Brake caliper bolts loose (Chapter 7).
4 Brake caliper shafts damaged or sticking, causing caliper to bind. Lube the shafts or replace them if they are corroded or bent (Chapter 7).
5 Wheel warped or otherwise damaged (Chapter 7).
6 Wheel bearings damaged or worn (Chapter 7).

52 Brakes drag

1 Master cylinder piston seized. Caused by wear or damage to piston or cylinder bore (Chapter 7).
2 Lever balky or stuck. Check pivot and lubricate (Chapter 7).
3 Brake caliper binds. Caused by inadequate lubrication or damage to caliper shafts (Chapter 7).
4 Brake caliper piston seized in bore. Caused by wear or ingestion of dirt past deteriorated seal (Chapter 7).
5 Brake pad damaged. Pad material separated from backing plate. Usually caused by faulty manufacturing process or from contact with chemicals. Replace pads (Chapter 7).
6 Pads improperly installed (Chapter 7).
7 Front brake lever or rear brake pedal freeplay insufficient (Chapter 1).

Electrical problems

53 Battery dead or weak

1 Battery faulty. Caused by sulfated plates which are shorted through sedimentation or low electrolyte level. Also, broken battery terminal making only occasional contact (Chapter 9).
2 Battery cables making poor contact (Chapter 9).
3 Load excessive. Caused by addition of high wattage lights or other electrical accessories.
4 Ignition switch defective. Switch either grounds internally or fails to shut off system. Replace the switch (Chapter 9).
5 Regulator/rectifier defective (Chapter 9).
6 Alternator defective (Chapter 9).
7 Wiring faulty. Wiring grounded or connections loose in ignition, charging or lighting circuits (Chapter 9).

54 Battery overcharged

1 Regulator/rectifier defective. Overcharging is noticed when battery gets excessively warm or boils over (Chapter 9).
2 Battery defective. Replace battery with a new one (Chapter 9).
3 Battery amperage too low, wrong type or size. Install manufacturer's specified amp-hour battery to handle charging load (Chapter 9).

Chapter 1
Tune-up and routine maintenance

Contents

	Section
Air filter element - servicing	13
Battery electrolyte level/specific gravity - check	4
Brake pads - wear check	5
Brake pedal position - check and adjustment	7
Brake system - general check	6
Carburetor synchronization - check and adjustment	18
Clutch - check and adjustment	10
Cooling system - draining, flushing and refilling	28
Cooling system - inspection	27
Crankcase breather - servicing	14
Cruise valve element (1987 Aspencade) - replacement	29
Cylinder compression - check	15
Engine oil/filter - change	11
Evaporative emission control system (California models) - check	21
Exhaust system - check	22
Fasteners - check	25
Final drive - oil change	30
Fluid levels - check	3
Forks	See Chapter 6
Fuel system - check and filter replacement	20
Headlight aim - check and adjust	31
Idle speed - check and adjustment	17
Introduction to tune-up and routine maintenance	1
Lubrication - general	19
On-board compressor system check and element cleaning	23
Pulse air system - inspection	12
Routine maintenance intervals	2
Spark plugs - replacement	16
Steering head bearings - check	24
Suspension	See Chapter 6
Suspension - check	26
Throttle and choke operation and freeplay - check and adjustment	9
Tires/wheels - general check	8

Specifications

Engine

Spark plugs
  Type
    Standard .... NGK DPR8EA-9 or ND X24EPR-U9
    Cold weather (below 5-degrees C/41-degrees F) .... NGK DPR7EA-9 or ND X22EPR-U9
    Extended high-speed riding .... NGK DPR9EA-9 or ND X27EPR-U9
  Gap .... 0.8 to 0.9 mm (0.031 to 0.035 inch)
  Firing order 1-3-2-4
Engine idle speed .... 800 +/- 80 rpm
Cylinder compression pressure (at sea level) .... 185 psi
Carburetor synchronization - maximum vacuum difference between cylinders .... 40 mm Hg (1.6 inch Hg)
Cylinder numbering (from front to rear of bike)
  Right side 1-3
  Left side 2-4

Miscellaneous

Brake pad material minimum thickness .... To wear groove - see text
Brake pedal position .... Zero to 5 mm (zero to 3/16-inch) above the top of the footpeg
Freeplay adjustments
  Throttle grip .... 2 to 6 mm (1/8 to 1/4 inch)
  Clutch lever .... Not adjustable
  Front brake lever .... Not adjustable
Battery electrolyte specific gravity .... 1.280 at 20-degrees C (68 degrees F)

Minimum tire tread depth	
Front	1.5 mm (0.06 inch)
Rear	2.0 mm (0.08 inch)
Tire pressures (cold)	
Front	32 psi
Rear	
All except 1987 Aspencade	
Up to 90 kg (200 lbs)	32 psi
Above 90 kg (200 lbs)	40 psi
1987 Aspencade	
Up to 90 kg (200 lbs)	36 psi
Above 90 kg (200 lbs)	40 psi
Tire sizes	
Front	130/90-16 67H
Rear	150/90-15 74H
Maximum load	
Overall	
1984	
Interstate	188 kg (415 lbs)
Aspencade	172 kg (380 lbs)
1985 through 1987	
Interstate	192 kg (425 lbs)
Aspencade	177 kg (390 lbs)
Trunk	9 kg (20 lbs)
Saddlebags (each)	9 kg (20 lbs)
Fairing pockets (each)	2 kg (5 lbs)
Torque specifications	
Engine oil drain plug	38 Nm (27 ft-lbs)
Oil filter bolt	30 Nm (22 ft-lbs)
Spark plugs	16 Nm (12 ft-lbs)
Final drive filler and drain plugs	12 Nm (9 ft-lbs)

Recommended lubricants and fluids

Engine/transmission oil	
Type	API grade SE or SF
Viscosity	SAE 10W-40
Capacity (with filter change)	
Routine oil change	3.2 liters (3.4 qt)
After engine overhaul	4.0 liters (4.2 qt)
Coolant	
Type	50/50 mixture of water and ethylene glycol antifreeze containing corrosion inhibitors for aluminum engines
Capacity	3.4 liters (3.6 qt)
Final drive oil	
Type	SAE 80 hypoid gear oil, API GL-5
Capacity	130 cc (4-1/2 fl oz)
Brake fluid	DOT 4
Fork oil	See Chapter 6

Miscellaneous

Wheel bearings	Medium weight, lithium-based multi-purpose grease
Swingarm pivot bearings	Medium weight, lithium-based multi-purpose grease
Cables and lever pivots	Chain and cable lubricant or 10W30 motor oil
Sidestand/centerstand pivots	Medium-weight, lithium-based multi-purpose grease
Brake pedal/shift lever pivots	Medium-weight, lithium-based multi-purpose grease
Throttle grip	Medium-weight, lithium-based multi-purpose grease

1 Introduction to tune-up and routine maintenance

Refer to illustrations 1.3a through 1.3e

This Chapter covers in detail the checks and procedures necessary for the tune-up and routine maintenance of your motorcycle. Section 1 includes the routine maintenance schedule, which is designed to keep the machine in proper running condition and prevent possible problems. The remaining Sections contain detailed procedures for carrying out the items listed on the maintenance schedule, as well as additional maintenance information designed to increase reliability.

Since routine maintenance plays such an important role in the safe and efficient operation of your motorcycle, it is presented here as a comprehensive check list. For the rider who does all his own maintenance, these lists outline the procedures and checks that should be done on a routine basis.

Chapter 1 Tune-up and routine maintenance

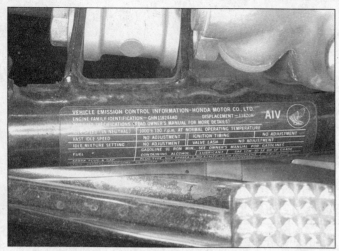

1.3a Maintenance information printed on decals includes tune-up data . . .

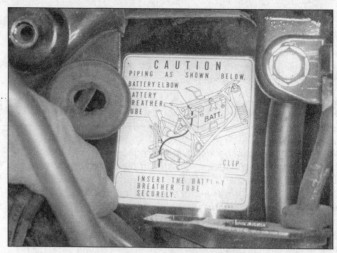

1.3b . . . battery vent tube routing . . .

1.3c . . . tire pressure specifications . . .

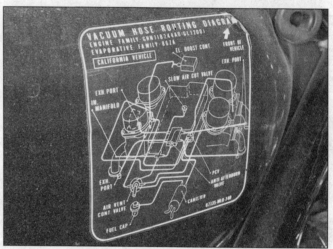

1.3d . . . vacuum hose connections . . .

1.3e . . . and safety information

Maintenance information is printed on labels attached to the motorcycle **(see illustrations)**. If the information on the labels differs from that included here, use the information on the label.

Deciding where to start or plug into the routine maintenance schedule depends on several factors. If you have a motorcycle whose warranty has recently expired, and if it has been maintained according to the warranty standards, you may want to pick up routine maintenance as it coincides with the next mileage or calendar interval. If you have owned the machine for some time but have never performed any maintenance on it, then you may want to start at the nearest interval and include some additional procedures to ensure that nothing important is overlooked. If you have just had a major engine overhaul, then you may want to start the maintenance routine from the beginning. If you have a used machine and have no knowledge of its history or maintenance record, you may desire to combine all the checks into one large service initially and then settle into the maintenance schedule prescribed.

The Sections which outline the inspection and maintenance procedures are written as step-by-step comprehensive guides to the performance of the work. They explain in detail each of the routine inspections and maintenance procedures on the check list. References to additional information in applicable Chapters is also included and should not be overlooked.

Before beginning any maintenance or repair, the machine should be cleaned thoroughly, especially around the oil filter, spark plugs, cylinder head covers, side covers, carburetors, etc. Cleaning will help ensure that dirt does not contaminate the engine and will allow you to detect wear and damage that could otherwise easily go unnoticed.

2 Honda GL1200 Routine maintenance intervals

Note: *The pre-ride inspection outlined in the owner's manual covers checks and maintenance that should be carried out on a daily basis. It's condensed and included here to remind you of its importance. Always perform the pre-ride inspection at every maintenance interval (in addition to the procedures listed). The intervals listed below are the shortest intervals recommended by the manufacturer for each particular operation during the model years covered in this manual. Your owner's manual may have different intervals for your model.*

Daily or before riding

Check the engine oil level
Check the coolant level
Check the fuel level and inspect for leaks
Check the operation of both brakes - also check the fluid level and look for leakage
Check the tires for damage, the presence of foreign objects and correct air pressure
Check the throttle for smooth operation and correct freeplay
Check the operation of the clutch - check the fluid level and look for leakage
Make sure the steering operates smoothly, without looseness and without binding
Check for proper operation of the headlight, taillight, brake light, turn signals, indicator lights, speedometer and horn
Make sure the sidestand returns to its fully up position and stays there under spring pressure
Make sure the engine kill switch works properly

After the initial 1000 km/600 miles

Perform all of the daily checks plus:
Check/adjust the engine idle speed
Change the engine oil and oil filter
Check the tightness of all fasteners
Check the steering
Check the brake fluid level
Check/adjust the brake pedal position
Check the operation of the brake light

Every 6000 km/4000 miles or 6 months

Replace the spark plugs
Inspect the crankcase breather system
Check idle speed
Check the battery electrolyte level and specific gravity; inspect the breather tube
Check the brake fluid level
Check the brake discs and pads
Check the clutch for fluid level and leaks

Every 12,000 km/8,000 miles or 12 months

Change the engine oil and filter
Replace the air filter element
Inspect the cooling system hoses
Check/adjust throttle cable freeplay
Check choke operation
Check/adjust the carburetor synchronization
Check/adjust the brake pedal position
Check the operation of the brake light
Lubricate the clutch and front brake lever pivots
Lubricate the throttle cables
Lubricate the shift/brake pedal pivots and the sidestand pivots
Check the operation of the sidestand switch
Check the steering for looseness or binding
Check the front forks for proper operation and fluid leaks
Check the tires, wheels and wheel bearings
Check the exhaust system for leaks and check the tightness of the fasteners
Check the cleanliness of the fuel system and the condition of the fuel lines and vacuum hoses
Inspect the evaporative emission control system (California models)
Inspect the secondary air induction system
Check rear suspension operation and swingarm play
Check the final drive oil level
Check all nuts, bolts and other fasteners for tightness
Inspect the air drier (on-board air compressor)
Check headlight aim

Every 18,000 km/12,000 miles or 18 months

Change the brake and clutch fluid*

Every 24,000 km/16,000 miles

Clean the air pump element (onboard compressor system)

Every 36,000 km/24,000 miles

Replace the fuel filter (1984 and 1985 models)
Replace the cruise valve element (if equipped)

*Or every two years, whichever comes first.

Chapter 1 Tune-up and routine maintenance

1-5

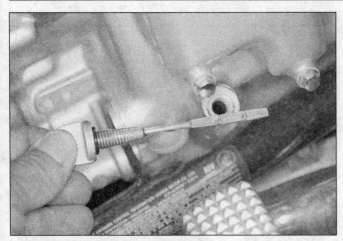

3.3 Check oil level on the dipstick; it should be between the Minimum and Maximum marks

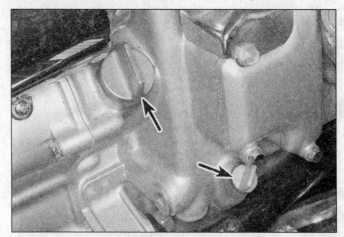

3.4 The dipstick (lower arrow) and oil filler cap (upper arrow) are located on the right side of the engine

3 Fluid levels - check

Engine oil

Refer to illustrations 3.3 and 3.4

1 Run the engine and allow it to reach normal operating temperature. **Warning:** *Do not run the engine in an enclosed space such as a garage or shop.*
2 Stop the engine and allow the machine to sit undisturbed for about five minutes.
3 Hold the motorcycle level. With the engine off, unscrew the dipstick located at the right crankcase cover. Wipe the dipstick with a clean rag, reinsert it (don't screw it in; just let it rest on the threads). Pull the dipstick out and check the oil level; it should be between the Maximum and Minimum marks on the dipstick **(see illustration)**.
4 If the level is below the Minimum mark, remove the oil filler cap from the right side of the crankcase **(see illustration)** and add enough oil of the recommended grade and type to bring the level up to the Maximum mark. Do not overfill.
5 Inspect the filler cap and dipstick O-rings. Replace them if they're cut, flattened or deteriorated. Install the filler cap and dipstick and tighten them securely with fingers.

Brake and clutch fluid

6 In order to ensure proper operation of the hydraulic disc brakes and the hydraulic clutch if equipped, the fluid level in the master cylinder reservoirs must be properly maintained.

Right front brake and clutch

Refer to illustrations 3.8a and 3.8b

7 With the motorcycle on its centerstand, turn the handlebars until the tops of the handlebar master cylinders are as level as possible.
8 Look closely at the inspection window in the master cylinder reservoirs. The right handlebar reservoir supplies the right front brake; the left handlebar reservoir supplies the clutch. Make sure that the fluid level is above the Lower mark on the reservoir **(see illustrations)**.
9 If the level is low, the fluid must be replenished. Before removing the master cylinder cap, wrap the reservoir with a rag to protect the surrounding area from brake fluid spills (which will damage the paint) and remove all dust and dirt from the area around the cap.
10 To top up left front brake or clutch fluid, remove the screws and lift off the cap and rubber diaphragm. **Note:** *Do not operate the brakes or clutch with the cap removed.*
11 Add new, clean brake fluid of the recommended type until the level is up to the upper level line, which is cast inside the reservoir body. Do not mix different brands of brake fluid in the reservoir, as they may not be compatible.

3.8a With the master cylinder in a level position, check fluid level in the inspection window (be sure the fluid level in the window is above the Lower mark) - this is the master cylinder for the right front brake . . .

3.8b . . . and this is the clutch master cylinder, mounted on the left handlebar - screws secure the cover

12 Replace the rubber diaphragm and the cover. Tighten the screws evenly, but do not overtighten them.
13 Wipe any spilled fluid off the reservoir body. If the brake fluid level was low, inspect the brake or clutch system for leaks.

Chapter 1 Tune-up and routine maintenance

3.15 The fluid level in the rear brake master cylinder can be checked by looking through the plastic reservoir - fluid must be above the Lower mark

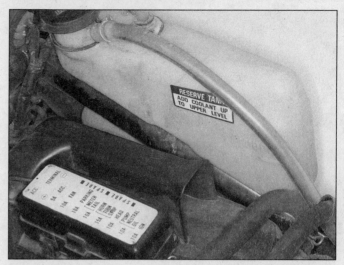

3.20 Coolant should be between the Lower and Upper marks on the reservoir

Left front and rear brakes

Refer to illustration 3.15

14 Remove the right rear side cover for access to the brake pedal reservoir (see Chapter 8). This reservoir supplies the right front brake and the rear brake.

15 The fluid level should be visible through the translucent reservoir **(see illustration)**. If it's below the Lower mark, clean the area around the cap, then place rags around the reservoir to protect painted parts from brake fluid spills. Unscrew the cap.

16 Add new, clean brake fluid of the recommended type until the level is up to the Upper mark cast in the reservoir body. Do not mix different brands of brake fluid in the reservoir, as they may not be compatible.

17 Replace the cap. If the brake fluid level was low, inspect the brake system for leaks.

Coolant

Refer to illustrations 3.20 and 3.21

18 The engine must be at normal operating temperature for the results to be accurate, so warm it up before performing this check. The measurement is taken with the bike on the centerstand and the engine running.

19 Remove the tool tray from the top compartment so you can see the reservoir tank.

20 Pull back the tab and lift the dipstick out of the filler hole (the dipstick is attached to the reservoir filler cap) **(see illustration)**. **Warning:** *Never remove the radiator cap when the engine is hot. Scalding coolant will spray out and may cause serious burns.*

21 The coolant level is satisfactory if it is between the Low and Full marks on the dipstick. If the level is at or below the Low mark, detach the fuse block and move it out of the way so it won't get spilled on **(see illustration)**. Add the recommended coolant mixture (see this Chapter's Specifications) until the Full level is reached. If the coolant level seems to be consistently low, start by checking around the reservoir tank mounting bolt hole for cracks. If there aren't any, check the entire cooling system for leaks.

Final drive oil

Refer to illustration 3.22

Warning: *Be sure the exhaust system is cool before starting this procedure. You'll be working close to the right muffler and touching it may cause serious burns.*

3.21 Move the fuse block aside so it isn't spilled on

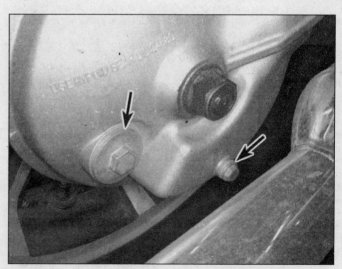

3.22 Final drive filler plug (left arrow) and drain plug (right arrow)

Chapter 1 Tune-up and routine maintenance

4.3 Battery electrolyte level can be seen through the battery case; it should be between the Upper level and Lower level marks

22 Place the motorcycle on its centerstand. Clean any dirt from around the filler plug, then unscrew the filler plug from the right side of the final drive **(see illustration)**. Look or reach into the filler hole and note the oil level. It should be up to the bottom of the hole.

23 If the oil level is low, add oil of the type recommended in this Chapter's Specifications, using a funnel with a flexible tube if necessary.

24 Thread the filler plug into the hole and tighten it to the torque listed in this Chapter's Specifications.

4 Battery electrolyte level/specific gravity - check

Refer to illustrations 4.3, 4.6 and 4.11

Caution: *Be extremely careful when handling or working around the battery. The electrolyte is very caustic and an explosive gas (hydrogen) is given off when the battery is charging.* **Note:** *The first Steps describe battery removal. If the electrolyte level is known to be sufficient it won't be necessary to remove the battery.*

1 This procedure applies to batteries that have removable filler caps, which can be removed to add water to the battery. This type is original equipment on the motorcycles covered in this manual. The sealed maintenance-free batteries used on some models can't be topped up.

2 Remove the left side cover for access to the battery (see Chapter 8).

3 The electrolyte level is visible through the translucent battery case. It should be between the Upper and Lower level marks **(see illustration)**.

4 If the electrolyte is low, remove the cell caps and fill each cell to the upper level mark with distilled water. Do not use tap water (except in an emergency), and do not overfill. The cell holes are quite small, so it may help to use a plastic squeeze bottle with a small spout to add the water. If the level is within the marks on the case, additional water is not necessary.

5 Next, check the specific gravity of the electrolyte in each cell with a small hydrometer made especially for motorcycle batteries. These are available from most dealer parts departments or motorcycle accessory stores.

6 Remove the caps, draw some electrolyte from the first cell into the hydrometer **(see illustration)** and note the specific gravity. Compare the reading to the Specifications listed in this Chapter. **Note:** *Add 0.004 points to the reading for every 10-degrees F above 20-degrees C (68-degrees F) - subtract 0.004 points from the reading for every 10-degrees below 20-degrees C (68-degrees F). Return the electrolyte to the appropriate cell and repeat the check for the remaining cells. When the check is complete, rinse the hydrometer thoroughly with clean water.*

7 If the specific gravity of the electrolyte in each cell is as specified, the battery is in good condition and is apparently being charged by the machine's charging system.

8 If the specific gravity is low, the battery is not fully charged. This may be due to corroded battery terminals, a dirty battery case, a malfunctioning charging system, or loose or corroded wiring connections. On the other hand, it may be that the battery is worn out, especially if the machine is old, or that infrequent use of the motorcycle prevents normal charging from taking place.

9 Be sure to correct any problems and charge the battery if necessary. Refer to Chapter 9 for additional battery maintenance and charging procedures.

10 Install the battery cell caps, tightening them securely.

11 Make sure the battery vent tube is secure in its retainer **(see illustration)**. Be very careful not to pinch or otherwise restrict the battery vent tube, as the battery may build up enough internal pressure during normal charging system operation to explode. Refer to the vent tube routing decal on the motorcycle to make sure the vent tube is routed correctly **(see illustration 1.3b)**.

12 Install the side cover.

4.6 Check the specific gravity with a hydrometer

4.11 The battery vent tube slips over a fitting on the battery case; it's secured by a grommet to a bracket on the battery box

Chapter 1 Tune-up and routine maintenance

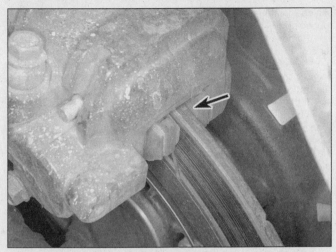

5.2a Inspect the groove between the friction material and the metal backing (arrow) (this is a front pad) . . .

5.2b . . . if the friction material is worn near the groove (arrow), replace the pads (this is a rear pad)

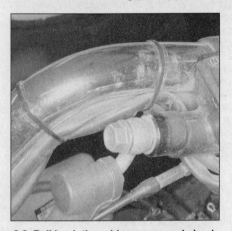

6.3 Pull back the rubber cover and check the hose fitting for leaks

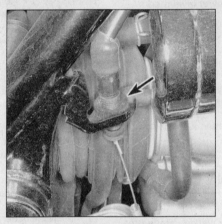

6.6 Hold the switch body and turn the nut (arrow) to adjust the switch

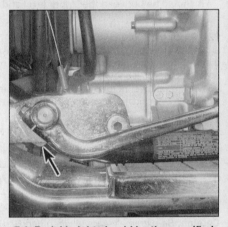

7.1 Pedal height should be the specified distance from the top of the footpeg; to adjust pedal height, loosen the locknut and turn the adjusting rod (arrow) (hidden behind pedal bracket)

5 Brake pads - wear check

Refer to illustrations 5.2a and 5.2b

1 The front and rear brake pads should be checked at the recommended intervals and replaced with new ones when worn beyond the limit listed in this Chapter's Specifications.
2 To check the brake pads, look at them from the edges **(see illustrations)**. There's a small gap between the edge of the friction material and the metal backing. If the friction material is worn near or all the way to the gap, the pads are worn excessively and must be replaced with new ones (see Chapter 7).

6 Brake system - general check

Refer to illustrations 6.3 and 6.6

1 A routine general check of the brakes will ensure that any problems are discovered and remedied before the rider's safety is jeopardized.
2 Check the brake lever and pedal for loose connections, excessive play, bends, and other damage. Replace any damaged parts with new ones (see Chapter 7).
3 Make sure all brake fasteners are tight. Check the brake pads for wear (see Section 5) and make sure the fluid level in the reservoirs is correct (see Section 3). Look for leaks at the hose connections and check for cracks in the hoses **(see illustration)**. If the lever or pedal is spongy, bleed the brakes as described in Chapter 7.
4 Make sure the brake light operates when the brake lever is depressed. The front brake light switch is not adjustable. If it doesn't work, check and replace it if necessary (see Chapter 9).
5 Press the brake pedal and make sure the brake light is activated just as the brake takes effect.
6 If adjustment is necessary, remove the right chamber protector and inner cover (see Chapter 8). Hold the switch and turn the adjusting nut on the switch body **(see illustration)** until the brake light is activated when required (don't turn the switch body). If the switch doesn't operate the brake lights, check it as described in Chapter 9.

7 Brake pedal position - check and adjustment

Refer to illustration 7.1

1 The rear brake pedal should be positioned above the top of the original equipment footpeg the distance listed in this Chapter's Specifications **(see illustration)**. **Note:** *If the stock footpegs have been replaced with floorboards (a common aftermarket accessory), adjust the pedal height so there's no brake drag.*

Chapter 1 Tune-up and routine maintenance

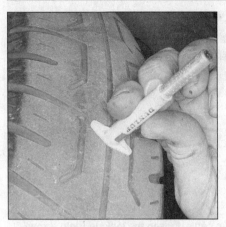

8.2 Measure tread depth; if the raised wear indicators (arrow) are even with the tread surface, the tire needs to be replaced

8.4 Use an accurate gauge to check the air pressure in the tires

9.2 Check for a small amount of freeplay at the throttle grip (arrows)

2 To adjust the position of the pedal, loosen the locknut on the adjuster, turn the adjuster to set the pedal position and tighten the locknut.
3 If necessary, adjust the brake light switch (see Section 6).

8 Tires/wheels - general check

Refer to illustrations 8.2 and 8.4

1 Routine tire and wheel checks should be made with the realization that your safety depends to a great extent on their condition.
2 Check the tires carefully for cuts, tears, embedded nails or other sharp objects and excessive wear. Operation of the motorcycle with excessively worn tires is extremely hazardous, as traction and handling are directly affected. Measure the tread depth at the center of the tire and replace worn tires with new ones when the tread depth is less than specified **(see illustration)**.
3 Repair or replace punctured tires as soon as damage is noted. Do not try to patch a torn tire, as wheel balance and tire reliability may be impaired.
4 Check the tire pressures when the tires are cold and keep them properly inflated **(see illustration)**. Proper air pressure will increase tire life and provide maximum stability and ride comfort. Keep in mind that low tire pressures may cause the tire to slip on the rim or come off, while high tire pressures will cause abnormal tread wear and unsafe handling.
5 The cast wheels used on this machine are virtually maintenance free, but they should be kept clean and checked periodically for cracks and other damage. Never attempt to repair damaged cast wheels; they must be replaced with new ones.
6 Check the valve stem locknuts to make sure they are tight. Also, make sure the valve stem cap is in place and tight. If it is missing, install a new one made of metal or hard plastic.

9 Throttle and choke operation and freeplay - check and adjustment

Throttle

Refer to illustrations 9.2, 9.3 and 9.4

1 Make sure the throttle grip rotates easily from fully closed to fully open with the front wheel turned at various angles. The grip should return automatically from fully open to fully closed when released. If the throttle sticks, check the throttle cables for cracks or kinks in the housings. Also, make sure the inner cables are clean and well-lubricated.

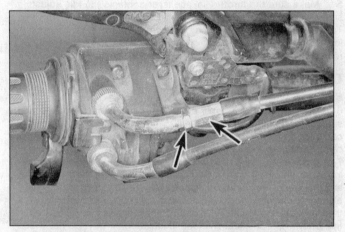

9.3 To make minor throttle cable adjustments, loosen the locknut (left arrow) and turn the adjuster (right arrow)

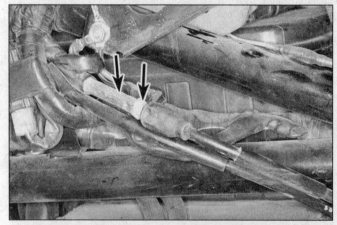

9.4 To make major adjustments, loosen the locknut (right arrow) and turn the adjuster (left arrow)

2 Check for a small amount of freeplay at the grip and compare the freeplay to the value listed in this Chapter's Specifications **(see illustration)**. If adjustment is necessary, adjust idle speed first as described in Section 17.
3 To make fine adjustments, loosen the upper locknut on the handlebar cable adjuster **(see illustration)**. Turn the adjuster until the desired freeplay is obtained, then retighten the locknut.
4 To make major adjustments, loosen the locknut on the middle cable adjuster **(see illustration)**. Turn the adjuster until the desired

1-10   Chapter 1 Tune-up and routine maintenance

9.7 Measure the stroke of the choke valves

9.8 To adjust the choke cable, loosen the locknut (right arrow) and turn the adjuster (left arrow)

freeplay is obtained, then retighten the locknut.
5   Make sure the throttle linkage lever contacts the idle adjusting screw when the throttle grip is in the closed throttle position. **Warning:** *Turn the handlebars all the way through their travel with the engine idling. Idle speed should not change. If it does, the cables may be routed incorrectly. Correct this condition before riding the bike.*

Choke

Refer to illustrations 9.7 and 9.8

6   Operate the choke lever on the left handlebar. It should move smoothly, without sticking or binding. If it doesn't, check the choke cable for cracks or kinks in the housing. Also, make sure the inner cable is clean and well-lubricated.
7   If you're working on an Interstate or Aspencade, remove the fairing lower and inner covers (see Chapter 8). Operate the choke lever and make sure the starting enrichment valve on the carburetor assembly moves smoothly from fully closed to fully open and back. Measure the travel of each choke valve and compare it with the value listed in this Chapter's Specifications **(see illustration).** If travel is not within the specified range, adjust the cable as described below.
8   Loosen the locknut on the cable adjuster at the left handlebar **(see illustration).** Turn the adjuster to get the correct enrichment valve travel, then tighten the locknut.

10 Clutch - check and adjustment

1   The hydraulic clutch release mechanism eliminates the need for freeplay adjustment. No means of manual adjustment is provided.
2   Check the fluid level (see Section 3). Check for fluid leaks around the master cylinder on the left handlebar. Pull back the rubber cover and inspect the fluid line connection, then follow the fluid line to the release cylinder on the rear of the engine. If leaks are found, refer to Chapter 2 for repair procedures.
3   Start the bike, release the clutch and ride off, noting the position of the clutch lever when the clutch begins to engage. If it's too close to the handlebar, there may be air in the clutch fluid (the air compresses, rather than transmitting lever force to the release mechanism). Refer to Chapter 2 and bleed the system.

11 Engine oil/filter - change

Refer to illustrations 11.4, 11.5a, 11.5b, 11.5c and 11.7

1   Consistent routine oil and filter changes are the single most important maintenance procedure you can perform on a motorcycle. The oil not only lubricates the internal parts of the engine, transmission and clutch, but it also acts as a coolant, a cleaner, a sealant, and a protectant. Because of these demands, the oil takes a terrific amount of abuse and should be replaced often with new oil of the recommended grade and type. Saving a little money on the difference in cost between a good oil and a cheap oil won't pay off if the engine is damaged.
2   Before changing the oil and filter, warm up the engine so the oil will drain easily. Be careful when draining the oil, as the exhaust pipes, the engine, and the oil itself can cause severe burns.
3   Place the bike on its centerstand. Remove the oil filler cap to vent the crankcase and act as a reminder that there is no oil in the engine.
4   Place a clean drain pan under the drain plug and oil filter. Remove the drain plug from the engine and allow the oil to drain into the pan **(see illustration).** Discard the sealing washer on the drain plug; it should be replaced whenever the plug is removed.
5   Unscrew the filter bolt partway and let the oil drain from the filter

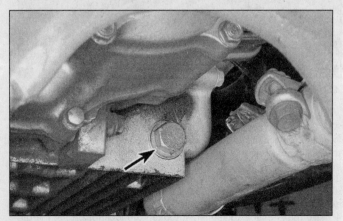

11.4 Remove the oil pan drain plug (arrow) and sealing washer

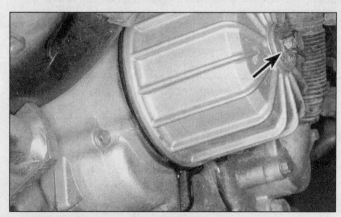

11.5a Partially loosen the oil filter bolt (arrow) and let the filter housing drain

Chapter 1 Tune-up and routine maintenance

11.5b Remove the filter housing and take out the filter

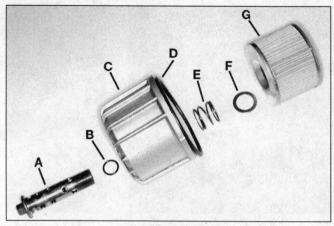

11.5c Oil filter details

A	Filter bolt	E	Spring
B	Small O-ring	F	Washer
C	Filter housing	G	Filter element
D	Large O-ring		

housing **(see illustration)**. Once it's stopped draining, remove the filter bolt, take off the housing and remove the element **(see illustrations)**.

6   Apply a film of oil to the small O-ring **(see illustration 11.5c)**. Install the small O-ring on the filter bolt, then install the filter bolt in the housing and slip the spring and washer over it.

7   Coat the large O-ring with oil and install it in the groove of the filter housing. Position the filter housing on the engine with its tabs on either side of the locating boss on the water pump cover **(see illustration)**. Tighten the filter bolt to the torque listed in this Chapter's Specifications.

8   Slip a new sealing washer over the oil drain plug, then install and tighten it to the torque listed in this Chapter's Specifications. Avoid overtightening, as damage to the engine case will result.

9   Before refilling the engine, check the old oil carefully. If the oil was drained into a clean pan, small pieces of metal or other material can be easily detected. If the oil is very metallic colored, then the engine is experiencing wear from break-in (new engine) or from insufficient lubrication. If there are flakes or chips of metal in the oil, then something is drastically wrong internally and the engine will have to be disassembled for inspection and repair.

10 If there are pieces of fiber-like material in the oil, the clutch is experiencing excessive wear and should be checked.

11 If the inspection of the oil turns up nothing unusual, refill the crankcase to the proper level with the recommended oil and install the filler cap. Start the engine and let it idle for a few minutes (do not rev the engine). Shut it off, wait a few minutes, then check the oil level. If necessary, add more oil to bring the level up to the Maximum mark. Check around the drain plug and filter for leaks.

12 The old oil drained from the engine cannot be reused in its present state and should be disposed of. Check with your local refuse disposal company, disposal facility or environmental agency to see whether they will accept the used oil for recycling. Don't pour used oil into drains or onto the ground. After the oil has cooled, it can be drained into a suitable container (capped plastic jugs, topped bottles, milk cartons, etc.) for transport to one of these disposal sites.

12 Pulse air system - inspection

1   If you're working on an Interstate or Aspencade, remove the lower and inner covers from the left side of the fairing (see Chapter 8).

2   Position the fan shroud toward the front of the bike to gain access (see Chapter 3).

3   Using an inspection mirror where necessary, check the rubber hoses that connect the metal lines, check valves and control valve. Refer to Chapter 4 for complete details of the system.

13 Air filter element - servicing

Refer to illustrations 13.3a, 13.3b and 13.3c

1   Open the top compartment and remove the tool tray (see Chapter 8).

2   Detach the fuse block and move it out of the way **(see illustration 3.21)**.

3   Pull the breather tube fitting out of the air cleaner housing **(see illustration)**. Remove the wing nut, lift off the cover and remove the

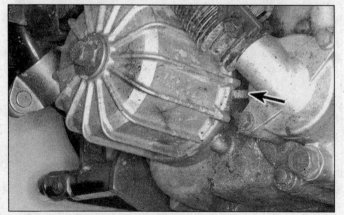

11.7 Position the filter tabs on either side of the water pump cover boss (arrow)

13.3a Undo the wing nut . . .

Chapter 1 Tune-up and routine maintenance

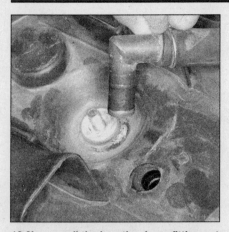

13.3b ... pull the breather hose fitting out of the filter element grommet inside the case ...

13.3c ... and lift out the element

14.1 The crankcase breather (arrow) is located forward of the left swingarm pivot

element **(see illustrations)**.
4   Clean the inside of the filter housing.
5   Install the new filter element by reversing the removal procedure. Make sure the element is seated properly in the filter housing before installing the cover.
6   Install all components removed for access. When you reconnect the breather hose, push the fitting securely into the grommet in the filter element.

14 Crankcase breather - servicing

Refer to illustration 14.1
1   At the specified interval, squeeze the clamp at the bottom of the drain tube and disconnect it from the storage tank **(see illustration)**.
2   Remove the tank and dump out accumulated deposits.
3   Installation is the reverse of the removal step.

15 Cylinder compression - check

Refer to Illustration 15.8
1   Among other things, poor engine performance may be caused by leaking valves, incorrect valve clearances, leaking head gaskets, or worn pistons, rings and/or cylinder walls. A cylinder compression check will help pinpoint these conditions and can also indicate the presence of excessive carbon deposits in the cylinder heads.
2   The only tools required are a compression gauge and a spark plug wrench. Depending on the outcome of the initial test, a squirt-type oil can may also be needed.
3   Start the engine and allow it to reach normal operating temperature.
4   Place the bike on its centerstand.
5   Remove the spark plug cap covers for access to the spark plugs.
6   Remove the spark plugs (see Section 16, if necessary). Work carefully; don't strip the spark plug hole threads and don't burn your hands.
7   Disable the ignition by unplugging the primary wires from the coils (see Chapter 5). Be sure to mark the locations of the wires before detaching them.
8   Install the compression gauge in one of the spark plug holes **(see illustration)**.
9   Hold or block the throttle wide open.
10 Crank the engine over a minimum of four or five revolutions (or until the gauge reading stops increasing) and observe the initial movement of the compression gauge needle as well as the final total gauge reading. Repeat the procedure for the other cylinders and compare the results to the value listed in this Chapter's Specifications.
11 If the compression in all cylinders built up quickly and evenly to the specified amount, you can assume the engine upper end is in reasonably good mechanical condition. Worn or sticking piston rings and worn cylinders will produce very little initial movement of the gauge needle, but compression will tend to build up gradually as the engine spins over. Valve and valve seat leakage, or head gasket leakage, is indicated by low initial compression which does not tend to build up.
12 To further confirm your findings, add a small amount of engine oil to each cylinder by inserting the nozzle of a squirt-type oil can through the spark plug holes. The oil will tend to seal the piston rings if they are leaking. Repeat the test for the other cylinders.
13 If the compression increases significantly after the addition of the oil, the piston rings and/or cylinders are definitely worn. If the compression does not increase, the pressure is leaking past the valves or the head gasket. Leakage past the valves may be due to insufficient valve clearances, burned, warped or cracked valves or valve seats or valves that are hanging up in the guides.
14 If compression readings are considerably higher than specified, the combustion chambers are probably coated with excessive carbon deposits. It is possible (but not very likely) for carbon deposits to raise the compression enough to compensate for the effects of leakage past rings or valves. Remove the cylinder head and carefully decarbonize the combustion chambers (see Chapter 2).

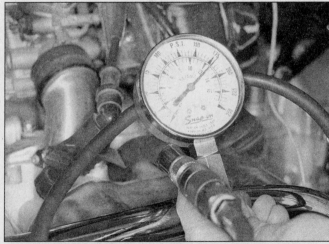

15.8 A compression gauge with a threaded fitting for the spark plug hole is preferred over the type that requires hand pressure to maintain the seal

Chapter 1 Tune-up and routine maintenance

16.2 Remove the spark plug cap covers

16.3a Rotate the spark plug caps back and forth to loosen them, then pull them off the plugs and check them for brittleness and cracking; there's a cylinder number on each wire (arrow)

16.3b Use an extension and a swivel-headed deep socket (preferably one with a rubber insert to prevent damage to the plug) to remove the spark plugs; a deep socket and universal joint will also work

16.7a Spark plug manufacturers recommend using a wire type gauge when checking the gap - if the wire doesn't slide between the electrodes with a slight drag, adjustment is required

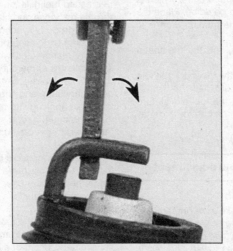

16.7b To change the gap, bend the side electrode only, as indicated by the arrows, and be very careful not to crack or chip the ceramic insulator surrounding the center electrode

16.7c A small dab of anti-seize compound will make the plugs easier to remove later

16 Spark plugs - replacement

Refer to illustrations 16.2, 16.3a, 16.3b, 16.7a, 16.7b, 16.7c and 16.8

1 Make sure your spark plug socket is the correct size before attempting to remove the plugs.
2 Remove the spark plug cap covers for access to the plugs **(see illustration)**.
3 Disconnect the spark plug caps from the spark plugs **(see illustration)**. If available, use compressed air to blow any accumulated debris from around the spark plugs. Remove the plugs **(see illustration)**.
4 Inspect the electrodes for wear. Both the center and side electrodes should have square edges and the side electrode should be of uniform thickness. Look for excessive deposits and evidence of a cracked or chipped insulator around the center electrode. Compare your spark plugs to the color spark plug reading chart. Check the threads, the washer and the ceramic insulator body for cracks and other damage.
5 If the electrodes are not excessively worn, and if the deposits can be easily removed with a wire brush, the plugs can be regapped and reused (if no cracks or chips are visible in the insulator). If in doubt concerning the condition of the plugs, replace them with new ones, as the expense is minimal.
6 Cleaning spark plugs by sandblasting is permitted, provided you clean the plugs with a high flash-point solvent afterwards.
7 Before installing new plugs, make sure they are the correct type and heat range. Check the gap between the electrodes, as they are not preset. For best results, use a wire-type gauge rather than a flat gauge to check the gap **(see illustration)**. If the gap must be adjusted, bend the side electrode only and be very careful not to chip or crack the insulator nose **(see illustration)**. Make sure the washer is in place before installing each plug. A small amount of anti-seize compound on the threads will make the plugs easy to remove later **(see illustration)**.
8 Since the cylinder head is made of aluminum, which is soft and easily damaged, thread the plugs into the heads by hand. Since the

plugs are recessed, slip a short length of hose over the end of the plug to use as a tool to thread it into place **(see illustration)**. The hose will grip the plug well enough to turn it, but will start to slip if the plug begins to cross-thread in the hole. This will prevent damaged threads and the accompanying repair costs.

9 Once the plugs are finger-tight, the job can be finished with a socket. Tighten the plugs an additional 1/2 turn to compress the washers. Do not over-tighten them.

10 Reconnect the spark plug caps and reinstall all removed components.

17 Idle speed - check and adjustment

Refer to illustration 17.3

1 The idle speed should be checked and adjusted before and after the carburetors are synchronized and when it is obviously too high or too low. Before adjusting the idle speed, make sure the spark plug gaps are correct. Also, turn the handlebars back-and-forth and see if the idle speed changes as this is done. If it does, the accelerator cable may not be routed correctly, or it may be worn out. This is a dangerous condition that can cause loss of control of the bike. Be sure to correct this problem before proceeding.

2 The engine should be at normal operating temperature, which is usually reached after 10 to 15 minutes of stop and go riding. Place the motorcycle on its centerstand and make sure the transmission is in Neutral.

3 Turn the throttle stop screw **(see illustration)** until the idle speed listed in this Chapter's Specifications is obtained.

4 Snap the throttle open and shut a few times, then recheck the idle speed. If necessary, repeat the adjustment procedure.

5 If a smooth, steady idle can't be achieved, the fuel/air mixture may be incorrect. Refer to Chapter 4 for additional carburetor information.

18 Carburetor synchronization - check and adjustment

Refer to illustrations 18.9, 18.10, 18.13a and 18.13b

Warning 1: *Gasoline is extremely flammable, so take extra precautions when you work on any part of the fuel system. Don't smoke or allow open flames or bare light bulbs near the work area, and don't work in a garage where a natural gas-type appliance (such as a water heater or clothes dryer) is present. If you spill any fuel on your skin, rinse it off immediately with soap and water. When you perform any kind of work on the fuel system, wear safety glasses and have a class B type fire extinguisher on hand.*

1 Carburetor synchronization is simply the process of adjusting the

16.8 Threading the plugs in with a piece of hose will save time and prevent damage

carburetors so they pass the same amount of fuel/air mixture to each cylinder. This is done by measuring the vacuum produced in each cylinder. Carburetors that are out of synchronization will result in decreased fuel mileage, increased engine temperature, less than ideal throttle response and higher vibration levels.

2 To properly synchronize the carburetors, you will need some sort of vacuum gauge setup, preferably with a gauge for each cylinder, or a mercury manometer, which is a calibrated tube arrangement that utilizes columns of mercury to indicate engine vacuum.

3 A manometer can be purchased from a motorcycle dealer or accessory shop and should have the necessary rubber hoses supplied with it for hooking into the vacuum hose fittings on the carburetors.

4 A vacuum gauge setup can also be purchased from a dealer or fabricated from commonly available hardware and automotive vacuum gauges.

5 The manometer is the more reliable and accurate instrument, and for that reason is preferred over the vacuum gauge setup; however, since the mercury used in the manometer is a liquid, and extremely toxic, extra precautions must be taken during use and storage of the instrument.

6 Because of the nature of the synchronization procedure and the need for special instruments, most owners leave the task to a dealer service department or a reputable motorcycle repair shop.

7 If you're working on an Interstate or Aspencade, remove both fairing lower covers and inner covers (see Chapter 8).

8 Start the engine and let it run until it reaches normal operating temperature, then shut it off.

9 Remove the screws from the vacuum ports and install vacuum hose fittings in their place **(see illustration)**.

17.3 This screw is used to set idle speed

18.9 Remove the vacuum port screws and install hose fittings (arrows)

Chapter 1 Tune-up and routine maintenance

18.10 A gauge setup like this one is used to synchronize the carburetors

18.13a These are the synchronizing screws for the no. 1 carburetor (A) and no. 3 carburetor (B)

10 Hook up the vacuum gauge set or the manometer according to the manufacturer's instructions **(see illustration)**. Make sure there are no leaks in the setup, as false readings will result.

11 Start the engine and make sure the idle speed is correct. If it isn't, adjust it (see Section 17).

12 The vacuum readings for all carburetors should be the same, or at least within the tolerance listed in this Chapter's Specifications. If the vacuum readings vary, adjust as necessary.

13 To perform the adjustment, synchronize the no. 1, 2 and 3 carburetors to the no. 4 carburetor by turning the synchronizing screws, as needed, until the vacuum is identical or nearly identical for all cylinders **(see illustrations)**. **Note:** *The no. 4 carburetor cannot be adjusted. It is the basis for adjusting the other three.* Snap the throttle open and shut 2 or 3 times, then recheck the adjustment and readjust as necessary.

14 When the adjustment is complete, recheck the vacuum readings and idle speed, then stop the engine. Remove the vacuum gauge or manometer and install the screw and vacuum hose.

15 Reinstall all components removed for access.

19 Lubrication - general

Refer to illustration 19.3

1 Since the controls, cables and various other components of a motorcycle are exposed to the elements, they should be lubricated periodically to ensure safe and trouble-free operation.

2 The footpegs, clutch and brake lever, brake pedal, shift lever and sidestand pivots should be lubricated frequently. In order for the lubricant to be applied where it will do the most good, the component should be disassembled. However, if chain and cable lubricant is being used, it can be applied to the pivot joint gaps and will usually work its way into the areas where friction occurs. If motor oil or light grease is being used, apply it sparingly as it may attract dirt (which could cause the controls to bind or wear at an accelerated rate). **Note:** *One of the best lubricants for the control lever pivots is a dry-film lubricant (available from many sources by different names).*

3 To lubricate the throttle and choke cables, disconnect the cable(s) at the lower end, then lubricate the cable with a pressure lube adapter **(see illustration)**.

4 The speedometer cable should be removed from its housing and lubricated with motor oil or cable lubricant.

5 Refer to Chapter 6 for the swingarm needle bearing lubrication procedures.

20 Fuel system - check and filter replacement

Warning: *Gasoline is extremely flammable, so take extra precautions when you work on any part of the fuel system. Don't smoke or allow open flames or bare light bulbs near the work area, and don't work in a garage where a natural gas-type appliance (such as a water heater or clothes dryer) is present. If you spill any fuel on your skin, rinse it off immediately with soap and water. When you perform any kind of work on the fuel system, wear safety glasses and have a class B type fire extinguisher on hand.*

Check

Refer to illustration 20.5

1 Check the fuel tank, the tank breather hose, the fuel tap, the lines and the carburetors for leaks and evidence of damage.

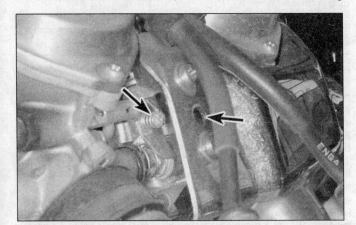

18.13b The synchronizing screw for the no. 2 carburetor (left arrow) is accessible through the hole in the bracket (right arrow)

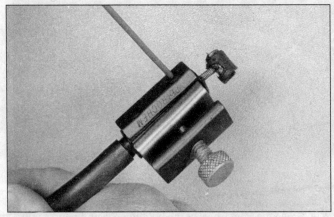

19.3 Lubricating a cable with a pressure lube adapter (make sure the tool seats around the inner cable)

1-16   Chapter 1 Tune-up and routine maintenance

20.5 Disconnect the inlet line (lower arrow) from the fuel pump and remove the mounting nut (upper arrow)

20.8 Pull the filter out, disconnect the hoses and remove the bracket

23.1 If the desiccant in the window is blue, it's in satisfactory condition; if it's pink or clear, it needs to be replaced

2 If carburetor gaskets are leaking, the carburetors should be disassembled and rebuilt (see Chapter 4).
3 If the fuel tap is leaking, tightening the screws may help. If leakage persists, the tap should be disassembled and repaired or replaced with a new one.
4 If the fuel lines are cracked or otherwise deteriorated, replace them with new ones.
5 Check the fuel filter for clogging **(see illustration)**. If there's visible sediment inside the filter, replace it. Honda doesn't specify a replacement interval for the filter on 1986 and 1987 models.

Filter replacement

Refer to illustration 20.8

6 Make sure the fuel tap and ignition switch are in the off position.
7 Disconnect the inlet hose from the fuel pump and remove the filter bracket's mounting nut **(see illustration 20.5)**.
8 Pull the inlet line and filter to the left so you can get at them, then remove the filter bracket and disconnect the hoses **(see illustration)**.
9 Install a new filter with the arrow molded into the filter case pointing toward the fuel pump. Reconnect the hoses. Run the engine and check for leaks.

21 Evaporative emission control system (California models) - check

1 Periodic checking of this system consists of inspecting the lines and tubes for wear, cracking, brittleness and loose connections.

2 Check the canister, mounted behind the engine on the right side, for obvious damage such as cracks. For further details of the system refer to Chapter 4.

22 Exhaust system - check

1 Periodically check all of the exhaust system joints for leaks and loose fasteners. The lower fairing panels will have to be removed to do this properly (see Chapter 8). If tightening the clamp bolts fails to stop any leaks, replace the gaskets with new ones (a procedure which requires disassembly of the system - see Chapter 4).
2 The exhaust pipe flange nuts at the cylinder heads are especially prone to loosening, which could cause damage to the head. Check them frequently and keep them tight.

23 On-board compressor system check and element cleaning

Refer to illustration 23.1

1 The desiccant in the compressor should be inspected **(see illustration)**.
2 For access, remove the right fairing pocket (see Chapter 8) and take the cover off the drier. If the desiccant is blue, it is in good condition. If it's colorless or pink, replace it following the procedure in Chapter 6.
3 Remove, clean and re-oil the filter element, following the procedure in Chapter 6.

24 Steering head bearings - check

Refer to illustration 24.4

1 This vehicle is equipped with tapered roller type steering head bearings which can become dented, rough or loose during normal use of the machine. In extreme cases, worn or loose steering head bearings can cause steering wobble that is potentially dangerous.
2 To check the bearings, support the motorcycle securely and block the machine so the front wheel is in the air.
3 Point the wheel straight ahead and slowly move the handlebars from side-to-side. Dents or roughness in the bearing races will be felt and the bars will not move smoothly.
4 Next, grasp the wheel and try to move it forward and backward **(see illustration)**. Any looseness in the steering head bearings will be felt as front-to-rear movement of the fork legs. If play is felt in the bearings, they should be adjusted, not a simple procedure on these models. Refer to Chapter 6 for details.

24.4 Grasp the front wheel or the bottom ends of the forks and try to pull the forks back and forth; if they move, the steering head bearings are loose and in need of adjustment

Chapter 1 Tune-up and routine maintenance

25 Fasteners - check

1 Since vibration of the machine tends to loosen fasteners, all nuts, bolts, screws, etc. should be periodically checked for proper tightness.
2 Pay particular attention to the following:
   Spark plugs
   Engine oil drain plug
   Oil filter cover bolt and drain plug
   Gearshift lever
   Footpegs, sidestand and centerstand
   Engine mount bolts
   Exhaust system mounts
   Shock absorber mount bolts
   Rear suspension linkage bolts
   Front axle and clamp bolt
   Rear axle nut
3 If a torque wrench is available, use it along with the torque specifications at the beginning of this, or other, Chapters.

26 Suspension - check

1 The suspension components must be maintained in top operating condition to ensure rider safety. Loose, worn or damaged suspension parts decrease the vehicle's stability and control.
2 While standing alongside the motorcycle, lock the front brake and push on the handlebars to compress the forks several times. See if they move up and down smoothly without binding. If binding is felt, the forks should be disassembled and inspected as described in Chapter 6.
3 Carefully inspect the area around the fork seals for any signs of fork oil leakage. If leakage is evident, the seals must be replaced as described in Chapter 6.
4 Check the tightness of all suspension nuts and bolts to be sure none have worked loose.
5 Inspect the rear shocks for fluid leakage and tightness of the mounting nuts. If leakage is found, the shocks should be replaced.
6 Support the bike securely so it can't be knocked over during this procedure. Grab the swingarm on each side, just ahead of the axle. Rock the swingarm from side to side. There should be no discernible movement at the rear. If there's a little movement or a slight clicking can be heard, make sure the pivot shaft nuts are tight. If the pivot nuts are tight but movement is still noticeable, the swingarm will have to be removed and the bearings replaced as described in Chapter 6.
7 Inspect the tightness of the rear suspension nuts and bolts.

27 Cooling system - inspection

Refer to illustrations 27.7 and 27.8
Warning: *The engine must be cool before beginning this procedure.*
Note: *Refer to Section 3 and check the coolant level before performing this check.*

1 The entire cooling system should be checked carefully at the recommended intervals. Look for evidence of leaks, check the condition of the coolant, check the radiator for clogged fins and damage and make sure the fan operates when required.
2 If you're working on a standard model, remove the left radiator side cover. If you're working on an Interstate or Aspencade, remove lower and inner left fairing covers for access to the cooling system components (see Chapter 8).
3 Examine each of the rubber coolant hoses along its entire length. Look for cracks, abrasions and other damage. Squeeze each hose at various points. They should feel firm, yet pliable, and return to their original shape when released. If they are dried out or hard, replace them with new ones.
4 Check for evidence of leaks at each cooling system joint. Tighten the hose clamps careful to prevent future leaks. If coolant has been leaking from the joints of steel or aluminum coolant tubes, remove the tubes and replace the O-rings (see Chapter 3).
5 Check the radiator for evidence of leaks and other damage. Leaks in the radiators leave telltale scale deposits or coolant stains on the outside of the core below the leak. If leaks are noted, remove the faulty radiator (see Chapter 3) and have it repaired by a radiator shop or replace it with a new one. **Caution:** *Do not use a liquid leak stopping compound to try to repair leaks.*
6 Check the radiator fins for mud, dirt and insects, which may impede the flow of air through the radiator. If the fins are dirty, force water or low pressure compressed air through the fins from the backside. If the fins are bent or distorted, straighten them carefully with a screwdriver.
7 Remove the pressure cap by turning it counterclockwise until it reaches a stop. If you hear a hissing sound (indicating there is still pressure in the system), wait until it stops. Now, press down on the cap with the palm of your hand and continue turning the cap counter-clockwise (anti-clockwise) until it can be removed. Check the condition of the coolant in the system. If it is rust colored or if accumulations of scale are visible, drain, flush and refill the system with new coolant. Check the cap gasket for cracks and other damage **(see illustration)**. Have the cap tested by a dealer service department or replace it with a new one. Install the cap by turning it clockwise until it reaches the first stop, then push down on the cap and continue turning until it can turn no further.
8 Check the antifreeze content of the coolant with an antifreeze hydrometer **(see illustration)**. Sometimes coolant may look like it's in good condition, but might be too weak to offer adequate protection. If the hydrometer indicates a weak mixture, drain, flush and refill the cooling system (see Section 28).

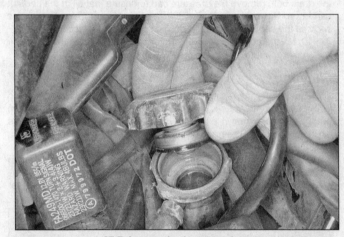

27.7 Inspect both cap gaskets

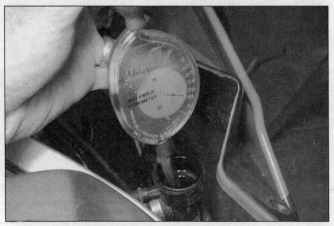

27.8 An antifreeze hydrometer is helpful in determining the condition of the coolant

9 Start the engine and let it reach normal operating temperature, then check for leaks again. As the coolant temperature increases, the fan should come on automatically and the temperature should begin to drop. If it doesn't, refer to Chapter 3 and check the fan and fan circuit carefully.
10 If the coolant level is consistently low, and no evidence of leaks can be found, have the entire system pressure checked by a Honda dealer service department, motorcycle repair shop or service station.

28 Cooling system - draining, flushing and refilling

Warning: *Allow the engine to cool completely before performing this maintenance operation. Also, don't allow antifreeze to come into contact with your skin or painted surfaces of the motorcycle. Rinse off spills immediately with plenty of water. Antifreeze is highly toxic if ingested. Never leave antifreeze lying around in an open container or in puddles on the floor; children and pets are attracted by its sweet smell and may drink it. Check with local authorities about disposing of used antifreeze. Many communities have collection centers which will see that antifreeze is disposed of safely. Antifreeze is also combustible, so don't store or use it near open flames.*

Draining

Refer to illustration 28.2

1 Place a large, clean drain pan under the water pump at the left front corner of the engine.
2 Remove the drain bolt from the bottom of the water pump **(see illustration)** and allow the coolant to drain into the pan. After removing the drain bolt, remove the pressure cap to ensure that all of the coolant can drain. **Note:** *The coolant will rush out with considerable force as soon as the cap is removed, so position the drain pan accordingly.*
3 Drain the coolant reservoir. Refer to Chapter 3 for the reservoir removal procedure. Wash the reservoir out with water.

Flushing

4 Flush the system with clean tap water by inserting a garden hose in the radiator filler neck. Allow the water to run through the system until it is clear when it exits the drain bolt holes. If the radiator is extremely corroded, remove it (see Chapter 3) and have it cleaned at a radiator shop.
5 Honda recommend flushing the cooling system with a flushing compound compatible with aluminum engines. However, these compounds are generally toxic. Check with local authorities to see whether it's necessary to collect the drained compound and take it to a hazardous waste disposal facility.
6 Check the drain bolt gasket. Replace it with a new one if necessary.
7 Clean the drain hole, then install the drain bolt and tighten it securely, but don't overtighten it and strip the threads.
8 Fill the cooling system with clean water mixed with a flushing compound. Make sure the flushing compound is compatible with aluminum components, and follow the manufacturer's instructions carefully.
9 Start the engine and let it run for about ten minutes.
10 Stop the engine. Let the machine cool for a while, then cover the pressure cap with a heavy rag and turn it counterclockwise to the first stop, releasing any pressure that may be present in the system. Once the hissing stops, push down on the cap and remove it completely.
11 Drain the system once again.
12 Fill the system with clean water, then repeat Steps 8 through 11 two more times (that is, run the engine for 10 minutes, drain it, then run it with clean water again and drain it again).

Refilling

13 Fill the system with the proper coolant mixture (see this Chapter's Specifications). When the system is full (all the way up to the top of the radiator cap filler neck), start the engine. Watch the coolant and level as the engine runs, and add coolant when the level drops. When the coolant level stabilizes, shut the engine off.
14 Fill the system with coolant to the top of the filler neck.
15 Allow the engine to cool, then check the coolant level in the reservoir (see Section 3). If the coolant level is low, add the specified mixture until it reaches the Full mark in the reservoir.
16 Check the system for leaks.
17 Do not dispose of the old coolant by pouring it down a drain. Instead, pour it into a heavy plastic container, cap it tightly and take it to an authorized disposal site or a service station.

29 Cruise valve element (1987 Aspencade) - replacement

1 Remove the seat, top compartment and side covers (see Chapter 8).
2 Pull the cover off one end of the cruise valve and the cap off the other end. Pull out the filter elements and install new ones.
3 Installation is the reverse of the removal steps.

30 Final drive - oil change

1 Place the bike on its centerstand and place a drain pan beneath the final drive **(see illustration 3.22)**.
2 Remove the filler plug, then the drain plug and let the oil drain into the pan for 10 minutes or more.
3 Reinstall the drain plug and tighten it to the torque listed in this Chapter's Specifications.
4 Add oil of the type and amount listed in this Chapter's Specifications. **Note:** *The specified capacity is approximate. Fill the final drive until the oil is at the bottom of the filler hole.*
5 Install the filler plug and tighten it to the torque listed in this Chapter's Specifications.

31 Headlight aim - check and adjust

The headlight aim should be adjusted periodically so it conforms with local regulations, for the safety of the rider as well as oncoming drivers. Some of the procedures require removal of the headlight trim or front grille. For detailed adjustment procedures, refer to Chapter 9.

28.2 Remove the drain bolt from the water pump and let the coolant drain

Chapter 2
Engine, clutch and transmission

Contents

	Section		Section
Alternator drive unit	See Chapter 9	Main and connecting rod bearings - general note	28
Camshafts, rocker arms and lash adjusters- removal, inspection and installation	9	Main oil pump - removal, inspection and installation	19
Clutch - removal, inspection and installation	14	Major engine repair - general note	4
Clutch release mechanism - bleeding, removal, inspection and installation	13	Oil and filter change	See Chapter 1
Connecting rod bearings - removal, inspection and installation	29	Operations possible with the engine in the frame	2
Crankcase - disassembly and reassembly	21	Operations requiring engine removal	3
Crankcase components - inspection and servicing	22	Output shaft - removal, inspection and installation	16
Crankshaft and main bearings - removal, inspection, main bearing selection and installation	30	Piston rings - installation	27
Cylinder head and valves - disassembly, inspection and reassembly	12	Piston/connecting rod assemblies - removal, connecting rod inspection and installation	24
Cylinder head covers - removal and installation	8	Pistons - inspection, removal and installation	26
Cylinder heads - removal and installation	10	Primary chain and gears - removal, inspection and installation	34
Cylinders - inspection	25	Rear case cover - removal, bearing inspection and installation	15
Engine - removal and installation	5	Recommended break-in procedure	36
Engine disassembly and reassembly - general information	6	Scavenging oil pump - removal, inspection and installation	17
External shift mechanism - removal, inspection and installation	20	Shift drum and forks - inspection	32
Front case cover - removal and installation	18	Spark plug replacement	See Chapter 1
General information	1	Starter clutch	See Chapter 9
Initial start-up after overhaul	35	Timing belts - removal, inspection and installation	7
Internal shift linkage - removal, inspection and installation	23	Transmission shafts - disassembly, inspection and reassembly	33
		Transmission shafts, shift drum and forks - removal and installation	31
		Valves/valve seats/valve guides - servicing	11

Specifications

Timing belts
Belt slack .... 3 to 5 mm (1/8 to 3/16 inch)

Camshaft holders
Rocker arm inside diameter
    Standard .... 1400 to 14.018 mm (0.5512 to 0.5519 inch)
    Limit .... 14.05 mm (0.553 inch)
Rocker arm shaft diameter
    Standard .... 13.973 to 13.984 mm (0.5501 to 0.5506 inch)
    Limit .... 13.84 mm (0.545 inch)
Lash adjuster stroke
    Standard .... Zero to 0.20 mm (zero to 0.10 inch)
    Limit .... 0.3 mm (0.12 inch)
Assist spring .... free length
    Standard .... 17.5 mm (0.69 inch)
    Limit .... 16.0 mm (0.63 inch)
Camshaft holder center collar clearance
    1984 and 1985 .... 0.10 mm (0.004 inch) minimum
    1986 and 1987 .... 0.30 to 0.35 mm (0.12 to 0.014 inch)

Chapter 2 Engine, clutch and transmission

Lash adjusters
Intake
- 8.5 to 9.5 mm (0.33 to 0.37 inch) .... No shims
- 9.5 to 10.5 mm (0.37 to 0.41 inch) .... 1 shim
- 10.5 to 11.5 mm (0.41 to 0.45 inch) .... 2 shims

Exhaust
- 10.5 to 11.5 mm (0.41 to 0.45 inch) .... No shims
- 11.5 to 12.5 mm (0.45 to 0.49 inch) .... 1 shim
- 12.5 to 13.5 mm (0.49 to 0.53 inch) .... 2 shims

Camshafts
Lobe height (1984 and 1985)
- Standard .... 35.8 mm (1.41 inches)
- Minimum .... 35.6 mm (1.40 inches)

Bearing oil clearance
- Center journals
  - Standard .... 0.050 to 0.087 mm (0.0020 to 0.0034 inch)
  - Limit .... 0.14 mm (0.006 inch)
- Forward and rear journals
  - Standard .... 0.030 to 0.067 mm (0.0012 to 0.0026 inch)
  - Limit .... 0.014 mm (0.006 inch)

Journal diameter
- Center journals
  - Standard .... 24.934 to 24.950 mm (0.9817 to 0.9823 inch)
  - Limit .... 24.91 mm (0.981 inch)
- Forward and rear journals
  - Standard .... 26.954 to 26.970 mm (1.0612 to 1.0618 inches)
  - Limit .... 26.91 mm (1.059 inch)

Bearing bore
- Center
  - Standard .... 25.000 to 25.021 mm (0.9843 to 0.9851 inch)
  - Limit .... 25.05 mm (0.986 inch)
- Front and rear
  - Standard .... 27.000 to 27.021 mm (1.0630 to 1.0638 inches)
  - Limit .... 27.05 mm (1.065 inch)

Camshaft runout limit .... Not specified

Cylinder head, valves and valve springs
Cylinder head warpage limit .... 0.10 mm (0.004 inch)
Valve stem bend limit .... Not specified
Valve stem diameter
- Standard
  - Intake .... 6.580 to 6.590 mm (0.2591 to 0.2594 inch)
  - Exhaust .... 6.550 to 6.560 mm (0.2579 to 0.2583 inch)
- Limit .... 6.54 mm (0.257 inch)

Valve guide inside diameter (intake and exhaust)
- Standard .... 6.600 to 6.615 mm (0.2598 to 0.2604 inch)
- Limit .... 6.64 mm (0.261 inch)

Stem-to-guide clearance
- Intake
  - Standard .... 0.010 to 0.035 mm (0.0004 to 0.0014 inch)
  - Limit .... 0.08 mm (0.003 inch)
- Exhaust
  - Standard .... 0.04 to 0.065m (0.0016 to 0.0026 inch)
  - Limit .... 0.10 mm (0.004 inch)

Valve seat width (intake and exhaust) .... 1.4 mm (0.06 inch)
Valve face width (intake and exhaust) .... Not specified

Valve spring free length (intake and exhaust)
- Inner springs
  - Standard .... 40.2 mm (1.58 inches)
  - Minimum .... 39.0 mm (1.54 inches)
- Outer springs
  - Standard .... 43.75 mm (1.2 inches)
  - Limit .... 42.5 mm (1.67 inches)

Valve spring bend limit .... Not specified

Cylinders
Bore diameter
- Standard .... 75.500 to 75.515 mm (2.9724 to 2.9730 inches)
- Limit .... 75.60 mm (2.976 inches)

Chapter 2 Engine, clutch and transmission

Bore measuring point	Top, center and bottom of ring travel
Out-of-round limit	0.15 mm (0.006 inch)
Taper limit	0.05 mm (0.002 inch)
Surface warp limit	0.10 mm (0.004 inch)

Pistons

Piston diameter
    Standard .... 75.470 to 75.490 mm (2.9713 to 2.9720 inches)
    Limit .... 75.35 mm (2.967 inches)
Diameter measuring point .... 10 mm (0.4 inch) from bottom of skirt
Piston-to-cylinder clearance
    Standard .... 0.010 to 0.045 mm (0.0004 to 0.0018 inch)
    Maximum .... 0.15 mm (0.006 inch)
Ring side clearance
    Standard .... 0.015 to 0.045 mm (0.0006 to 0.0018 inch)
    Limit .... 0.12 mm (0.005 inch)
Ring end gap
    Top and second rings
        Standard .... 0.10 to 0.30 mm (0.004 to 0.012 inch)
        Limit .... 0.6 mm (0.02 inch)
    Oil ring
        Standard .... 0.20 to 0.90 mm (0.008 to 0.035 inch)
        Limit .... 1.1 mm (0.004 inch)

Output shaft

Spring installed length
    1984 and 1985 .... 84.5 mm (3.33 inches)
    1986 .... 84.1 mm (3.31 inches)
    1987 .... 71.1 mm (2.80 inches)
Spring free length
    1984 and 1985
        Standard .... 110.9 mm (4.37 inches)
        Limit .... 100.0 mm (3.9 inches)
    1986
        Standard .... 100.2 mm (3.95 inches)
        Limit .... 94 mm (3.7 inches)
    1987
        Standard .... 87.8 mm (3.46 inches)
        Limit .... 82 mm (3.2 inches)

Crankshaft, connecting rods and bearings

Main bearing oil clearance
    Standard .... 0.020 to 0.044 mm (0.0008 to 0.0017 inch)
    Maximum .... 0.08 mm (0.003 inch)
Connecting rod side clearance
    Standard .... 0.15 to 0.30 mm (0.006 to 0.012 inch)
    Maximum .... 0.40 mm (0.016 inch)
Connecting rod bearing oil clearance
    Standard .... 0.020 to 0.044 mm (0.0008 to 0.003 inch)
    Maximum .... 0.08 mm (0.003 inch)
Crankshaft runout limit .... 0.05 mm (0.002 inch)
Crankshaft journal taper limit .... 0.004 mm (0.0002 inch)
Crankshaft journal out-of-round limit .... 0.008 mm (0.0003 inch)
Connecting rod weight selection
    Old weight code A, B or C .... New weight code B
    Old weight code D, E or F .... New weight code E
Connecting rod bearing selection
    If connecting rod ID number is 1
        With crankshaft journal ID letter A .... Yellow
        With crankshaft journal ID letter B .... Green
        With crankshaft journal ID letter C .... Brown
    If connecting ID number is 2
        With crankshaft journal ID letter A .... Green
        With crankshaft journal ID letter B .... Brown
        With crankshaft journal ID letter C .... Black
    If connecting rod ID number is 3
        With crankshaft journal ID letter A .... Brown
        With crankshaft journal ID letter B .... Black
        With crankshaft journal ID letter C .... Blue

Main bearing selection
If crankcase ID number is I
    With crankshaft journal ID number 1 .... Yellow
    With crankshaft journal ID number 2 .... Green
    With crankshaft journal ID number 3 .... Brown
If crankcase ID number is II
    With crankshaft journal ID number 1 .... Green
    With crankshaft journal ID number 2 .... Brown
    With crankshaft journal ID number 3 .... Black
If crankcase ID number is III
    With crankshaft journal ID number 1 .... Brown
    With crankshaft journal ID number 2 .... Black
    With crankshaft journal ID number 3 .... Blue

Oil pumps

Inner to outer rotor clearance
    Standard .... Less than 0.15 mm (0.006 inch)
    Limit .... 0.35 mm (0.014 inch)
Outer rotor to housing clearance
    Standard .... 0.15 to 0.21 mm (0.006 to 0.008 inch)
    Limit .... 0.41 mm (0.016 inch)
Rotor to straightedge clearance
    Standard .... 0.02 to 0.07 mm (0.001 to 0.003 inch)
    Limit .... 0.12 mm (0.005 inch)

Clutch

Friction plate thickness
    Standard .... 3.45 to 3.55 mm (0.136 to 0.140 inch)
    Minimum .... 3.2 mm (0.13 inch)
Metal plate warpage limit .... 0.30 mm (0.012 inch)
Spring finger free height
    Standard .... 5.80 mm (0.228 inch)
    Minimum .... 5.5 mm (0.22 inch)
Master cylinder bore diameter
    Standard .... 15.870 to 15.913 mm (0.6248 to 0.6265 inch)
    Limit .... 15.925 mm (0.6270 inch)
Master cylinder piston diameter
    Standard .... 15.827 to 15.854 mm (0.6231 to 0.6242 inch)
    Limit .... 15.815 mm (0.6226 inch)

Transmission

Countershaft gear inside diameter
  First gear
    Standard .... 31.000 to 31.0256 mm (1.2205 to 1.2215 inches)
    Limit .... 31.05 mm (1.222 inches)
  Second and third gears
    Standard .... 31.000 to 31.033 mm (1.2205 to 1.2215 inches)
    Limit .... 31.06 mm (1.223 inches)
Mainshaft gear inside diameter
  Fourth gear
    1984 through 1986
      Standard .... 25.020 to 25.041 mm (0.9850 to 0.9859 inch)
      Limit .... 25.06 mm (0.987 inch)
    1987
      Standard .... 28.000 to 28.021 mm (1.1023 to 1.1031 inches)
      Limit .... 28.04 mm (1.104 inches)
  Fifth gear
    Standard .... 28.020 to 28.041 mm (1.1031 to 1.1040 inches)
    Limit .... 28.06 mm (1.105 inches)
Countershaft bushing outside diameter
    Standard .... 30.950 to 30.975 mm (1.2185 to 1.2195 inches)
    Limit .... 30.90 mm (1.217 inches)
Mainshaft bushing outside diameter
  Fourth gear (1987 only) and fifth gear (all)
    Standard .... 27.959 to 27.980 mm (1.1007 to 1.1016 inches)
    Limit .... 27.90 mm (1.1098 inches)
Gear-to-bushing clearance
  Countershaft first
    Standard .... 0.025 to 0.075 mm (0.0010 to 0.0030 inch)
    Limit .... 0.15 mm (0.006 inch)

Chapter 2 Engine, clutch and transmission

    Countershaft second and third
        Standard .... 0.025 to 0.083 mm (0.0010 to 0.0033 inch)
        Limit .... 0.16 mm (0.006 inch)
    Mainshaft fourth
        Standard .... 0.020 to 0.062 mm (0.0008 to 0.0024 inch)
        Limit .... 0.15 mm (0.006 inch)
    Mainshaft fifth
        Standard .... 0.040 to 0.082 mm (0.0016 to 0.0032 inch)
        Limit .... 0.16 mm (0.006 inch)
    Gear-to-shaft clearance (1984 through 1986 mainshaft fourth gear only)
        Standard .... 0.040 to 0.082 mm (0.0016 to 0.0032 inch)
        Limit .... 0.15 mm (0.006 inch)
Mainshaft assembled length .... 177.4 mm (6.98 inches)
Mainshaft diameter .... Not specified
Shift forks
    Bore diameter
        Left and center forks
            Standard .... 13.000 to 13.018 mm (0.5118 to 0.5125 inch)
            Limit .... 13.04 mm (0.513 inch)
        Right fork
            Standard .... 13.000 to 13.027 mm (0.5118 to 0.5129 inch)
            Limit .... 13.05 mm (0.514 inch)
    Finger thickness
        Standard .... 6.4 to 6.5 mm (0.25 to 0.26 inch)
        Limit .... 6.1 mm (0.24 inch)
    Fork shaft diameter
        Standard .... 12.966 to 12.984 mm (0.5105 to 0.5112 inch)
        Limit .... 12.90 mm (0.508 inch)

Torque specifications

Engine mounting bolts and nuts
    12 mm .... 60 Nm (43 ft-lbs)
    10 mm .... 35 Nm (25 ft-lbs)
    8 mm .... 22 Nm (16 ft-lbs)
Cylinder head main bolts .... 55 Nm (40 ft-lbs) (1)
Cylinder head cover bolts .... 12 Nm (9 ft-lbs)
Timing belt cover bolts .... 12 Nm (9 ft-lbs)
Timing belt tensioner bolts .... 26 Nm (19 ft-lbs)
Timing belt pulley bolts
    On crankshaft .... 75 Nm (54 ft-lbs)
    On camshafts .... 27 Nm (20 ft-lbs)
Camshaft holder bolts
    All except bottom center bolt .... 20 Nm (14 ft-lbs)
    Bottom center bolt .... 25 Nm (18 ft-lbs)
    Camshaft holder dowel bolts .... 20 Nm (14 ft-lbs)
Lash adjuster stopper plugs .... 25 Nm (18 ft-lbs)
Rocker arm assist spring bolts .... 12 Nm (9 ft-lbs)
Oil pressure switch .... 12 Nm (9 ft-lbs) (2)
Oil pipe union bolts .... 14 Nm (10 ft-lbs) (3)
Clutch master cylinder clamp bolts .... 12 Nm (9 ft-lbs)
Clutch hose union bolts .... 30 Nm (22 ft-lbs)
Slave cylinder bleed valve .... Not specified
Clutch cover bolts .... 12 Nm (9 ft-lbs)
Clutch cover nuts .... 10 Nm (7 ft-lbs)
Clutch housing locknut .... 60 Nm (43 ft-lbs) (3)
Rear case cover bolts .... 10 Nm (7 ft-lbs)
Output shaft gear bolt .... 12 Nm (9 ft-lbs)
Output shaft locknut .... 70 Nm (51 ft-lbs)
Oil pump driven sprocket bolt .... 18 Nm (13 ft-lbs)
Crankcase bolts
    10 mm .... 35 Nm (25 ft-lbs)
    8 mm .... 26 Nm (19 ft-lbs)
    6 mm .... 12 Nm (9 ft-lbs)
Shift arm return spring post .... Not specified
Internal shift linkage lockbolt .... 25 Nm (18 ft-lbs)
Shift fork lockbolt .... 16 Nm (12 ft-lbs)
Shift drum center bolt .... Not specified
Stopper arm nut .... 10 Nm (7 ft-lbs)
Positive stopper bolt .... 10 Nm (7 ft-lbs)
Connecting rod cap nuts .... 32 Nm (23 ft-lbs) (4)

Chapter 2 Engine, clutch and transmission

Torque specifications

Main bearing cap bolts
- 12 mm .... 70 Nm (51 ft-lbs) (1)
- 10 mm .... 50 Nm (36 ft-lbs) (1)

Countershaft bearing locknut .... 70 Nm (51 ft-lbs)

1 Apply molybdenum disulfide grease to the threads and the undersides of the bolt heads.
2 Apply sealant to the threads.
3 Use new sealing washers.
4 Apply engine oil to the threads and the nut seating surfaces.

1 General information

The engine/transmission unit is a liquid-cooled, horizontally opposed four. The valves are operated by single overhead camshafts which are belt driven off the crankshaft. The engine/transmission assembly is constructed from aluminum alloy. The crankcase is divided vertically.

The crankcase incorporates a wet sump, pressure-fed lubrication system which uses two chain-driven oil pumps, an oil filter, relief valve and an oil pressure switch. The scavenge pump draws oil from the clutch well and the main pump supplies oil under pressure to friction points in the engine.

Power from the crankshaft is routed to the transmission via the clutch, which is of the diaphragm spring, wet multi-plate type and rides on the rear end of the mainshaft. The transmission is a five-speed, constant-mesh unit.

2 Operations possible with the engine in the frame

The components and assemblies listed below can be removed without having to remove the engine from the frame. If, however, a number of areas require attention at the same time, removal of the engine is recommended.

- Starter motor
- Alternator
- Clutch assembly
- Timing belts
- Valve covers, rocker arms, camshafts and lifters
- Cylinder heads

3 Operations requiring engine removal

It is necessary to remove the engine/transmission assembly from the frame and remove the rear engine cover or separate the crankcase halves to gain access to the following components:

- Scavenging oil pump
- Main oil pump
- Starter clutch
- Primary gears and chain
- Output shaft and final drive gear
- External and internal shift mechanisms
- Crankshaft, connecting rods and bearings
- Transmission shafts

4 Major engine repair - general note

1 It is not always easy to determine when or if an engine should be completely overhauled, as a number of factors must be considered.
2 High mileage is not necessarily an indication that an overhaul is needed, while low mileage, on the other hand, does not preclude the need for an overhaul. Frequency of servicing is probably the single most important consideration. An engine that has regular and frequent oil and filter changes, as well as other required maintenance, will most likely give many miles of reliable service. Conversely, a neglected engine, or one which has not been broken in properly, may require an overhaul very early in its life.
3 Exhaust smoke and excessive oil consumption are both indications that piston rings and/or valve guides are in need of attention. Make sure oil leaks are not responsible before deciding that the rings and guides are bad. Refer to Chapter 1 and perform a cylinder compression check to determine for certain the nature and extent of the work required.
4 If the engine is making obvious knocking or rumbling noises, the connecting rod and/or main bearings are probably at fault.
5 Loss of power, rough running, excessive valve train noise and high fuel consumption rates may also point to the need for an overhaul, especially if they are all present at the same time. If a complete tune-up does not remedy the situation, major mechanical work is the only solution.
6 An engine overhaul generally involves restoring the internal parts to the specifications of a new engine. During an overhaul the piston rings are replaced and the cylinder walls are bored and/or honed. If a rebore is done, then new pistons are also required. The main and connecting rod bearings are generally replaced with new ones and, if necessary, the crankshaft is also replaced. Generally the valves are serviced as well, since they are usually in less than perfect condition at this point. While the engine is being overhauled, other components such as the carburetors and the starter motor can be rebuilt also. The end result should be a like-new engine that will give as many trouble free miles as the original.
7 Before beginning the engine overhaul, read through all of the related procedures to familiarize yourself with the scope and requirements of the job. Overhauling an engine is not all that difficult, but it is time consuming. Plan on the motorcycle being tied up for a minimum of two weeks. Check on the availability of parts and make sure that any necessary special tools, equipment and supplies are obtained in advance.
8 Most work can be done with typical shop hand tools, although a number of precision measuring tools are required for inspecting parts to determine if they must be replaced. Often a dealer service department or motorcycle repair shop will handle the inspection of parts and offer advice concerning reconditioning and replacement. As a general rule, time is the primary cost of an overhaul so it doesn't pay to install worn or substandard parts.
9 As a final note, to ensure maximum life and minimum trouble from a rebuilt engine, everything must be assembled with care in a spotlessly clean environment.

5 Engine - removal and installation

Note: *Engine removal and installation should be done with the aid of an assistant to avoid damage or injury that could occur if the engine is dropped. A hydraulic floor jack should be used to support and lower the engine if possible (they can be rented at low cost).*

Removal

Refer to illustrations 5.10, 5.17a, 5.17b, 5.17c, 5.18a, 5.18b, 5.18c, 5.19, 5.20a, 5.20b, 5.20c and 5.22

1 Support the bike securely so it can't be knocked over during this procedure.
2 Disconnect the negative cable from the battery and unhook the spring from the brake pedal switch (see Chapter 1).

Chapter 2 Engine, clutch and transmission

5.10 Disconnect the breather hose from the crankcase

5.17a Remove the front mount upper bolts (there's one on each side of the bike) . . .

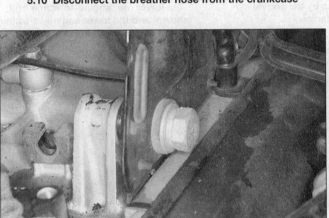

5.17b . . . and the front mount lower bolts (there's also one of these on each side) . . .

5.17c . . . and tilt the front mount (arrow), which is combined with the radiator shroud, backward to free it

3   If you're working on an Interstate or Aspencade, remove the fairing lower and inner covers (see Chapter 8).
4   Remove the air filter housing (see Chapter 4).
5   Drain the engine oil and coolant (see Chapter 1).
6   Remove the radiator (see Chapter 3).
7   Remove the left and right engine guards (see Chapter 8).
8   Locate the electrical connectors for the pulse generators and alternator just forward of the battery, then disconnect them. **Note:** *The alternator connector on many Gold Wing 1200s was replaced with soldered wires due to burning. If this is the case, cut the wires and resolder them on installation.*
9   Remove the exhaust system (see Chapter 4).
10 Disconnect the crankcase breather tube from the engine **(see illustration)**.
11 Remove the right timing belt cover (see Section 7).
12 Refer to Chapter 9 and disconnect the starter cable.
13 Locate the electrical connectors for the gearshift sensor and cooling fan to the left of the ignition coils, then disconnect them. Free the wiring harnesses from their retainers.
14 Remove the fuel filter, fuel pump and carburetor assembly (Chapters 1 and 4).
15 Refer to Section 13 and detach the clutch slave cylinder from the engine. Free the clutch hose from its retainer. **Note:** *It isn't necessary to disconnect the fluid line from the slave cylinder. However, to prevent the slave cylinder piston from being forced out of its bore, squeeze the clutch lever all the way to the handlebar and tie it securely. Don't release the clutch lever until the slave cylinder is reinstalled.*
16 Support the engine from below with a jack. **Note:** *At all times while the engine mounts and subframe are being unbolted, use the jack*

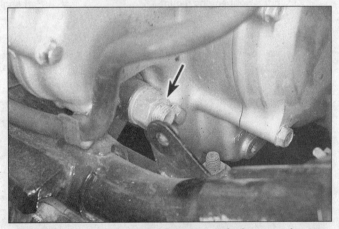

5.18a On the left side of the bike, remove the lower engine-to-subframe nut/bolt (shown) and the lower engine-to-subframe bolt that's below the cylinder head

to relieve pressure on the mounts. You may need to raise or lower it slightly.
17 Unbolt the front engine mount bracket and fan shroud at top and bottom (four bolts), then tilt the bracket back onto the engine **(see illustrations)**. Use a socket, universal and long extension for the top bolts.
18 Remove the mounting bolt and nut at the lower left rear of the engine that attach the engine to the subframe **(see illustration)**.

5.18b Remove the cap nuts from these studs at the rear end of the subframe . . .

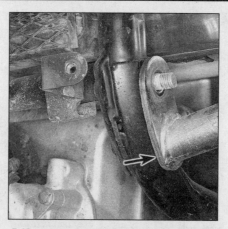

5.18c . . . and at the front; the lower front cap nut is hidden by the engine guard (arrow)

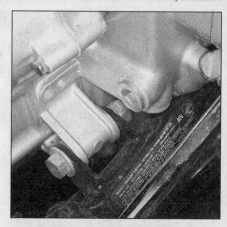

5.19 On the right side of the bike, remove the lower rear engine-to-frame bolt (shown) and the lower engine-to-frame bolt that's beneath the cylinder head

5.20a Remove the two bolts and cap nut from the right engine mount . . .

5.20b . . . remove two small bolts from the left engine mount . . .

5.20c . . . the through-bolt, which connects the left and right engine mounts, secures a ground cable (arrow) on the left side

Remove the other subframe to engine mounting bolt (it's underneath the cylinder head). Remove the cap nuts at each end of the subframe, then take the subframe off (see illustrations).

19 Remove two engine mounting bolts along the lower right side of the frame (see illustration).

20 Remove the upper engine mount from each side of the bike (see illustrations). The through-bolt secures a ground cable on the left side (see illustration).

21 Make sure no wires or hoses are still attached to the engine assembly. **Warning:** *The engine weighs nearly 300 pounds and may cause injury if it falls. Be sure it's securely supported. Have an assistant help you steady the engine on the jack as you remove it.*

22 Slide the front end of the driveshaft off of the output shaft splines (see Chapter 6). Slowly and carefully lower the engine assembly to the floor, then guide it out from under the bike (see illustration).

Installation

23 Installation is the reverse of removal. Note the following points.

24 Tighten all of the mounting bolts finger-tight in the following order:

   a) Right rear lower
   b) Right front lower
   c) Right front upper
   d) Left front and rear brackets
   e) Upper rear (don't forget the collar)
   f) Subframe Allen bolts
   g) Subframe hex bolt on right side
   h) Engine guards
   i) Left lower rear
   j) Left lower front

5.22 Use a jack to lower the engine and have an assistant help guide it out of the frame

Chapter 2 Engine, clutch and transmission

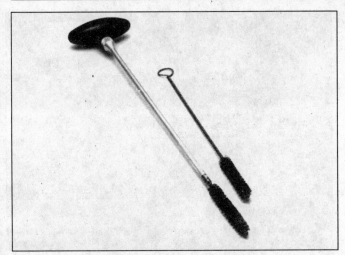

6.2a A selection of brushes is required for cleaning holes and passages in the engine components

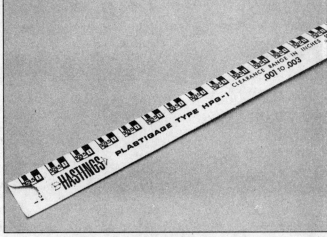

6.2b Type HPG-1 Plastigage is needed to check the crankshaft, connecting rod and camshaft oil clearances

25 Tighten the mounting bolts and nuts to the torque listed in this Chapter's Specifications, in the following order:
  a) *Subframe Allen bolts (front and rear)*
  b) *Subframe right side hex bolt*
  c) *Lower right engine guard bolt*
  d) *Left lower rear mounting bolt*
  e) *Right lower rear mounting bolt*
  f) *Left lower front mounting bolt*
  g) *Right lower front mounting bolt*
  h) *Left front and rear upper brackets to frame (but not to engine yet)*
  i) *Left upper rear bracket through-bolt*
  j) *Right upper front bracket bolt*
  k) *Left upper front bracket to engine*

26 Use new gaskets at all exhaust pipe connections.
27 Adjust the throttle and choke cables following the procedures in Chapter 1.
28 Be sure to refill the cooling system and engine oil before starting the engine.

6 Engine disassembly and reassembly - general information

Refer to illustrations 6.2a, 6.2b and 6.3

1 Before disassembling the engine, clean the exterior with a degreaser and rinse it with water. A clean engine will make the job easier and prevent the possibility of getting dirt into the internal areas of the engine.
2 In addition to the precision measuring tools mentioned earlier, you will need a torque wrench, a valve spring compressor, oil gallery brushes, a piston ring removal and installation tool and special Honda piston ring compressors (which are described in Section 21). Some new, clean engine oil of the correct grade and type, some engine assembly lube (or moly-based grease) and a tube of RTV (silicone) sealant will also be required. Although it may not be considered a tool, some Plastigage (type HPG-1) should also be obtained to use for checking bearing oil clearances **(see illustrations)**.
3 An engine support stand made from short lengths of 2 x 4's bolted together will facilitate the disassembly and reassembly procedures **(see illustration)**. The perimeter of the mount should be just big enough to accommodate the engine oil pan. If you have an automotive-type engine stand, an adapter plate can be made from a piece of plate, some angle iron and some nuts and bolts.
4 When disassembling the engine, keep "mated" parts together

6.3 An engine stand can be made from short lengths of 2 x 4 lumber and lag bolts or nails

(including gears, cylinders, pistons, etc. that have been in contact with each other during engine operation). These "mated" parts must be reused or replaced as an assembly.
5 Engine/transmission disassembly should be done in the following general order with reference to the appropriate Sections.

  Remove the timing belts
  Remove the cylinder head covers
  Remove the camshaft holders, rocker arms and camshafts
  Remove the cylinder heads
  Remove the front case cover
  Remove the rear case cover
  Remove the clutch
  Remove the scavenging oil pump
  Remove the alternator and starter clutch
  Remove the external shift mechanism
  Separate the crankcase halves
  Remove the main oil pump
  Remove the pistons and connecting rods
  Remove the crankshaft and main bearings
  Remove the transmission shafts/gears
  Remove the shift drum/forks

6 Reassembly is accomplished by reversing the general disassembly sequence.

2-10 Chapter 2 Engine, clutch and transmission

7.3a Each timing belt cover has two bolts; this is the right cover . . .

7.3b . . . and this is the left cover . . .

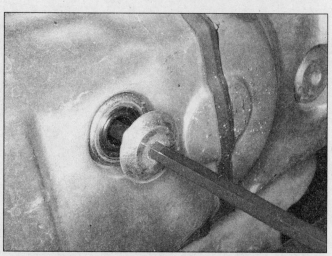

7.3c . . . remove the bolts with an Allen wrench and inspect the O-rings

7.4a With the engine at top dead center on its compression stroke, the line next to the T-1 mark on the crankshaft pulley will align with the lines in the crankcase . . .

7 Timing belts - removal, inspection and installation

Note: *The timing belts can be removed with the engine in the frame. If the engine has been removed, ignore the steps which don't apply.*

Removal

Refer to illustrations 7.3a, 7.3b, 7.3c, 7.4a, 7.4b, 7.4c, 7.5a, 7.5b and 7.6

1 Support the bike securely on its centerstand.
2 Remove the top compartment. If you're working on an Interstate or Aspencade, remove the lower fairing covers (see Chapter 8). Remove the radiator (see Chapter 3).
3 Unbolt the timing belt covers from the engine **(see illustrations)**.
4 Remove the plug from the timing mark access hole on top of the engine. Place a wrench on the crankshaft pulley and turn it clockwise (viewed from the front of the engine) until the line next to the T-1 mark on the flywheel aligns with the line cast in the crankcase **(see illustration)**. The engine should be at top dead center on its compression stroke at this point. To verify that it is, check the alignment marks on the timing belt pulleys; they should be next to the pointers cast in the front of the engine **(see illustrations)**.
5 Mark the belts with LEFT and RIGHT and an arrow to indicate their direction of rotation (clockwise, viewed from the front of the

7.4b . . . and the index mark on each camshaft pulley will align with its pointer in the cylinder head (arrows) - this is the right camshaft pulley; its R mark and hub offset face away from the engine . . .

Chapter 2 Engine, clutch and transmission

7.4c . . . and this is the left camshaft pulley

7.5a Label each belt with Left or Right marks and an arrow indicating direction of rotation

7.5b A holder tool like this can be used to keep the camshaft pulley from turning while you loosen its bolt

7.6 There's a separate tensioner for each belt; they're secured by bolts (arrows)

7.11a Remove the camshaft pulley bolts and washers

7.11b The R mark and hub offset on the left camshaft pulley face the engine

7.11c Remove the crankshaft pulley bolt and washer; the dished side of the front belt guide faces away from the engine

7.11d The F mark on the 1985 and later center belt guide faces away from the engine; the dished side of the rear belt guide faces toward the engine

engine) **(see illustration)**. *Note: If you plan to remove the crankshaft pulley or either of the camshaft pulleys, loosen the pulley bolts now, before the belts are removed. If you decide to remove the pulleys later and the bolts haven't been loosened, you'll need a holder tool to keep the pulleys from turning while you loosen the bolts* **(see illustration)**.

6 Loosen the tensioner mounting and adjusting bolts **(see illustration)**. Slide the right timing belt off the pulleys with fingers only; don't pry it off or the belt may be damaged. **Caution:** *Once either timing belt has been removed, don't turn the crankshaft pulley or either camshaft pulley. If this happens, the valves may be forced against the pistons, bending the valves.*

7 If you're working on a 1985 or later model, refer to Chapter 5 and remove the pulse generators.

8 Slide the left timing belt off the pulleys.

Inspection

Refer to illustrations 7.11a, 7.11b, 7.11c, 7.11d, 7.14a and 7.14b

9 Check the belts for worn, broken or missing teeth. If the teeth are worn more on one side that the other, replace the belt.

10 Look at both edges of the belt, all along the length, to see if the plies have separated. Replace the belt if there's any visible separation.

11 Check the pulley teeth for wear or damage. If the teeth are worn on one side, or if the plating is worn off, replace the pulleys **(see illustrations)**. Try to rotate the pulleys on the crankshaft with fingers. If

2-12 Chapter 2 Engine, clutch and transmission

7.14a Check around the crankshaft seal for oil leaks

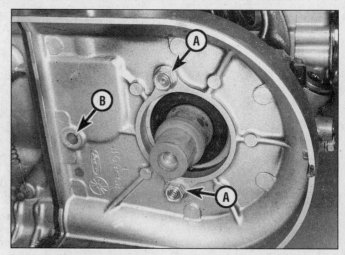

7.14b If oil has been leaking past the camshaft seal, the camshaft will need to be removed to install a new one

A Heat shield bolts   B Alignment hole

either pulley moves separately from the crankshaft, remove the pulleys and check their key slots for wear.

12 Spin the tensioners and make sure they rotate freely. If rotation is rough, loose, or noisy, or if a tensioner pulley binds, replace the tensioner. **Caution:** *Don't try to free a sticking tensioner by lubricating it. The lubricant will fly off and damage the timing belt. Also, don't clean the tensioners in solvent; it will break down the lubricant inside the tensioner.*

13 Check the tensioner springs for breakage or corrosion and replace them if any problems are found. Make sure the tensioner spring posts are securely attached to the engine.

14 Check for leaks around the crankshaft and camshaft seals **(see illustrations)**. If oil has been leaking from the crankshaft seal, pry it out and drive in a new one. If a camshaft seal has been leaking, remove the camshaft and install a new seal (see Section 9).

Installation

Refer to illustrations 7.19a and 7.19b

15 If you removed the pulleys and related components from the crankshaft, install them in the correct order **(see illustrations 7.11d and 7.11c)**. Be sure the cupped edges of the front and rear guide plates face away from the timing belt and the F mark on the center guide plate faces away from the engine.

16 If the timing belt pulleys were removed, install them with their UP marks facing away from the engine. Install the washer on the pulley bolt with its chamfered side toward the bolt head, then thread the bolt into the camshaft. Keep the pulley from turning with a holder tool **(see illustration 7.5b)** and tighten the pulley bolt to the torque listed in this Chapter's Specifications.

17 Make sure the pulley timing marks are still aligned correctly **(see illustrations 7.4a, 7.4b and 7.4c)**.

18 Clean the threads of the left tensioner bolts, then coat them with non-permanent thread-locking agent.

19 Install the belt tensioners on the engine. Tighten the bolts just enough so the tensioners can still move in its slot. Install the tensioner springs with their hooked end at the tensioner facing toward the engine **(see illustrations)**.

20 Install the left timing belt. Place a wrench on the timing belt pulley and turn it counterclockwise (viewed from the front of the engine) so the loosest point of the belt will be at the tensioner. Don't tighten the tensioner bolts yet.

21 If you're working on a 1986 or 1987 model, refer to Chapter 5 and install the pulse generators.

22 Repeat Steps 17 through 20 above to install the right timing belt.

23 Place a wrench on the crankshaft pulley bolt. Turn the engine 30 to 40-degrees counterclockwise, then the same distance clockwise. Make sure all of the timing marks are still aligned correctly **(see illustrations 7.4a, 7.4b and 7.4c)**. If they aren't, find out why and fix the problem before continuing further; the valves could be bent if the engine is run while the timing marks are misaligned.

7.19a The left tensioner's spring is installed like this . . .

7.19b . . . and the right spring is installed like this

Chapter 2 Engine, clutch and transmission

8.2 The camshaft end cover protects the rubber camshaft end plug

8.3a Unscrew the cover bolts (arrows) . . .

24 Tighten the left tensioner bolts to the torque listed in this Chapter's Specifications.
25 Check belt tension by pressing down on the top run of the belt between the pulleys. Tension should be within the range listed in this Chapter's Specifications. **Note:** *If the left belt is too tight, it will whine.*
26 Turn the crankshaft pulley one full turn clockwise, so the T-1 mark on the flywheel again lines with the crankcase lines **(see illustration 7.4a)**. The UP marks on the camshaft pulleys should now be downward.
27 Tighten the right tensioner bolts to the torque listed in this Chapter's Specifications.
28 Check belt tension by pressing down on the top run of the belt between the pulleys. Tension should be within the range listed in this Chapter's Specifications. **Note:** *If a right belt is loose, it will hit the cover and make a tapping noise when the engine idles. If it's too tight, it will whine.*

8 Cylinder head covers - removal and installation

Refer to illustrations 8.2, 8.3a, 8.3b and 8.4

1 Remove the engine guard from the side of the bike you'll be working on (see Chapter 8).
2 Remove the camshaft end cover from the left cylinder head (see illustration).
3 Remove the cover bolts, washers and seals **(see illustrations)**.
4 Pull the cover off the engine **(see illustration)**. If it's stuck, tap it gently with a soft faced mallet. Don't pry between the cover and engine or the gasket surfaces will be damaged.
5 Peel the rubber gasket from the cover. If it's cracked, hardened, has soft spots or shows signs of general deterioration, replace it with a new one.
6 Clean the mating surfaces of the cylinder head and cover with lacquer thinner, acetone or brake system cleaner. Apply a thin film of RTV sealant to the gasket groove in the cover, but don't put any on the head.
7 Install the gasket to the cover. Make sure it fits completely into the cover groove.
8 Position the cover on the cylinder head, making sure the gasket doesn't slip out of place.
9 Check the rubber seals on the valve cover bolts, replacing them if necessary **(see illustration 8.3b)**. Coat the seals with engine oil, then install the bolts with their seals, tightening them evenly to the torque listed in this Chapter's Specifications.
10 Install the camshaft end cover on the rear of the cylinder head, using a new gasket. Align the tabs on the gasket with the holes in the cover.
11 Install the engine guard.

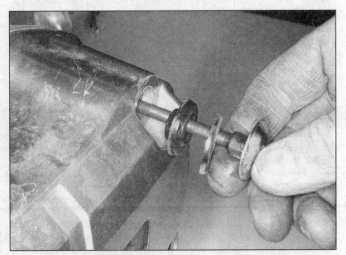

8.3b . . . and replace the rubber seals if they're brittle or deteriorated; on installation, coat the seal with oil

8.4 Take the cover and gasket off the cylinder head

9.2 Take the timing belt heat shield off and clean away the old gasket

9.3a Remove the bolts and sealing washers and take the covers off the defoaming chambers

9.3b The upper two oil distribution plate bolts secure springs and assist shafts

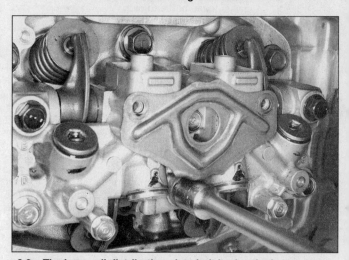

9.3c The lower oil distribution plate bolt is also the lower center bolt for the camshaft holder

9.4 The deeper sides of the oil distribution plate O-rings (arrows) face the camshaft holder

9 Camshafts, rocker arms and lash adjusters- removal, inspection and installation

Note: *This procedure can be performed with the engine in the frame.*

Camshafts

Removal

Refer to illustrations 9.2, 9.3a, 9.3b, 9.3c, 9.4, 9.5a, 9.5b, 9.5c, 9.6 and 9.7

1 Remove the timing belt (Section 7) and cylinder head cover (Section 8).
2 Remove the timing belt shield bolts and remove the shield **(see illustration 7.14b and the accompanying illustration)**.
3 Remove the defoaming chamber covers and the oil distribution plate **(see illustrations)**. The upper two oil distribution plate bolts also retain the assist shafts and springs.
4 Remove the O-rings from behind the oil distribution plate **(see illustration)**.
5 Unscrew the camshaft holder bolts in two or three stages in a criss-cross pattern **(see illustrations)**. Take the holder off, together with the camshaft and rocker arms **(see illustration)**.
6 Locate the holder dowels **(see illustration)**. They may have come off with the holder or remained in the cylinder head.
7 Remove the camshaft from the holder, then remove the end plug, orifice plate and camshaft seal **(see illustration)**.

Chapter 2 Engine, clutch and transmission 2-15

9.5a Camshaft holder bolts (arrows); all except the lower center bolt are loosened and tightened in stages

9.5b The upper camshaft holder bolts are shouldered; the lower ones are plain

9.5c Take off the holder and camshaft (or remove the camshaft separately if it stays in the engine)

9.6 The dowels (arrows) may stay in the cylinder head or come off with the holder

Inspection

Refer to illustrations 9.8, 9.9a, 9.9b, 9.11, 9.14a and 9.14b

Note: *Before replacing camshafts or the cylinder head and camshaft holder because of damage, check with local machine shops specializing in motorcycle engine work. In the case of the camshafts, it may be possible for cam lobes to be welded, reground and hardened, at a cost far lower than that of a new camshaft. If the bearing surfaces in the cylinder head or holder are damaged, it may be possible for them to be bored out to accept bearing inserts. Due to the cost of a new cylinder head it is recommended that all options be explored before condemning it as trash!*

8 Inspect the cam bearing surfaces of the head and the camshaft holder **(see illustration 9.6 and the accompanying illustration)**. Look for score marks, deep scratches and evidence of spalling (a pitted appearance).

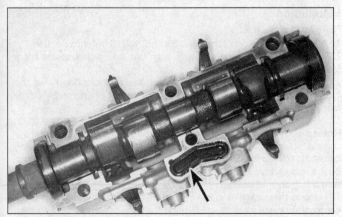

9.7 There's an oil seal on one end of the camshaft and a cap on the other end; be sure the orifice plate (arrow) is in place on installation

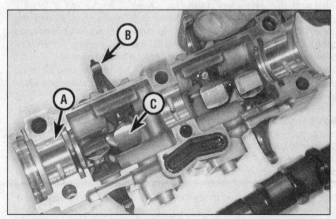

9.8 Check the three camshaft bearing surfaces (A) for wear and damage; also inspect the rocker arm valve contact surfaces (B) and cam contact surfaces (C)

2-16 Chapter 2 Engine, clutch and transmission

9.9a Check the lobes of the camshaft for wear - here's a good example of damage which will require replacement (or repair) of the camshaft

9.9b Measure the height of the camshaft lobes with a micrometer

9.11 Lay a strip of Plastigage lengthwise along each journal

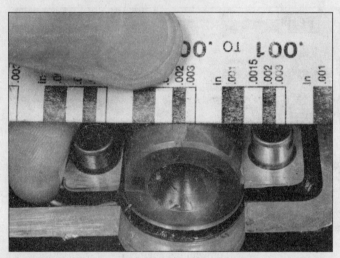

9.14a Compare the width of the crushed Plastigage to the scale printed on the Plastigage container to obtain the clearance

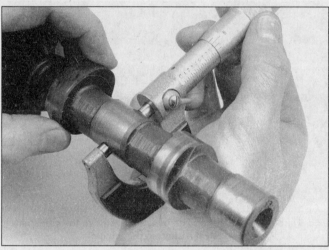

9.14b Measure the cam bearing journal diameter with a micrometer

9   Check the camshaft lobes for heat discoloration (blue appearance), score marks, chipped areas, flat spots and spalling (see illustration). Measure the height of each lobe with a micrometer (see illustration) and compare the results to the minimum lobe height listed in this Chapter's Specifications. If damage is noted or wear is excessive, the camshaft must be replaced.
10   Next, check the camshaft bearing oil clearances. Clean the camshafts, the bearing surfaces in the cylinder head and the bearing caps with a clean, lint-free cloth, then lay the cam in place in the cylinder head. Be sure the keyways in the camshafts are upward.
11   Cut three strips of Plastigage (type HPG-1) and lay one piece on each bearing journal, parallel with the camshaft centerline (see illustration).
12   Make sure the camshaft holder dowels are installed (see illustration 9.6). Install the camshaft holder (see Step 5). Tighten the bolts in two or three steps to the torque listed in this Chapter's Specifications. **Caution:** *Tighten the holder bolts evenly to specifications, starting with the inner bolt and working outward. While tightening, DO NOT let the camshaft rotate!*
13   Now unscrew the bolts, a little at a time, and carefully lift off the camshaft holder. Be sure to start with the outer bolts and work inward.
14   To determine the oil clearance, compare the crushed Plastigage (at its widest point) on each journal to the scale printed on the Plastigage container (see illustration). Compare the results to this Chapter's Specifications. If the oil clearance is greater than specified, mea-

sure the diameter of the cam bearing journal with a micrometer (see illustration). If the journal diameter is less than the specified limit, replace the camshaft with a new one and recheck the clearance. If the clearance is still too great, replace the cylinder head and camshaft with new parts (see the Note that precedes Step 8).

Installation

Refer to illustration 9.23

15   Make sure the crankshaft is still at no. 1 TDC (refer to Section 7).
16   If the camshaft holder dowels aren't in their holes, install them (see illustration 9.6).
17   Make sure the bearing surfaces in the cylinder head and the camshaft holder are clean, then apply a light coat of engine assembly lube or moly-based grease to each of them.
18   Apply a coat of moly-based grease to the lobes of the camshaft. **Note:** *If you've removed both camshafts, be sure to install them on the correct sides of the engine.* Install the seal over the front end of the camshaft with its open side facing the rear of the engine. Install the cap on the rear end. Wipe the outer circumferences of the seal and end cap with a thin layer of sealant.
19   Place the camshaft in the cylinder head bearing journals with the camshaft keyway straight up. Engage the seal and end cap with their bores in the cylinder head.
20   Position the camshaft holder on the cylinder head, making sure the orifice plate is in place (see illustration 9.7). Install the three upper

Chapter 2 Engine, clutch and transmission

9.23 Fill the defoaming chamber pockets with clean engine oil

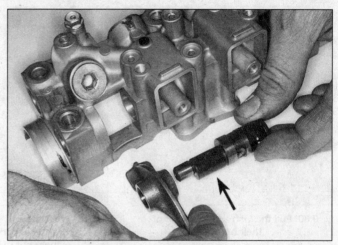

9.26a Each rocker arm pivots on the offset portion of its rocker shaft (arrow) . . .

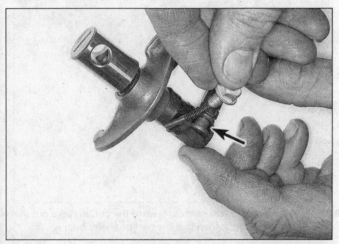

9.26b . . . the spring-loaded assist shaft and the lash adjuster (arrow) rotate the rocker shaft, moving the pivot point to eliminate valve clearance

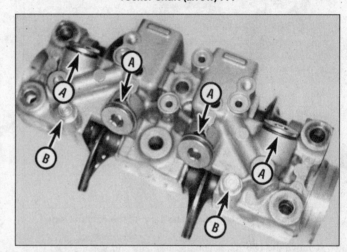

9.29 Lash adjuster position relative to the rocker shafts is determined by shims

A Lash adjuster shims B Assist shaft spring bolts

holder bolts and two outer lower ones (don't install the center lower bolt, which secures the oil distribution plate). Tighten the bolts in two or three stages to the torque listed in this Chapter's Specifications, starting with the center bolt and working outward.

21 Install new O-rings in the camshaft holder bores with their deep sides facing in (toward the camshaft holder) **(see illustration 9.4)**.

22 Install the oil distribution plate, the two assist shafts and their springs. Install the assist shaft bolt and the lower center camshaft holder bolt to secure the oil distribution plate.

23 Fill the defoaming chamber pockets with clean engine oil **(see illustration)**. Install the covers on the defoaming chambers with their vent holes toward the engine, then install the bolts with sealing washers and tighten them securely.

24 Install the timing belt heat shield, using a new gasket, and tighten the bolts finger-tight. Temporarily install a timing belt cover bolt through the alignment hole into the cylinder head, then tighten the heat shield bolts securely, but don't overtighten them and strip the threads **(see illustration 7.14b)**.

25 The remainder of installation is the reverse of removal.

Rocker arms and lash adjusters

Refer to illustrations 9.26a and 9.26b

26 The valves are opened and closed by rocker arms, which are operated directly by the camshafts. The rocker arms ride on eccentric spindles, which are mounted in the camshaft holder **(see illustration)**.

Valve clearance is controlled by hydraulic lash adjusters mounted in the camshaft holder. The adjusters extend, pressing against notches on the eccentric spindles, causing them to rotate **(see illustration)**. As the spindles rotate, they raise or lower the pivot point of their rocker arm, so that valve clearance is maintained at zero. Each spindle has a spring-loaded assist shaft, which adds spring pressure to the hydraulic pressure of the lash adjuster.

Removal

Refer to illustrations 9.29, 9.30, 9.31a, 9.31b, 9.31c and 9.32

27 Remove the camshaft holder following the procedure given above.

28 Make a holder with a separate section for each lash adjuster, spindle, assist shaft and rocker arm. The intake valve lash adjusters have small caps that fit between the adjuster and the spindle; exhaust valve lash adjusters don't have caps. Label the sections according to cylinder number (1 through 4), valve number (starting from the front of the engine) and whether the parts belong with an intake or exhaust valve. The parts form a wear pattern with each other and must be returned to their original locations if reused.

29 Note the number of shims used with each lash adjuster **(see illustration)**. It's important to install the same number of shims if the old parts are reinstalled (if parts are replaced with new ones, you'll need to select the number of shims as described below).

9.30 Pull the lash adjusters out of their bores

9.31a Twist the end collars to free them, using their screwdriver slots, then pull them out of their bores

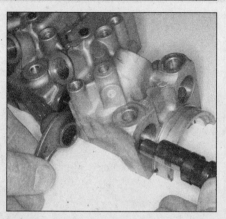

9.31b Pull out the rocker shafts and take the rocker arms out

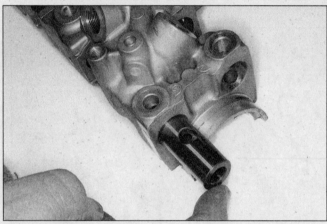

9.31c Pull the center rocker shaft out of the exhaust side

9.32 Push the intake rocker shafts toward the center, take out the rocker arms, then pull the rocker shafts out

30 Remove the two remaining assist shafts and springs (two were removed as part of camshaft holder removal) **(see illustration 9.29)**. Unscrew the stopper plugs and remove them from the adjuster bores, together with their shims. Pull the adjusters (and their caps if they're intake valve adjusters) out of the bores, using a magnet if necessary **(see illustration)**. If the adjusters are stuck, spray the area around them with carburetor cleaner and let it soak in. Place the adjusters in order in their holder.

31 On the exhaust side of the cylinder head, remove the collar from each end **(see illustration)**. Pull out the rocker shafts, remove the rocker arms and pull out the center collar **(see illustrations)**.

32 On the intake side, remove the collar from each end. Push the rocker shafts toward the center and take out the rocker arms, then pull the rocker shafts out of the camshaft holder **(see illustration)**.

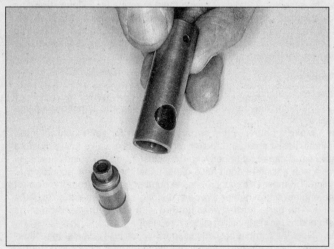

9.37 This tool opens the check valve in the lash adjuster so it can be filled with kerosene

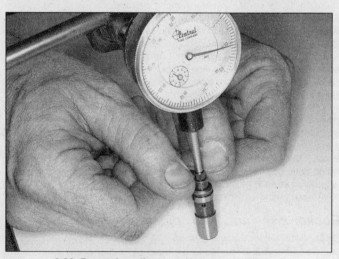

9.38 Pump the adjuster and measure its travel with a dial indicator

Chapter 2 Engine, clutch and transmission

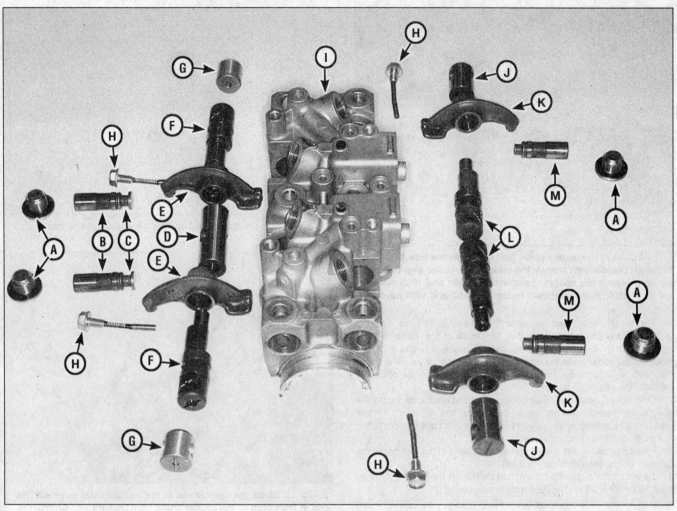

9.40a Camshaft holder details

A Lash adjuster stopper plugs and shims	F Exhaust rocker shafts	K Intake rocker arms
B Intake lash adjusters	G Exhaust rocker shaft end caps	L Intake rocker shafts
C Intake lash adjuster caps	H Assist shafts, springs and bolts	M Exhaust lash adjusters
D Exhaust rocker shaft center collar	I Camshaft holder	
E Exhaust rocker arms	J Intake rocker shaft end caps	

Inspection

Refer to illustrations 9.37 and 9.38

33 Check the contact surfaces of the rocker arms and for wear, scoring or pitting. If there's any visible damage, replace the worn parts.

34 Check the bores in the camshaft holder for wear or scoring. If you have precision measuring equipment, measure the bore and shaft diameters and compare them to the values listed in this Chapter's Specifications. Replace worn or damaged parts.

35 Make sure the oil holes in the hydraulic adjusters are clear. Check the adjusters and their bores for wear, scuff marks, scratches or other damage. Also check the caps used on the intake valve adjusters. Honda doesn't provide specifications or wear tolerances for the adjusters or their bores. If wear or damage is found, replace the worn parts.

36 Adjuster performance can be tested, but it requires a dial indicator and a special Honda fixture for which there is no good substitute. The fixture holds open the adjuster check valve, allowing it to be bled of air. The procedure is described below, but you can have it done by a Honda dealer or motorcycle service shop if you don't have the equipment.

37 Place the adjuster in a tappet bleeder (Honda part no. 07973-MJ00000) **(see illustration)**. Immerse the fixture in a pan of kerosene with the adjuster in its upright position. Slowly compress and extend the bleeder until no more air bubbles can be seen coming from the adjuster.

38 Take the adjuster out of the fixture and place it on a workbench with a dial indicator contacting its end **(see illustration)**. Compress the adjuster suddenly with a finger and measure its stroke. If it's more than listed in this Chapter's Specifications, repeat Step 37 to bleed the adjuster, then measure the stroke again. If the stroke is still more than the specification, replace the adjuster.

Installation

Refer to illustrations 9.40a and 9.40b

39 Coat the inner bores of the rocker arms and the outer bores of the shafts with Honda Moly 45 or equivalent moly-based grease.

40 Install the center collar in the exhaust side bore and align its bolt hole with the bolt in the camshaft holder **(see illustrations)**. Place the rocker arms in their installed positions and install the rocker shafts through them. Install the collars on the ends of the rocker shafts. Make sure the bolt holes in the collars align with the bolt holes in the camshaft holder. A screwdriver can be used to turn and push the end collars to line them up **(see illustration 9.31a)**.

2-20   **Chapter 2 Engine, clutch and transmission**

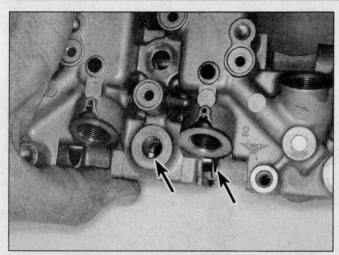

9.40b Align the center collar bolt hole with the hole in the camshaft holder (left arrow); the ends of the collar (right arrow) should protrude the specified distance on 1984 and 1985 models, or be flush with the camshaft holder on 1986 and 1987 models

41   The center collar must be perfectly centered in its bore. If you're working on a 1984 or 1985 model, the ends of the collar will be exposed slightly in the rocker arm cavities; make sure the exposed amount is the same on both ends of the center collar. If you're working on a 1986 or 1987 model, make sure the ends of the center collar are flush with the camshaft holder.
42   Coat the adjusters and their bores with clean engine oil. Install the caps on the intake valve adjusters, then install the adjusters in their bores. Install the stopper plugs with their shims and tighten them to the torque listed in this Chapter's Specifications.
43   Install the two assist shafts, springs and bolts in the bottom of the camshaft holder **(see illustration 9.29)**.
44   To install the assembled camshaft holder on the engine, refer to Steps 15 through 25 above. Also note the following:
 a) *If any parts were replaced, you'll need to select the correct number of shims as described below after the camshaft holder is installed.*
 b) *When you tighten the bottom center camshaft holder bolt (the one that secures the bottom of the oil distribution plate), make sure the center collar remains in its centered position. To do this, insert a feeler gauge between each end of the center collar and the rocker shaft next to it* **(see illustration 9.40b)**. *Leave the feeler gauges in place while you tighten the bolt. Feeler gauge thicknesses are listed in this Chapter's Specifications.*

Shim selection

Refer to illustrations 9.47a and 9.47b

45   This procedure requires a special Honda gauge and a vernier caliper. Have it done by a Honda dealer if you don't have the equipment.
46   Position the engine with no. 1 cylinder at top dead center on its compression stroke (see Section 7).
47   Starting with no. 1 cylinder, remove the stopper plugs, shims and adjusters. Insert the gauge in the adjuster bore **(see illustration)**. Make sure the rocker arm is touching the camshaft and the end of the gauge is touching the lever on the eccentric spindle. Measure the distance from the top of the gauge to the shim contact surface on the camshaft holder **(see illustration)**. Compare the measurement with the values listed in this Chapter's Specifications to determine how many shims are needed for that adjuster.
48   With no. 1 cylinder still at TDC compression, select shims for the no. 3 cylinder's exhaust valve and the no. 4 cylinder's intake valve as described in Step 40.
49   Turn the engine one full turn clockwise, so the T-1 mark again aligns with the marks on the crankcase. This places no. 1 cylinder at

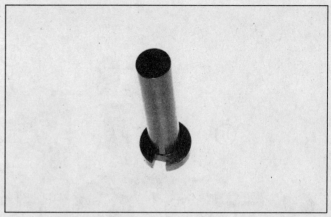

9.47a This gauge is used to select lash adjuster shims . . .

9.47b . . . place the narrow end in the lash adjuster bore with its end in the notch of the rocker shaft, then measure its protrusion; use the measurement to select the number of shims

TDC on its exhaust stroke. Don't turn the engine more than one turn; a second turn will put it back to TDC compression.
50   With no. 1 cylinder at TDC on its exhaust stroke, measure both valves of no. 2 cylinder, as well as no. 3 cylinder's intake valve and no. 4 cylinder's exhaust valve.

10 Cylinder heads - removal and installation

Caution: *The engine must be completely cool before beginning this procedure, or the cylinder head may become warped.*
Note: *This procedure can be performed with the engine in the frame. If the engine has been removed, ignore the steps which don't apply. If you're planning to remove the head just for gasket replacement, it can be removed as a unit with the camshaft holder.*

Removal

Refer to illustrations 10.8, 10.11a, 10.11b and 10.12

1   Place the bike on its centerstand.
2   Drain the cooling system and disconnect the spark plug wires (see Chapter 1).
3   Remove the cylinder head cover (see Section 8).
4   Remove the timing belt(s) (see Section 7).
5   Remove the camshaft holder and camshaft (see Section 9).
6   Detach the exhaust pipes and carburetor intake tubes from the head. Tie the intake tubes up so they won't be in the way (see Chapter 4).

Chapter 2 Engine, clutch and transmission 2-21

10.8 Cylinder head bolts TIGHTENING sequence

10.11a Locate both dowels; they may come away with the cylinder head (arrow)...

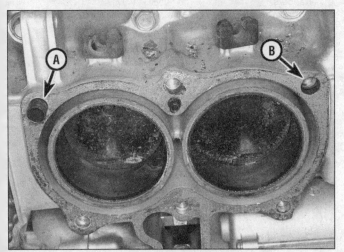

10.11b ... or remain in the crankcase

A Dowel B Dowel location

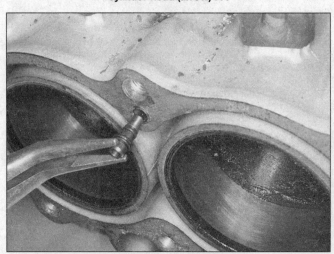

10.12 Lift the oil orifice out of its passage; its inner O-ring is smaller than the outer one

7 Detach the coolant tube from the top of the cylinder head (see Chapter 3).
8 Remove the single 6 mm bolt from beneath the cylinder head **(see illustration)**.
9 Loosen the main cylinder head bolts, 1/2 turn at a time, in the reverse of the tightening sequence **(see illustration 10.8)**. Once all of the bolts are loose, remove the bolts and washers.
10 Take the cylinder head off the crankcase. If the head is stuck, tap upward with a rubber mallet to jar it loose, or use two wooden dowels inserted into the intake or exhaust ports to rock the head back and forth slightly. Don't attempt to pry the head off by inserting a screwdriver between the head and the crankcase - you'll damage the sealing surfaces.
11 Lift the head gasket off the crankcase. Remove the dowel pins **(see illustrations)**.
12 Pull the oil orifice out of its bore in the crankcase **(see illustration)**.
13 Check the cylinder head gasket and the mating surfaces on the cylinder head and block for leakage, which could indicate warpage. Refer to Section 12 and check the flatness of the cylinder head and its mating surface on the crankcase.
14 Clean all traces of old gasket material from the cylinder head and crankcase. Be careful not to let any of the gasket material fall into the crankcase, the cylinder bores or the coolant passages.

Installation

15 Install the oil orifice and dowels in the crankcase **(see illustrations 10.12, 10.11a and 10.11b)**.
16 Lay the new gasket in place on the crankcase. Never reuse the old gasket and don't use any type of gasket sealant.
17 Carefully place the cylinder head on the crankcase, making sure the coolant tube fits into the fitting on the side of the head toward the center of the engine.
18 Coat the threads of the main bolts and the undersides of the bolt heads with Honda Moly 45 or equivalent moly-based grease. Install the main head bolts and washers. Starting with the inner bolts and working outward **(see illustration 10.8)**, tighten the bolts in three stages to the torque listed in this Chapter's Specifications.
19 Install the 6 mm bolt. Tighten it securely, but don't overtighten it and strip the threads.
20 The remainder of installation is the reverse of the removal steps.
21 Change the engine oil (see Chapter 1).

11 Valves/valve seats/valve guides - servicing

1 Because of the complex nature of this job and the special tools and equipment required, servicing of the valves, the valve seats and the valve guides (commonly known as a valve job) is best left to a professional.

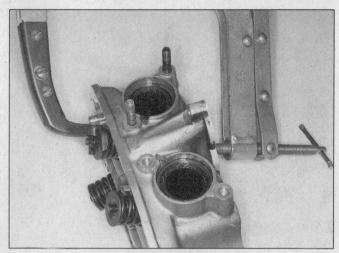

12.7a Compress the valve spring with a spring compressor and remove the keepers with a magnet

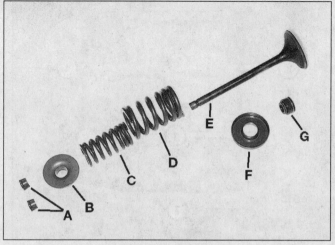

12.7b Valve components

A Keepers
B Upper spring retainer
C Inner valve spring
D Outer valve spring
E Valve
F Lower spring retainer
G Valve stem oil seal

2 The home mechanic can, however, remove and disassemble the head, do the initial cleaning and inspection, then reassemble and deliver the head to a dealer service department or properly equipped motorcycle repair shop for the actual valve servicing. Refer to Section 12 for those procedures.
3 The dealer service department will remove the valves and springs, recondition or replace the valves and valve seats, replace the valve guides, check and replace the valve springs, spring retainers and keepers (as necessary), replace the valve seals with new ones and reassemble the valve components.
4 After the valve job has been performed, the head will be in like-new condition. When the head is returned, be sure to clean it again very thoroughly before installation on the engine to remove any metal particles or abrasive grit that may still be present from the valve service operations. Use compressed air, if available, to blow out all the holes and passages.

12 Cylinder head and valves - disassembly, inspection and reassembly

1 As mentioned in the previous Section, valve servicing and valve guide replacement should be left to a dealer service department or motorcycle repair shop. However, disassembly, cleaning and inspection of the valves and related components can be done (if the necessary special tools are available) by the home mechanic. This way no expense is incurred if the inspection reveals that service work is not required at this time.
2 To properly disassemble the valve components without the risk of damaging them, a valve spring compressor is absolutely necessary. This special tool can usually be rented, but if it's not available, have a dealer service department or motorcycle repair shop handle the entire process of disassembly, inspection, service or repair (if required) and reassembly of the valves.

Disassembly

Refer to illustrations 12.7a, 12.7b and 12.7c

3 Remove the camshaft holder if you haven't already done so (see Section 9). Store the components in such a way that they can be returned to their original locations without getting mixed up.
4 Before the valves are removed, scrape away any traces of gasket material from the head gasket sealing surface. Work slowly and do not nick or gouge the soft aluminum of the head. Gasket removing solvents, which work very well, are available at most motorcycle shops and auto parts stores.
5 Carefully scrape all carbon deposits out of the combustion cham-

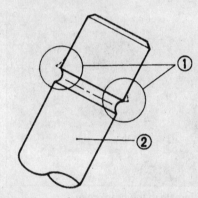

12.7c Take the valve out of the combustion chamber, but don't force it if it's stuck; check the area around the keeper groove for burrs and remove any that you find

1 Burrs (removed)
2 Valve stem

ber area. A hand held wire brush or a piece of fine emery cloth can be used once the majority of deposits have been scraped away. Do not use a wire brush mounted in a drill motor, or one with extremely stiff bristles, as the head material is soft and may be eroded away or scratched by the wire brush.
6 Before proceeding, arrange to label and store the valves along with their related components so they can be kept separate and reinstalled in the same valve guides they are removed from (labeled plastic bags work well for this).
7 Compress the valve spring on the first valve with a spring compressor, then remove the keepers and the spring retainer from the valve assembly **(see illustrations)**. Do not compress the springs any more than is absolutely necessary. Carefully release the valve spring compressor and remove the spring and the valve from the head. If the valve binds in the guide (won't pull through), push it back into the head and deburr the area around the keeper groove with a very fine file or whetstone **(see illustration)**.
8 Repeat the procedure for the remaining valves. Remember to keep the parts for each valve together so they can be reinstalled in the same location.
9 Once the valves have been removed and labeled, pull off the valve stem seals with pliers and discard them (the old seals should never be reused), then remove the spring seats.
10 Next, clean the cylinder head with solvent and dry it thoroughly. Compressed air will speed the drying process and ensure that all holes and recessed areas are clean.

Chapter 2 Engine, clutch and transmission

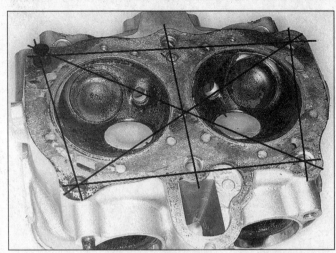

12.14a Measure the head along these lines with a feeler gauge and straightedge

12.14b Measure the top surface of the cylinders

12.15 Measure the valve seat width (A); measure the guide inner diameter (B) with a small hole gauge . . .

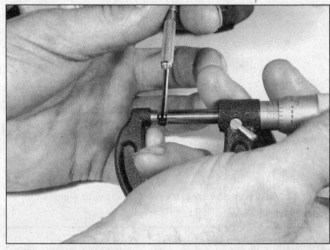

12.16 . . . then measure the small hole gauge with a micrometer

11 Clean all of the valve springs, keepers, retainers and spring seats with solvent and dry them thoroughly. Do the parts from one valve at a time so that no mixing of parts between valves occurs.

12 Scrape off any deposits that may have formed on the valve, then use a motorized wire brush to remove deposits from the valve heads and stems. Again, make sure the valves do not get mixed up.

Inspection

Refer to illustrations 12.14a, 12.14b, 12.15, 12.16, 12.17, 12.18a, 12.18b, 12.19a and 12.19b

13 Inspect the head very carefully for cracks and other damage. If cracks are found, a new head will be required. Check the cam bearing surfaces for wear and evidence of seizure. Check the camshafts for wear as well (see Section 9).

14 Using a precision straightedge and a feeler gauge, check the head gasket mating surface for warpage. Lay the straightedge lengthwise, across the head and diagonally (corner-to-corner), intersecting the head bolt holes, and try to slip a feeler gauge under it, on either side of each combustion chamber **(see illustration)**. The gauge should be the same thickness as the cylinder head warp limit listed in this Chapter's Specifications. If the feeler gauge can be inserted between the head and the straightedge, the head is warped and must either be machined or, if warpage is excessive, replaced with a new one. Minor surface imperfections can be cleaned up by sanding on a surface plate in a figure-eight pattern with 400 or 600 grit wet or dry sandpaper. Be sure to rotate the head every few strokes to avoid removing material unevenly. Also check the head mating surface on the cylinders **(see illustration)**.

15 Examine the valve seats in each of the combustion chambers. If they are pitted, cracked or burned, the head will require valve service that's beyond the scope of the home mechanic. Measure the valve seat width **(see illustration)** and compare it to this Chapter's Specifications. If it is not within the specified range, or if it varies around its circumference, valve service work is required.

16 Clean the valve guides to remove any carbon buildup, then measure the inside diameters of the guides (at both ends and the center of the guide) with a small hole gauge and a 0-to-1-inch micrometer **(see illustration 12.15 and the accompanying illustration)**. Record the measurements for future reference. These measurements, along with the valve stem diameter measurements, will enable you to compute the valve stem-to-guide clearance. This clearance, when compared to the Specifications, will be one factor that will determine the extent of the valve service work required. The guides are measured at the ends and at the center to determine if they are worn in a bell-mouth pattern (more wear at the ends). If they are, guide replacement is an absolute must.

17 Carefully inspect each valve face for cracks, pits and burned spots. Check the valve stem and the keeper groove area for cracks

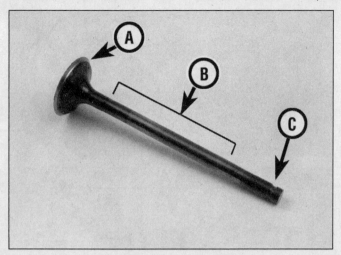

12.17 Check the valve face (A), stem (B) and keeper groove (C) for signs of wear and damage

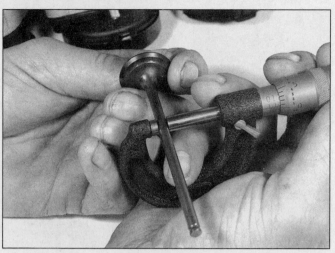

12.18a Measure the valve stem diameter with a micrometer

12.18b Check the valve stem for bends with V-blocks and a dial indicator

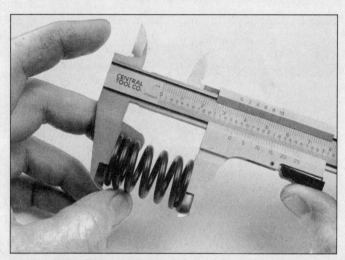

12.19a Measure the free length of the valve springs

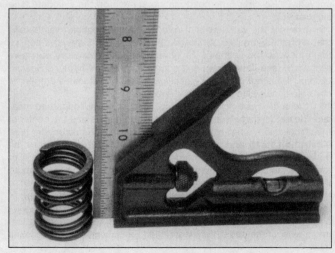

12.19b Check the valve springs for squareness

(see illustration). Rotate the valve and check for any obvious indication that it is bent. Check the end of the stem for pitting and excessive wear and make sure the margin is not too thin. The presence of any of the above conditions indicates the need for valve servicing.

18 Measure the valve stem diameter **(see illustration)**. By subtracting the stem diameter from the valve guide diameter, the valve stem-to-guide clearance is obtained. If the stem-to-guide clearance is greater than listed in this Chapter's Specifications, the guides and valves will have to be replaced with new ones. Also check the valve stem for bending. Set the valve in a V-block with a dial indicator touching the middle of the stem **(see illustration)**. Rotate the valve and note the reading on the gauge. If the stem is bent, replace the valve.

19 Check the end of each valve spring for wear and pitting. Measure the free length **(see illustration)** and compare it to this Chapter's Specifications. Any springs that are shorter than specified have sagged and should not be reused. Stand the spring on a flat surface and check it for squareness **(see illustration)**.

20 Check the spring retainers and keepers for obvious wear and cracks. Any questionable parts should not be reused, as extensive damage will occur in the event of failure during engine operation.

21 If the inspection indicates that no service work is required, the valve components can be reinstalled in the head.

Reassembly

Refer to illustrations 12.23, 12.24, 12.27, 12.28 and 12.29

22 Before installing the valves in the head, they should be lapped to ensure a positive seal between the valves and seats. This procedure requires coarse and fine valve lapping compound (available at auto parts stores) and a valve lapping tool. If a lapping tool is not available, a piece of rubber or plastic hose can be slipped over the valve stem (after the valve has been installed in the guide) and used to turn the valve.

Chapter 2 Engine, clutch and transmission

12.23 Apply the lapping compound very sparingly, in small dabs, to the valve face only

12.24 After lapping, the valve face should have a uniform, unbroken contact pattern (arrow)

12.27 A small dab of grease will help hold the keepers (collets) in place on the valve spring while the spring is released

12.28 Install the lower retainers and seals on the head

23 Apply a small amount of coarse lapping compound to the valve face **(see illustration)**, then slip the valve into the guide. **Note:** *Make sure the valve is installed in the correct guide and be careful not to get any lapping compound on the valve stem.*
24 Attach the lapping tool (or hose) to the valve and rotate the tool between the palms of your hands. Use a back-and-forth motion rather than a circular motion. Lift the valve off the seat and turn it at regular intervals to distribute the lapping compound properly. Continue the lapping procedure until the valve face and seat contact area is of uniform width and unbroken around the entire circumference of the valve face and seat **(see illustration)**.
25 Carefully remove the valve from the guide and wipe off all traces of lapping compound. Use solvent to clean the valve and wipe the seat area thoroughly with a solvent soaked cloth.
26 Repeat the procedure with fine valve lapping compound, then repeat the entire procedure for the remaining valves.
27 Lay the spring seats in place in the cylinder head, then install new valve stem seals on each of the guides **(see illustration)**. Use an appropriate size deep socket to push the seals into place until they are properly seated. Don't twist or cock them, or they will not seal properly against the valve stems. Also, don't remove them again or they will be damaged.
28 Coat the valve stems with assembly lube or moly-based grease, then install one of them into its guide. Next, install the springs and retainers, compress the springs and install the keepers. **Note:** *When compressing the springs with the valve spring compressor, depress them only as far as is absolutely necessary to slip the keepers into place.* Apply a small amount of grease to the keepers **(see illustration)**

12.29 Rest one hammer on the end of the valve stem and tap on it with another hammer to settle the keepers

to help hold them in place as the pressure is released from the springs. Make certain that the keepers are securely locked in their retaining grooves.
29 Support the cylinder head on blocks so the valves can't contact the workbench top, then very gently tap each of the valve stems with a soft-faced hammer **(see illustration)**. This will help seat the keepers in their grooves.

2-26 Chapter 2 Engine, clutch and transmission

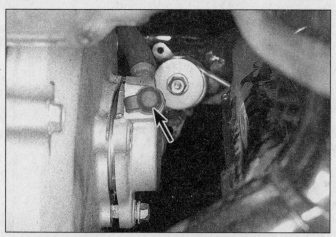

13.3 Pull back the rubber cap (arrow) and place a vinyl tube on the clutch bleed valve

30 Once all of the valves have been installed in the head, check for proper valve sealing by pouring a small amount of solvent into each of the valve ports. If the solvent leaks past the valve(s) into the combustion chamber area, disassemble the valve(s) and repeat the lapping procedure, then reinstall the valve(s) and repeat the check. Repeat the procedure until a satisfactory seal is obtained.

13 Clutch release mechanism - bleeding, removal, inspection and installation

Clutch bleeding

Refer to illustration 13.3

1 Place the motorcycle on its centerstand.
2 Remove the master cylinder cover and diaphragm. Place rags around the master cylinder to protect plastic and painted parts from being damaged by the clutch fluid. Top up the master cylinder with fluid to the upper level line cast inside the cylinder.
3 Remove the cap from the bleed valve **(see illustration)**. Place a box wrench over the bleed valve. Attach a vinyl tube to the valve fitting and put the other end of the tube in a container. Pour enough clean brake fluid into the container to cover the end of the tube.
4 Squeeze the clutch lever several times while you watch the bleed holes in the bottom of the reservoir. Once air bubbles stop rising from the bleed holes, hold the lever in. Tap on the master cylinder body several times to free any air bubbles that may be stuck to the sides of the fluid line. With the clutch lever held in, open the bleed valve 1/4-turn

13.11 Remove the baffle from the bottom of the master cylinder

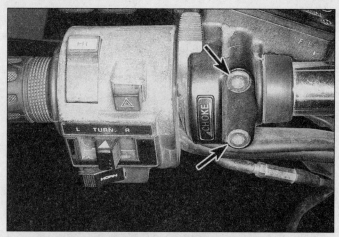

13.9 Remove the clamp bolts (arrows) to separate the master cylinder from the handlebar; on installation, tighten the top bolt first, then the bottom bolt

with the wrench, let air and fluid escape, then tighten the valve.
5 Slowly release the clutch lever.
6 Wait several seconds after releasing the lever, then repeat Steps 4 and 5 until there aren't any more bubbles in the fluid flowing into the container. Top off the master cylinder with fluid, then reinstall the diaphragm and cover and tighten the screws.

Master cylinder

Removal

Refer to illustration 13.9

7 Disconnect the electrical connector from the clutch switch beneath the master cylinder. If the bike has cruise control, disconnect the cruise cancel switch connector as well.
8 Place a towel under the master cylinder to catch any spilled fluid, then remove the union bolt from the master cylinder fluid line. **Caution:** *Brake fluid will damage paint. Wipe up any spills immediately and wash the area with soap and water.*
9 Remove the master cylinder clamp bolts and take the cylinder body off the handlebar **(see illustration)**.

Overhaul

Refer to illustrations 13.11, 13.12, 13.13a and 13.13b

10 Remove the lever pivot bolt and nut and take off the clutch lever. Remove the rearview mirror.
11 Remove the cover and rubber diaphragm from the reservoir.

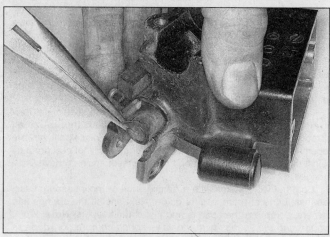

13.12 Pull out the rubber boot and remove the pushrod

Chapter 2 Engine, clutch and transmission

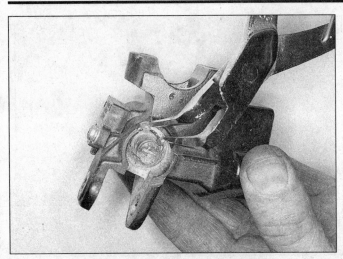

13.13a Remove the snap-ring and washer . . .

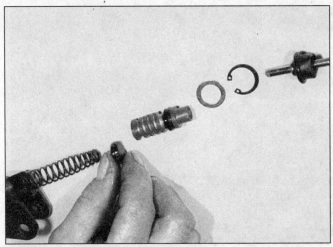

13.13b . . . then pull out the piston with secondary cup, primary cup and spring

Remove the baffle from the bottom of the master cylinder (see illustration).

12 Remove the rubber boot, bushing and pushrod from the master cylinder (see illustration).

13 Remove the snap-ring and retaining ring, then dump out the piston and primary cup, secondary cup and spring (see illustrations). If they won't come out, blow compressed air into the fluid line hole. **Warning:** *The piston may shoot out forcefully enough to cause injury. Point the piston at a block of wood or a pile of rags inside a box and apply air pressure gradually. Never point the end of the cylinder at yourself, including your fingers.*

14 Thoroughly clean all of the components in clean brake fluid (don't use any type of petroleum-based solvent).

15 Check the piston and cylinder bore for wear, scratches and rust. If the piston shows these conditions, replace it and both rubber cups as a set. If the cylinder bore has any defects, replace the entire master cylinder.

16 Install the spring in the cylinder bore, wide end first.

17 Coat a new cup with brake fluid and install it in the cylinder, wide side first.

18 Coat the piston with brake fluid and install it in the cylinder.

19 Install the retaining ring. Press the piston into the bore and install the snap-ring to hold it in place.

20 Install the rubber boot, pushrod and spring.

21 When you install the lever, align the hole in the lever bushing with the pushrod.

Installation

Refer to illustration 13.22

22 Installation is the reverse of the removal steps, with the following additions:

a) *The split between the clamp and master cylinder aligns with the punch mark on the handlebar* (see illustration).

b) *Tighten the clamp bolts to the torque listed in this Chapter's Specifications. Tighten the upper bolt first, then the lower bolt.* **Caution:** *If there's a gap between the lower ends of the clamp when the bolt is tightened to the correct torque, don't try to close it by tightening the lower bolt further. You'll only break the clamp.*

c) *Fill and bleed the clutch hydraulic system.*

d) *Operate the clutch lever and check for fluid leaks.*

Slave cylinder

Removal

Refer to illustrations 13.24 and 13.25

23 If you're removing the slave cylinder for access to other components and don't plan to disassemble it, leave the fluid hose connected during this procedure.

24 If you're planning to disconnect the fluid hose, place rags and a container beneath the slave cylinder to catch spilled fluid. Remove the union bolt and disconnect the clutch hose (see illustration). Place the end of the fluid hose in the container to let the fluid drain.

13.22 Align the split in the master cylinder clamp with the punch mark on the handlebar (arrow)

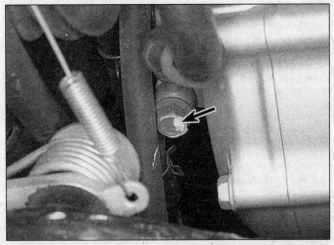

13.24 Remove the union bolt (arrow) to disconnect the clutch line

Chapter 2 Engine, clutch and transmission

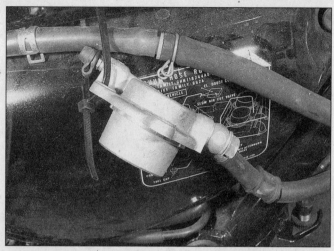

13.25 If you're removing the slave cylinder for access to other components, leave the fluid line connected and tie it up like this

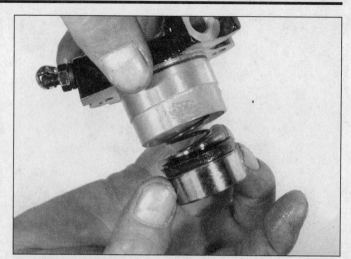

13.26 Take the piston and spring out of the cylinder and remove the seal from the piston; the wide side of the seal faces into the bore

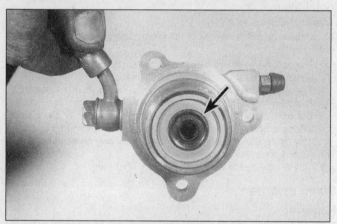

13.29 Replace the pushrod seal (arrow) if it's worn or damaged

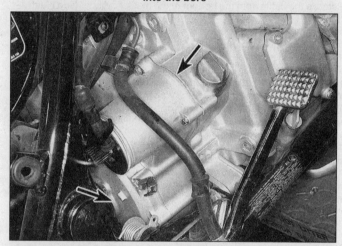

14.4 All clutch components except the housing can be reached by removing the clutch cover (left arrow) with the engine in the frame; to remove the clutch housing, you'll need to remove the engine and the rear crankcase cover (right arrow)

Caution: *Brake fluid will damage paint. Wipe up any spills immediately and wash the area with soap and water.*

25 Remove the slave cylinder mounting bolts and take it off the rear cover. If the hose is still connected, tie the cylinder up so it doesn't hang by the hose **(see illustration)**.

Overhaul

Refer to illustrations 13.26 and 13.29

26 Remove the piston and spring **(see illustration)**. If they won't come out, blow compressed air into the fluid line hole. **Warning:** *The piston may shoot out forcefully enough to cause injury. Point the piston at a block of wood or a pile of rags inside a box and apply air pressure gradually. Never point the end of the cylinder at yourself, including your fingers.*

27 Thoroughly clean all of the components in clean brake fluid (don't use any type of petroleum-based solvent).

28 Check the piston and cylinder bore for wear, scratches and rust. If the piston shows these conditions, replace it and the seal as a set. If the cylinder bore has any defects, replace the entire slave cylinder. If the piston and bore are good, carefully remove the seal from the piston and install a new one with its wide side facing into the cylinder bore.

29 Check the pushrod seal in the back of the piston and replace it if it's worn or damaged **(see illustration)**.

Installation

30 Installation is the reverse of the removal procedure, with the following additions:

a) Use new sealing washers on the fluid line.
b) Tighten the cylinder mounting bolts securely. Tighten the fluid line union bolt to the torques listed in this Chapter's Specifications.
c) Bleed the clutch (see above).
d) Operate the clutch and check for fluid leaks.

14 Clutch - removal, inspection and installation

Note: *All clutch components except the clutch housing can be removed with the engine in the frame.*

Removal

Refer to illustrations 14.4, 14.7, 14.8a, 14.8b, 14.8c, 14.8d, 14.9, 14.10a, 14.10b, 14.11a, 14.11b, 14.12a, 14.12b, 14.13a and 14.13b

1 Place the bike on its centerstand and drain the engine oil (see Chapter 1).
2 Remove the right rear side cover (see Chapter 8).
3 Refer to Section 13 and remove the slave cylinder.
4 Unbolt the clutch cover from the rear of the engine **(see illustration)**. If the cover is stuck, tap it gently with a soft-faced mallet to free it. Don't pry between the cover and engine or the gasket surfaces will be damaged.

Chapter 2 Engine, clutch and transmission

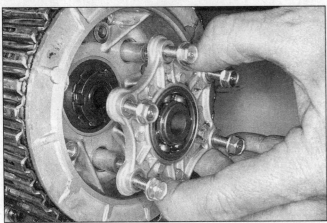

14.7 Pull out the pushrod, then remove the six bolts shown and take off the lifter plate with its lifter piece and bearing

14.8a Bend the lockwasher away from the nut; on installation, fit its slot over the tab on the clutch center (arrow)

14.8b Hold the clutch with a tool like this one and undo the nut . . .

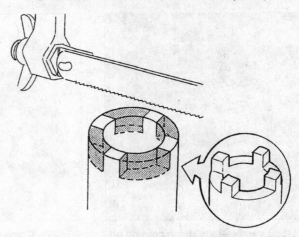

14.8c . . . a clutch nut tool can be made from a piece of thick-walled tubing

14.8d Remove the nut, lockwasher and thrust washer (arrow); on installation, the OUT SIDE mark on the thrust washer faces away from the engine and the tapered end of the nut faces toward the engine

14.9 Pull the clutch center and plates off as a pack

5 Locate the cover dowels and remove the old gasket.
6 If you're planning to remove the clutch housing, remove the engine from the bike and remove the rear crankcase cover (Sections 5 and 15).
7 Loosen the lifter plate bolts evenly in a criss-cross pattern, then remove the lifter plate (see illustration).
8 Bend back the lockwasher on the clutch nut (see illustration).

Remove the nut, using a special holding tool (Honda clutch center holder 07HGB-001000A or equivalent) to prevent the clutch housing from turning (see illustration). Remove the lockwasher and plain washer (see illustrations). Discard the lockwasher and use a new one during installation.
9 Thread a pair of bolts into two of the pressure plate posts and pull out the pressure plate, together with the clutch center and clutch plates (see illustration). The bolts aren't strictly necessary, but do make convenient handles.

14.10a Remove the spline washer from the mainshaft ...

14.10b ... and pry the snap-ring out of its groove

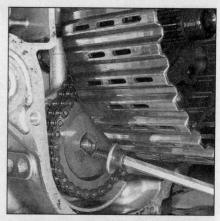
14.11a Unbolt the oil pump sprocket ...

14.11b ... and pull the clutch housing off, together with the oil pump sprocket and drive chain

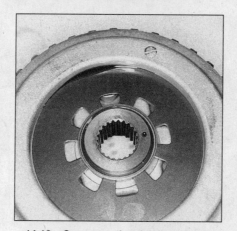
14.12a Compress the clutch pack in a vise just enough to provide removal clearance for the snap-ring

14.12b Remove the snap-ring, washer and diaphragm spring

14.13a Check the pressure plate and clutch center friction surfaces, as well as the clutch center splines

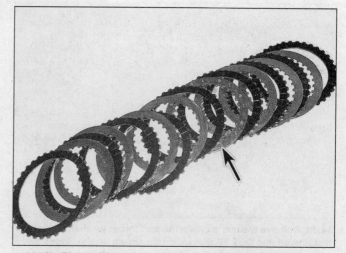
14.13b The clutch pack is made up of alternating friction and metal plates, with friction plates going on first and last; the clutch damper (arrow) is in the eighth position from the clutch center

10   Take the spline washer off the transmission mainshaft and pry the snap-ring out with a pointed tool **(see illustrations)**.

11   Unbolt the oil pump sprocket, then slide the clutch housing, oil pump chain and sprocket off together **(see illustrations)**.

12   Place the clutch center assembly in a vise. Tighten the vise just enough to take the pressure off the snap-ring that secures the diaphragm spring, then remove the spring, washer and diaphragm spring **(see illustrations)**. **Caution:** *Don't compress the spring any more than necessary or it will lose tension.*

13   Lift the pressure plate out of the clutch center, then remove the clutch plates and damper **(see illustrations)**.

Chapter 2 Engine, clutch and transmission

2-31

14.15 Check the clutch housing for worn splines or slots; check the oil pump drive chain and sprockets for wear or damage

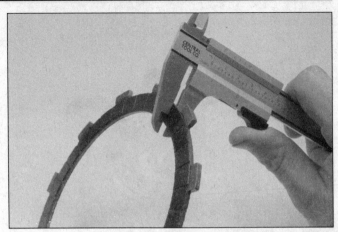

14.17 Measure the thickness of the friction plates

14.19 Check the metal plates for warpage

14.20a Check the clutch damper for warpage . . .

Inspection

Refer to illustrations 14.15, 14.17, 14.19, 14.20a, 14.20b and 14.22

14 Examine the splines on both the inside and the outside of the clutch center **(see illustration 14.13a)**. If any wear is evident, replace the clutch center with a new one. Check the friction surfaces on the clutch center and pressure plate for scoring, wear or signs of overheating.

15 Check the clutch housing splines for wear or damage. Check the edges of the slots in the clutch housing for indentations made by the friction plate tabs. If the indentations are deep they can prevent clutch release, so the housing should be replaced with a new one. If the indentations can be removed easily with a file, the life of the housing can be prolonged to an extent. Also check the oil pump chain and sprockets for damage **(see illustration)**. The chain, oil pump sprocket and clutch housing should be replaced as a set if problems are found.

16 Lay the diaphragm spring on a flat surface and measure the height of the spring fingers. Replace the spring if its free height is less than the value listed in this Chapter's Specifications.

17 If the lining material of the friction plates smells burnt or if it's glazed, new parts are required. If the metal clutch plates are scored or discolored, they must be replaced with new ones. Measure the thickness of each friction plate **(see illustration)** and compare the results to this Chapter's Specifications. Replace the friction plates as a set if any are near the wear limit.

18 Check the tabs on the friction plates for excessive wear and mushroomed edges. They can be cleaned up with a file if the deformation is not severe.

19 Lay the metal plates, one at a time, on a perfectly flat surface (such as a piece of plate glass) and check for warpage by trying to slip

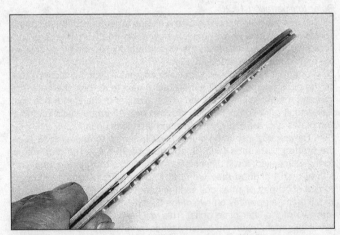

14.20b . . . and make sure its wave spring (between the plates) isn't broken

a feeler gauge between the flat surface and the plate **(see illustration)**. The feeler gauge should be the same thickness as the warpage limit listed in this Chapter's Specifications. Do this at several places around the plate's circumference. If the feeler gauge can be slipped under the plate, it is warped and should be replaced with a new one.

20 Check the clutch damper for warpage in the same manner as the metal plates **(see illustration)**. Also check the wave spring between the layers of the damper **(see illustration)**; if it's damaged, replace the damper.

2-32   Chapter 2   Engine, clutch and transmission

14.22 Pull the lifter piece out of the bearing and take the bearing out of the lifter plate

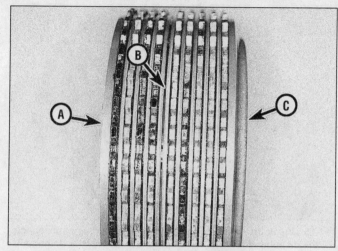

14.26 Clutch pack details

A   Clutch center   C   Pressure plate
B   Damper

21   Check the thrust washers and locknut for wear and damage. Replace any worn or damaged parts.

22   Make sure the clutch pushrod isn't bent (roll it on a perfectly flat surface or use V-blocks and a dial indicator). Check the pushrod and lifter piece for wear or damage and replace them if defects are visible **(see illustration)**.

23   Check the release bearing and lifter plate for wear, damage or roughness. Replace the bearing if its condition is uncertain or obviously bad. Drive it out with a bearing driver, then drive a new one in with a bearing driver or socket that presses against the outer race of the bearing. Don't apply pressure to the inner race or the bearing will be damaged.

24   Clean all traces of old gasket material from the clutch cover (and the rear cover if it was removed) and its mating surface on the crankcase.

Installation

Refer to illustration 14.26

25   Install the clutch housing on the engine together with the oil pump sprocket and drive chain. Install a new snap-ring with its sharp-cornered side facing away from the engine and its rounded side toward the engine **(see illustration 14.10b)**.

26   Coat the friction plates with clean engine oil. Install a friction plate on the clutch center. Install a metal plate next to it, then alternate friction and metal plates. Install the clutch damper in the eighth position, then install a friction plate **(see illustration)**. Alternate metal and friction plates until are installed; a friction plate goes on last.

27   Temporarily install the clutch pack in the clutch housing to align the friction plate tabs **(see illustration 14.9)**. Once the diaphragm spring is installed, it will difficult if not impossible to align the tabs, and if they aren't aligned they won't fit into the clutch housing slots. If you've got a pair of small coil springs and washers, it's a good idea to install them temporarily on two of the clutch center posts (secure them with two of the lifter plate bolts). This will keep the tabs from slipping out of alignment when the clutch pack is removed from the housing.

28   Install the clutch pack in a vise and reverse Steps 12 and 13 to install the diaphragm spring. Remove the clutch pack from the vise and take off the coil springs and washers (if used).

29   Install the clutch pack in the clutch housing. Install a new lockwasher with its oval hole over the tab on clutch center **(see illustration 14.8a)**. Hold the clutch from turning with the tools described in Step 8 and tighten the nut to the torque listed in this Chapter's Specifications. Bend the lockwasher against the flats on the nut.

30   Install the lifter plate. Tighten its bolts securely, but don't overtighten them and strip the threads.

31   Lubricate the lifter piece and pushrod with multipurpose grease, then install them in the clutch.

15.4 Remove the output gear access cover from the right side of the engine . . .

32   Make sure the clutch cover dowels are in position, then install a new gasket. Install the cover and tighten its bolts evenly; tighten them securely, but don't strip the threads.

33   The remainder of installation is the reverse of the removal steps.

34   Fill the crankcase with the recommended type and amount of engine oil (see Chapter 1).

15   Rear case cover - removal, bearing inspection and installation

Removal

Refer to illustrations 15.4, 15.5, 15.6a and 15.b

1   Remove the engine from the motorcycle (see Section 5).

2   If you're working on a 1984 model, remove the pulse generators (see Chapter 5).

3   Refer to Section 14 and remove the clutch cover.

4   Remove the output gear access plate from the right side of the engine **(see illustration)**.

5   If you're working on a 1986 or 1987 model, remove the retaining bolt from one side of the output shaft gear, then turn it 1/2 turn and

Chapter 2 Engine, clutch and transmission 2-33

15.5 ... and remove the gear (1984 and 1985 shown)

15.6a Unbolt the cover and take it off ...

15.6b ... then locate the dowels (arrows) and remove the old gasket

15.8 Replace the output shaft bearing if it's rough, loose or noisy

15.9 Pry out the output shaft seal and tap in a new one

remove the bolt from the other side. Take the gear out of the engine **(see illustration)**.
6 Undo the rear case cover bolts. Tap the cover loose and take it off the engine, then locate the dowel pins and remove the old gasket **(see illustrations)**.

Inspection

Refer to illustrations 15.8 and 15.9

7 Check the cover for obvious problems, such as warpage, cracks or a damaged gasket surface, and replace it if problems are found.
8 Rotate the output shaft bearing in the cover and check for roughness, looseness or noise **(see illustration)**. If the bearing is in bad or doubtful condition, replace it. Tap the bearing out of its bore with a bearing driver or a socket the same diameter as the bearing outer race. Drive in a new bearing, using the same tool.
9 Pry the output shaft oil seal out of the cover and tap in a new one, using a bearing driver or socket the same diameter as the seal **(see illustration)**.

Installation

Refer to illustration 15.10

10 Apply a dab of sealant to each of the crankcase parting lines **(see illustration)**. Be sure the dowels are in position, then install a new gasket.
11 Place the cover on the engine and finger-tighten its bolts. Then

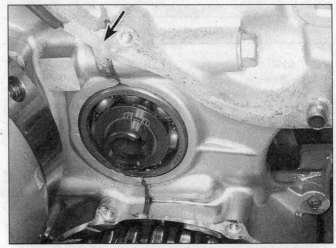

15.10 Apply a dab of sealant at each point where the gasket crosses a crankcase seam (arrow)

tighten the bolts evenly in stages to the torque listed in this Chapter's Specifications.
12 The remainder of installation is the reverse of the removal steps.

Chapter 2 Engine, clutch and transmission

16.4 Pull the output shaft assembly out of the engine

17.4 Remove the three bolts to detach the pump (the three Phillips screws hold the pump together)

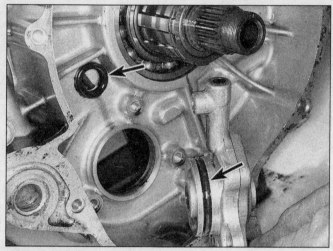

17.5 Pull the pump off; it's a good idea to replace the grommet and pump body O-ring (arrows) whenever the pump is removed

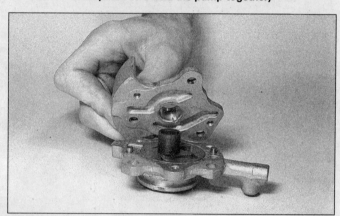

17.6 Remove the screws, separate the pump halves and locate the dowels

16 Output shaft - removal, inspection and installation

Removal

Refer to illustration 16.4

1 Remove the engine from the frame (Section 5).
2 If you're working on a 1986 or 1987 model, Pry the output shaft dust seal out of the rear case cover. Hold the output shaft with Honda tool 07923-6890101 and undo the locknut with Honda tool 07916-MB00000.
3 Remove the rear case cover from the engine (Section 15).
4 Pull the output shaft out of the engine **(see illustration)**. Take the output gear out through the access hole **(see illustration 15.5)**.

Inspection

5 Check the gears for worn or damaged teeth and replace them if problems are found.
6 Check the output shaft for wear or damage, such as a broken spring. Spin the bearing on the end of the output shaft and check it for roughness, looseness or noise.
7 Measure the assembled length of the damper spring and compare it with the value listed in this Chapter's Specifications.
8 If problems are found, take the shaft to a Honda dealer for disassembly and parts replacement.

Installation

9 Installation is the reverse of the removal steps, with the following additions:
   a) If you're working on a 1986 or 1987 model, secure the output gear with a new lockwasher.
   b) If you're working on a 1986 or 1987 model, hold the output shaft with the same tools used for removal. Use a new lockwasher on the output shaft locknut and tighten it to the torque listed in this Chapter's Specifications.

17 Scavenging oil pump - removal, inspection and installation

Removal

Refer to illustrations 17.4 and 17.5

1 The scavenging oil pump, which picks up oil from the clutch cavity, can be removed without separating the crankcase halves.
2 Remove the engine from the motorcycle (see Section 5).
3 Remove the clutch housing, together with the oil pump chain and sprockets (see Section 14).
4 Unbolt the scavenging pump from the engine **(see illustration)**.
5 Pull the pump out and locate the grommet **(see illustration)**.

Inspection

Refer to illustrations 17.6, 17.7, 17.9a, 17.9b and 17.9c

6 Remove the three Phillips screws and separate the pump halves **(see illustration)**.

Chapter 2 Engine, clutch and transmission

17.7 Remove the drive piece and the rotors; if scoring like this is found, replace the pump

17.9a Measure the gap between inner and outer rotors (this is the main pump; the measurement is done in the same way for the scavenge pump) . . .

17.9b . . . and between the inner and outer rotors

17.9c Lay a straightedge across the rotors and pump body and measure the gap

7 Take the rotors and drive guide out of the pump **(see illustration)**. Wash the oil pump in solvent, then dry it off.

8 Check the pump body and rotors for scoring and wear. If any damage or uneven or excessive wear is evident, replace the pump (individual parts aren't available). If you are rebuilding the engine, it's a good idea to install a new oil pump.

9 Measure the clearance between the inner and outer rotor tips and between the outer rotor and housing **(see illustrations)**. Place a straightedge across the pump body and measure the gap between the straightedge and rotors with a feeler gauge **(see illustration)**. Replace the pump if any of the clearances is excessive.

10 Inspect the rubber grommet **(see illustration 17.5)**. Since there's a good deal of labor required to remove the pump, it's a good idea to replace the grommet whenever the pump is removed.

11 If the pump is good, reverse the disassembly steps to reassemble it. Make sure the pin is centered in the rotor shaft so it will align with the slot in the inner rotor.

Installation

12 Before installing the pump, prime it by pouring oil into it while turning the shaft by hand - this will ensure that it begins to pump oil quickly.

13 Installation is the reverse of removal, with the following additions:
  a) Align the flat on the pump drive shaft with the flat in the drive guide.
  b) Be sure the pump-to-engine dowel and rubber grommet are in position.
  c) Tighten the mounting bolts securely, but don't overtighten them and strip the threads.

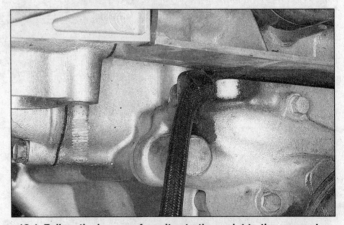

18.4 Follow the harness from its starting point to the connector and unplug it

18 Front case cover - removal and installation

Refer to illustrations 18.4, 18.5a, 18.5b, 18.5c, 18.8 and 18.9

1 Place the transmission in neutral.
2 Drain the engine oil and coolant (see Chapter 1).
3 Remove the water pump cover and disconnect the lower hose from the radiator (see Chapter 3).
4 Follow the gear position sensor harness from the rubber grommet in the cover to the electrical connector and unplug it **(see illustration)**.

Chapter 2 Engine, clutch and transmission

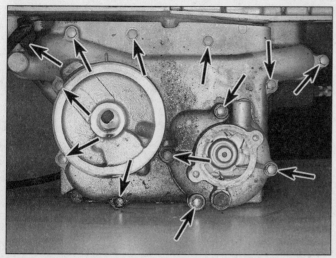

18.5a Loosen the cover bolts evenly, in two or three stages

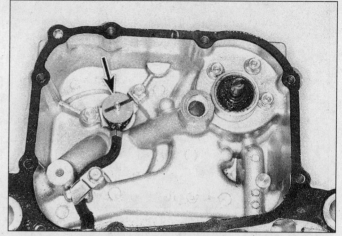

18.5b Pull the cover away from the crankcase and remove the gasket; if necessary, unbolt the gearshift sensor (arrow) and its harness retainer from the cover

5   Remove the cover bolts and take the cover off the engine, locate the dowels and remove the gasket (see illustrations).
6   Pull out the oil pump tube (see illustration 18.5b). Replace its O-rings with new ones if there's any doubt about their condition. It's a good idea to replace these O-rings, as well as the cover O-rings, whenever the cover is removed.
7   Thoroughly clean the gasket from the cover and crankcase.
8   Turn the pin on the gearshift position sensor to align with the tab on the switch (see illustration).
9   Make sure all O-rings and the wiring harness grommet are in position (see illustration). Install the oil pump tube in the oil pump.
10 Place a quarter-inch wide dab of sealant across the crankcase parting lines at top center and bottom center of the gasket surface, then install a new gasket over the dowels.
11 Position the cover on the engine and install its bolts. Tighten the bolts evenly, in two or three stages, in a criss-cross pattern. Tighten the bolts securely, but don't overtighten them and damage the threads.

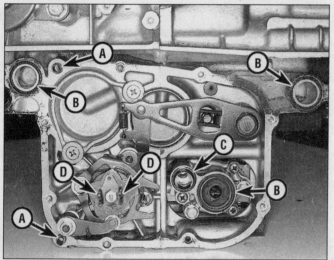

18.5c Front crankcase details

A   Dowels
B   O-rings
C   O-ring and oil pump tube
D   Slots for gearshift sensor pin

19 Main oil pump - removal, inspection and installation

Refer to illustrations 19.2a through 19.2g

1   Refer to Section 18 and remove the front case cover.
2   To remove and disassemble the pump, refer to the accompanying

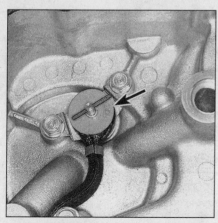

18.8 Align the gearshift sensor pin with the tab on the sensor body (arrow) so the pin will fit into the slots of the external shift mechanism when the cover is installed

18.9 The wiring harness grommet fits under the gasket like this

19.2a Remove two mounting bolts and three cover screws . . .

Chapter 2 Engine, clutch and transmission

2-37

19.2b ... pull the cover off the oil pump, locate the dowels (arrows) and remove the outer rotor

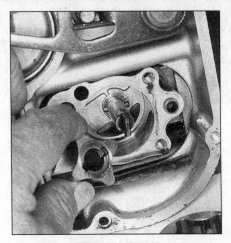

19.2c Pull out the inner rotor; on installation, its slot fits over the drive pin

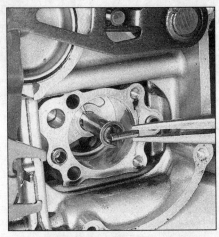

19.2d Pull out the drive pin and remove the thrust washer

illustrations (see illustrations).

3   Check the pressure relief valve for scoring or wear and replace the pump if problems are found.

4   The remainder of inspection is the same as for the scavenging oil pump (see Section 17).

5   Assembly is the reverse of disassembly. Make sure the drive pin engages the inner rotor (see illustration 19.2c). Use a new cotter pin to secure the relief valve.

6   Installation is the reverse of the removal steps. Tighten the mounting bolts securely, but don't overtighten them and strip the threads.

20 External shift mechanism - removal, inspection and installation

Shift pedal - removal and installation

Refer to illustrations 20.2 and 20.3

1   Place the bike on its centerstand.

2   Look for alignment marks on the shift pedal and its outer shaft (see illustration). If there aren't any, make your own. Remove the pinch bolt and take the pedal off the shaft.

19.2e Pull the pump body off the crankcase, remove the old gasket and locate the dowels; you'll need to remove the engine from the frame to remove the pump driveshaft

19.2f Remove the relief valve cotter pin; use a new one on assembly

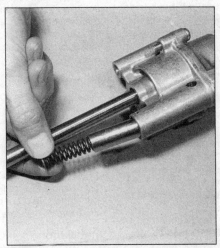

19.2g Pull out the spring and relief valve and check the valve for wear or damage

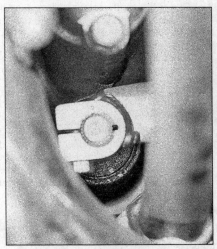

20.2 Check for alignment marks on the pedal and shaft, then remove the pinch bolt and take the pedal off

2-38   Chapter 2 Engine, clutch and transmission

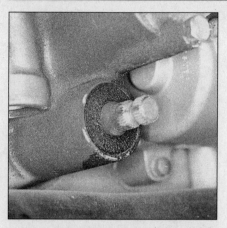

20.3 Check the shift shaft seal and replace it if it leaks

20.7 Pull the shift arm away from the linkage

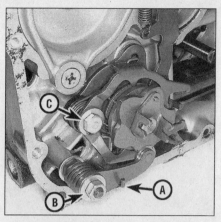

20.8 Note how the spring fits over the stopper arm (A), then remove the bolt (B), washer, arm and spring; remove the positive stopper bolt and washer (C) . . .

20.9 . . . and take off the positive stopper, its spring and collar

A Drum joint
B Stopper plate
C Positive stopper post
D Stopper pins

20.13 Remove the drum center (lower arrow) and the bearing retainer (upper arrow) for access to the bearing

3   Check the shaft seal for leakage (see illustration). It it's been leaking, pry it out and tap in a new one with a socket the same diameter as the seal. You may need to remove the left side of the exhaust system for access (see Chapter 4).
4   Installation is the reverse of the removal steps. Tighten the pinch bolts securely, but don't overtighten them and strip the threads.

Shift mechanism
Removal

Refer to illustrations 20.7, 20.8 and 20.9

5   The stopper arm(s), positive stopper, drum joint and stopper plate(s) are the only parts of the external shift linkage that can be removed without disassembling the crankcase. The shift arm, generally considered part of the external linkage, is bolted to components on the inside of the crankcase, so the crankcase must be disassembled to remove it.
6   Remove the front case cover from the engine (see Section 18).
7   Pull the shift arm away from the shift drum center (see illustration).
8   Remove the nut and washer from the stopper arm, then remove the stopper arm, spring and collar (see illustration). If you're working on a 1984 or 1985 model, there are two stopper arms pivoting on the same collar. The lower one is the neutral stopper arm; the upper one is the stopper arm.
9   Remove the positive stopper bolt and washer, then remove the positive stopper with its spring and collar (see illustration 20.8 and the accompanying illustration).
10   Remove the bolt from the center of the shift drum, then take off the drum joint and stopper plate (two stopper plates on 1984 and 1985 models).

Inspection

Refer to illustration 20.13

11   Check the condition of the stopper lever(s) and spring. Replace the stopper lever if it's worn where it contacts the shift drum. Replace the spring if it's distorted.
12   Inspect the stopper pins plate and the pins on the end of the shift drum (see illustration 20.9). If they're worn or damaged, replace them. If their holes in the end of the shift drum are enlarged, you'll have to disassemble the crankcase to replace the shift drum.
13   If the shift drum bearing is worn, remove the bearing retainer (see illustration). Take the bearing out of the case and install a new one.

Installation

14   If the stopper pin plate was removed from the shift drum, install it. Be sure to reinstall the dowel pins.
15   Apply non-permanent thread locking agent to the threads of the stopper arm bolt, then install the stopper arm (both stopper arms on

Chapter 2 Engine, clutch and transmission

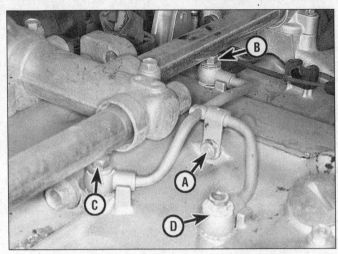

21.11 Crankcase oil line details

- A Mounting bolt
- B Long union bolt
- C Union bolt with large oil hole
- D Union bolt with small oil hole

21.12a Upper left side crankcase bolts

- A 10 mm bolts
- B 8 mm bolts

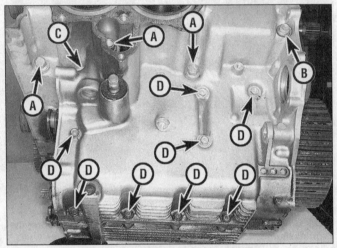

21.12b Lower left side crankcase bolts

- A 10 mm bolts
- B 8 mm bolt
- C 6 mm bolt (hidden)
- D 6 mm bolts

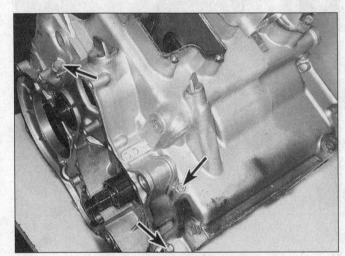

21.12c Right side crankcase bolts

1984 and 1985 models) and return spring. Make sure the stopper arm engages the neutral detent in the shift drum. Tighten the bolt securely, but don't overtighten it and damage the threads.

16 The remainder of installation is the reverse of the removal steps, plus the following additions:
 a) Before installing the front case cover, operate the shift linkage by hand to make sure it works properly.
 b) Fill the engine with oil and coolant (see Chapter 1).

21 Crankcase - disassembly and reassembly

1 To examine and repair or replace the pistons, connecting rods, bearings, main oil pump, crankshaft, primary chain and gears, internal shift linkage or transmission components, the crankcase must be split into two parts.

Disassembly

Refer to illustrations 21.11, 21.12a, 21.12b, 21.12c, 21.14, 21.15a and 21.15b

2 Remove the engine from the motorcycle (see Section 5).
3 If you're working on a 1984 model, refer to Chapter 5 and remove the pulse generators.
4 Remove the rear engine cover (Section 15). If you're working on a 1984 model, remove the pulse generator shaft (see Chapter 5).
5 It's not necessary to remove the clutch to separate the case halves, but if you're planning to do clutch work, it will be easier to remove at this stage (Section 14). If you don't remove the clutch, you'll need to unscrew the scavenge oil pump sprocket bolt, then slip the sprocket off the pump and let it hang by the chain (see illustration 14.11a).
6 Remove the starter motor (see Chapter 9).
7 Remove the carburetors and intake tubes (see Chapter 4).
8 Refer to Chapter 3 and remove the coolant tubes and thermostat housing.
9 Remove the timing belts and front engine cover (see Sections 7 and 18).
10 Remove the cylinder head(s). You can remove just the left cylinder head if you're not planning to work on the right cylinder head, pistons or connecting rods (see Section 10).

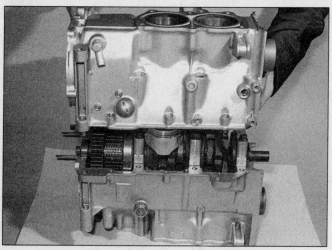

21.14 Lift the left case off; don't let the pistons fall

21.15a Locate the dowel at the rear corner . . .

21.15b . . . and the one at the front

21.20 Be sure the primary chain oiler (left arrow) is in its bore; the crankshaft ball bearing (right arrow) should be replaced if it's rough, loose or noisy when spun

11 Remove the oil distribution line from the top of the crankcase (see illustration).

12 Remove 19 crankcase bolts from the left side of the case and three bolts from the right side (see illustrations).

13 Place a couple of wooden blocks and some shop rags where you can reach them easily while holding onto the crankcase. **Note:** *This step will be easier if you have an assistant.* Lift the left case half partway off the right case half. When you can see the connecting rods, let the left case half rest on the wooden support blocks. Stuff the shop rags around the connecting rods so they won't fall when the left case half is pulled off the pistons.

14 Carefully separate the crankcase halves, guiding the external shift linkage pawl clear of the drum center as you do so (see illustration 20.7 and the accompanying illustration). If they won't separate easily, make sure all fasteners have been removed. Don't pry against the crankcase mating surfaces or they will leak.

15 Look for the case dowels (see illustrations). If they're not in one of the crankcase halves, locate them.

16 Refer to Sections 22 through 34 for information on the internal components of the crankcase.

Reassembly

Refer to illustration 21.20

17 Make sure the transmission shafts are correctly positioned in the right crankcase half (see Section 31). Make sure the crankshaft is fully installed, with all connecting rods, pistons and rings.

18 You'll need to support the left side pistons and connecting rods perfectly upright later in the procedure. The easiest way to do this is have an assistant hold the pistons and rods for you while you lower the left case half over them. Another way is to make a pair of wooden support blocks that fit beneath the pistons and hold them upright. These can be slipped out after the case half has been installed far enough that the cylinder are over the piston rings.

19 Conventional ring compressors can't be used because there's no way to remove them once the case half is over the rings. Honda uses special ring compressors made in two halves, which are secured together by Velcro strips. After the case half is installed far enough to compress the rings, the compressor halves are separated by pulling on a string. You can order the special compressors from a Honda dealer. However, if you're very careful, the chamfered bottom edges of the cylinders will allow the cylinders to be fitted over the pistons and rings without the use of ring compressors.

20 Remove all traces of sealant from the crankcase mating surfaces. Be careful not to let any fall into the case as this is done. Check to make sure the dowel pins and the primary chain oiler are in place (see illustrations 21.15a, 21.15b and the accompanying illustration).

21 Apply a thin, even bead of sealant to the crankcase mating surfaces.

22 Lubricate the threads and the undersides of the heads of the 10 mm bolts with moly-based grease. Install the case bolts (see illustrations 21.12a, 21.12b and 21.12c). Tighten the 10 mm bolts first, in two

Chapter 2 Engine, clutch and transmission

2-41

22.3a Remove the oil strainer for cleaning (late design shown; early design similar)

22.3b Unbolt the oil guide plate from the crankcase wall

23.2 Bend the lockwasher tab away from the shift arm bolt and undo the bolt

23.3a Note how the ends of the return spring fit over the post (arrow)

23.3b Pull the outer shift arm shaft out of the crankcase . . .

23.3c . . . and remove the inner shift arm

or three stages and a criss-cross pattern, to the torque listed in this Chapter's Specifications. Then tighten the remaining bolts evenly to their specified torques.

23   Turn the mainshaft and make sure it turns freely. Also make sure the crankshaft turns freely.

24   The remainder of assembly is the reverse of disassembly.

22 Crankcase components - inspection and servicing

Refer to illustrations 22.3a and 22.3b

1   After the crankcases have been separated and the crankshaft, shift cam and forks and transmission components removed, the crankcases should be cleaned thoroughly with new solvent and dried with compressed air.

2   Remove any oil passage plugs that haven't already been removed. All oil passages should be blown out with compressed air.

3   Remove the oil strainer screen and the oil guide plate (see illustrations). Clean the screen thoroughly in solvent and let it dry completely.

4   If you're working on a 1984 through 1986 model, inspect the countershaft rear bearing (it's a press fit in the right case half). If the bearing is rough, loose or noisy when spun, remove it with a slide hammer. Drive in a new bearing with a driver that applies pressure to the bearing outer race.

5   All traces of old gasket sealant should be removed from the mating surfaces. Minor damage to the surfaces can be cleaned up with a fine sharpening stone or grindstone. **Caution:** *Be very careful not to nick or gouge the crankcase mating surfaces or leaks will result. Check both crankcase halves very carefully for cracks and other damage.*

6   If any damage is found that can't be repaired, replace the crankcase halves as a set.

23 Internal shift linkage - removal, inspection and installation

Removal

Refer to illustrations 23.2, 23.3a, 23.3b and 23.3c

1   Refer to Section 21 and disassemble the crankcase.

2   In the left case half, bend back the lockwasher tab and remove the shift arm bolt (see illustration).

3   On the outside of the case at the front, note how the return spring ends fit over the return spring post (see illustration). Pull the outer shift arm shaft out of the case and lift out the inner shift arm (see illustrations).

Inspection

4   Inspect the return spring post (see illustration 23.3a). If it's worn or damaged, replace it. If it's loose, unscrew it, apply a non-permanent thread locking compound to the threads, reinstall the post and tighten it securely.

5   Check the shift arm shaft for bends. If the shaft is bent, you can attempt to straighten it. Inspect the pawls and springs on the shift shaft and replace the shaft if they're worn or damaged.

24.3 The number on each connecting rod is a bearing selection code; the letter indicates weight grade

24.4a Lay the left side connecting rods down so the nuts are accessible, then remove them

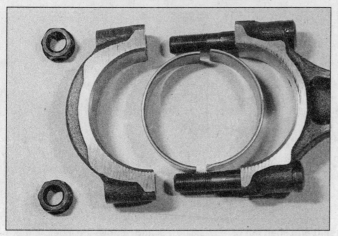

24.4b Separate the caps from the connecting rods and remove the bearing inserts from rod and cap

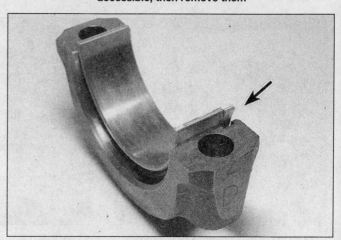

24.8 The tab on the bearing insert fits into the notch in the cap or connecting rod

6 Check the inner shift arm and shift spindle for wear at their contact points. Replace worn parts.

Installation

7 Installation is the reverse of the removal steps. Use a new lockwasher on the shift arm bolt. Tighten the bolt to the torque listed in this Chapter's Specifications and bend the lockwasher tab against the bolt.

24 Piston/connecting rod assemblies - removal, connecting rod inspection and installation

Removal

Refer to illustrations 24.3, 24.4a and 24.4b

1 Remove both cylinder heads and disassemble the crankcase (Sections 10 and 21).
2 Before removing the connecting rods from the crankshaft, insert a feeler gauge between the side of each connecting rod and the crankshaft. If the clearance on any rod (connecting rod side clearance) is greater than that listed in this Chapter's Specifications, that rod will have to be replaced with a new one. If the clearance is still excessive after replacing the rod, the crankshaft will have to be replaced.
3 There aren't any cylinder numbers marked on the connecting rods and caps, and it's important to reinstall them in their original locations. Using a felt pen or a center punch, mark the cylinder number on each rod and cap. Number the pistons as well; if they're reused, they must be returned to their original cylinders. The letter marks on the rods refer to connecting rod weight grades; the number marks are used for bearing selection **(see illustration)**.
4 Unscrew the left side bearing cap nuts, separate the caps from the rods, then detach the rods from the crankshaft **(see illustrations)**. If the cap is stuck, tap on the ends of the rod bolts with a soft face hammer to free them.
5 Temporarily reassemble the rods to the caps so the rods and caps don't get mixed up.
6 Unscrew the right side bearing cap nuts and separate the caps from the rods. If the engine is still on a workbench with its right side facing down, lay it flat. Tap gently on the studs of the connecting rods with a wooden hammer handle to push the pistons out of their bores, then carefully remove the rods without scratching the cylinders. Temporarily reassemble the rods to the caps so the rods and caps don't get mixed up.

Connecting rod inspection

7 Check the connecting rods for cracks and other obvious damage. Have the rods checked for twisting and bending at a dealer service department or other motorcycle repair shop.

Installation

Refer to illustrations 24.8, 24.10a, 24.10b and 24.12

8 Wipe off the bearing inserts, connecting rods and caps. Install the inserts into the rods and caps, using your hands only, making sure the tabs on the inserts engage with the notches in the rods and caps **(see illustration)**. When all the inserts are installed, lubricate them with engine assembly lube or moly-based grease. Don't get any lubricant on the mating surfaces of the rod or cap.

Chapter 2 Engine, clutch and transmission

24.10a Place ring compressors on the no. 1 and no. 3 pistons

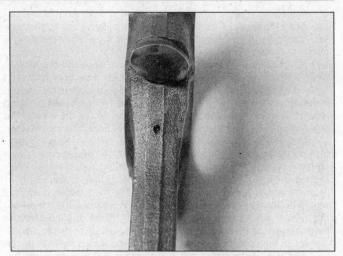

24.10b Be sure the connecting rod oil hole faces the proper direction when installed (see text); align the oil hole in the bearing insert with the oil hole in the rod

14   As a final step, recheck the connecting rod side clearances (see Step 1). If the clearances aren't correct, find out why before proceeding with engine assembly.

25 Cylinders - inspection

Refer to illustration 25.3

1   Don't attempt to separate the liners from the cylinder block.
2   Check the cylinder walls carefully for scratches and score marks.
3   Using the appropriate precision measuring tools, check each cylinder's diameter. Measure parallel to the crankshaft axis and across the crankshaft axis, at the top, center and bottom of the cylinder **(see illustration)**. Average the measurements and compare the results to this Chapter's Specifications. If the cylinder walls are tapered, out-of-round, worn beyond the specified limits, or badly scuffed or scored, have them rebored and honed by a dealer service department or a motorcycle repair shop. If a rebore is done, oversize pistons and rings will be required as well.
4   As an alternative, if the precision measuring tools are not available, a dealer service department or motorcycle repair shop will make the measurements and offer advice concerning servicing of the cylinders.

24.12 Tighten the connecting rod nuts to the specified torque

9   Place short pieces of vinyl hose over the connecting rod studs to prevent them from damaging the crankshaft.
10   On the right side of the engine, place the ring compressors over the rings **(see illustration)**. Insert the connecting rods into the correct bores, making sure the oil holes and piston top marks are in the correct relationship. The IN mark on the top of the no. 1 and no. 3 pistons goes toward the top of the engine; the oil hole in the no. 1 and no. 3 connecting rods faces down **(see illustration)**. The no. 2 and no. 4 piston IN marks go toward the top of the engine; the no. 2 and no. 4 connecting rod oil holes also go toward the top of the engine.
11   Assemble each connecting rod to its proper journal, referring to the previously applied cylinder numbers. The number stamped across the rod/cap seam on one side of the connecting rod should fit together perfectly when the rod and cap are assembled. If it doesn't, the wrong cap is on the rod. Fix this problem before assembling the engine any further.
12   When you're sure the rods are positioned correctly, lubricate the threads of the rod bolts and the undersides of the rod nuts with engine oil and tighten the nuts to the torque listed in this Chapter's Specifications **(see illustration)**. **Note:** *Snug both nuts evenly, in several stages, to the specified torque.*
13   Turn the rods on the crankshaft. If any of them feel tight, tap on the bottom of the connecting rod caps with a hammer - this should relieve stress and free them up. If it doesn't, recheck the bearing clearance.

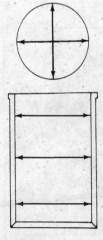

25.3 Measure bore diameter with a bore gauge in two directions, at top, center and bottom of the ring travel

5   If they are in reasonably good condition and not worn to the outside of the limits, and if the piston-to-cylinder clearances can be maintained properly, then the cylinders do not have to be rebored; honing is all that is necessary.

6   To perform the honing operation you will need the proper size flexible hone with fine stones, or a "bottle brush" type hone, plenty of light oil or honing oil, some shop towels and an electric drill motor. Hold the crankcase half in a vise (cushioned with soft jaws or wood blocks) when performing the honing operation. Mount the hone in the drill motor, compress the stones and slip the hone into the cylinder. Lubricate the cylinder thoroughly, turn on the drill and move the hone up and down in the cylinder at a pace which will produce a fine crosshatch pattern on the cylinder wall with the crosshatch lines intersecting at approximately a 60-degree angle. Be sure to use plenty of lubricant and do not take off any more material than is absolutely necessary to produce the desired effect. Do not withdraw the hone from the cylinder while it is running. Instead, shut off the drill and continue moving the hone up and down in the cylinder until it comes to a complete stop, then compress the stones and withdraw the hone. Wipe the oil out of the cylinder and repeat the procedure on the remaining cylinders. Remember, do not remove too much material from the cylinder wall. If you do not have the tools, or do not desire to perform the honing operation, a dealer service department or motorcycle repair shop will generally do it for a reasonable fee.

7   Next, the cylinders must be thoroughly washed with warm soapy water to remove all traces of the abrasive grit produced during the honing operation. Be sure to run a brush through the bolt holes and coolant passages and flush them with running water. After rinsing, dry the cylinders thoroughly and apply a coat of light, rust-preventative oil to all machined surfaces.

26 Pistons - inspection, removal and installation

1   The pistons are attached to the connecting rods with piston pins that are a tight press fit in the rods and a light slip fit in the pistons.
2   Refer to Section 24 and remove the piston/connecting rod assemblies.

Inspection

Refer to illustrations 26.4, 26.11 and 26.12

3   Before the inspection process can be carried out, the pistons must be cleaned and the old piston rings removed.
4   Using a piston ring installation tool, carefully remove the rings from the pistons **(see illustration)**. Do not nick or gouge the pistons in the process.
5   Scrape all traces of carbon from the tops of the pistons. A handheld wire brush or a piece of fine emery cloth can be used once most of the deposits have been scraped away. **Caution:** *Do not, under any circumstances, use a wire brush mounted in a drill motor to remove deposits from the pistons; the piston material is soft and will be eroded away by the wire brush.*
6   Use a piston ring groove cleaning tool to remove any carbon deposits from the ring grooves. If a tool is not available, a piece broken off the old ring will do the job. Be very careful to remove only the carbon deposits. Do not remove any metal and do not nick or gouge the sides of the ring grooves.
7   Once the deposits have been removed, clean the pistons with solvent and dry them thoroughly. Make sure the oil return holes below the oil ring grooves are clear.
8   If the pistons are not damaged or worn excessively and if the cylinders are not rebored, new pistons will not be necessary. Normal piston wear appears as even, vertical wear on the thrust surfaces of the piston and slight looseness of the top ring in its groove. New piston rings, on the other hand, should always be used when an engine is rebuilt.
9   Carefully inspect each piston for cracks around the skirt, at the pin bosses and at the ring lands.
10 Look for scoring and scuffing on the thrust faces of the skirt, holes in the piston crown and burned areas at the edge of the crown. If the skirt is scored or scuffed, the engine may have been suffering from overheating and/or abnormal combustion, which caused excessively high operating temperatures. The oil pump and cooling system should be checked thoroughly. A hole in the piston crown, an extreme to be sure, is an indication that abnormal combustion (pre-ignition) was occurring. Burned areas at the edge of the piston crown are usually evidence of spark knock (detonation). If any of the above problems exist, the causes must be corrected or the damage will occur again.
11 Measure the piston ring-to-groove clearance by laying a new piston ring in the ring groove and slipping a feeler gauge in beside it **(see illustration)**. Check the clearance at three or four locations around the groove. Be sure to use the correct ring for each groove; they are different. If the clearance is greater than specified, new pistons will have to be used when the engine is reassembled.
12 Check the piston-to-bore clearance by measuring the bore (see Section 25) and the piston diameter. Make sure that the pistons and cylinders are correctly matched. Measure the piston across the skirt on the thrust faces at a 90-degree angle to the piston pin, at the distance from the bottom of the skirt listed in this Chapter's Specifications **(see illustration)**. Subtract the piston diameter from the bore diameter to obtain the clearance. If it is greater than specified, the cylinders will have to be rebored and new oversized pistons and rings installed. If the appropriate precision measuring tools are not available, the piston-to-cylinder clearances can be obtained, though not quite as accurately, using feeler gauge stock. Feeler gauge stock comes in 12-inch lengths and various thicknesses and is generally available at auto parts stores. To check the clearance, select a feeler gauge of the same thickness as the piston clearance listed in this Chapter's Specifications and slip it into the cylinder along with the appropriate piston. The cylin-

26.4 Remove the piston rings with a ring removal and installation tool

26.11 Measure the piston ring-to-groove clearance with a feeler gauge

26.12 Measure the piston diameter with a micrometer

Chapter 2 Engine, clutch and transmission

27.3 Check the ring end gap at the bottom of the cylinder

27.5 If the end gap is too small, clamp a file in a vise and file the ring ends (from the outside in only) to enlarge the gap slightly

der should be upside down and the piston must be positioned exactly as it normally would be. Place the feeler gauge between the piston and cylinder on one of the thrust faces (90-degrees to the piston pin bore). The piston should slip through the cylinder (with the feeler gauge in place) with moderate pressure. If it falls through, or slides through easily, the clearance is excessive and a new piston will be required. If the piston binds at the lower end of the cylinder and is loose toward the top, the cylinder is tapered, and if tight spots are encountered as the feeler gauge is placed at different points around the cylinder, the cylinder is out-of-round. Repeat the procedure for the remaining pistons and cylinders. Be sure to have the cylinders and pistons checked by a dealer service department or a motorcycle repair shop to confirm your findings before purchasing new parts.

13 Hold the rod securely with one hand and try to rock the piston side-to-side, at right angles to its normal direction of rotation around the piston pin. Any noticeable play indicates excessive wear, which must be corrected.

Removal and installation

14 Take the piston/connecting rod assemblies to a Honda dealer or machine shop to have the pistons removed from the rods and new ones installed. **Note:** *Unless new pistons or connecting rods must be installed, do not disassemble the pistons from the rods.*

27 Piston rings - installation

Refer to illustrations 27.3, 27.5, 27.9a, 27.9b, 27.11 and 27.15

1 Before installing the new piston rings, the ring end gaps must be checked.

2 Lay out the pistons and the new ring sets so the rings will be matched with the same piston and cylinder during the end gap measurement procedure and engine assembly.

3 Insert the top (No. 1) ring into the bottom of the first cylinder and square it up with the cylinder walls by pushing it in with the top of the piston. The ring should be about one inch above the bottom edge of the cylinder. To measure the end gap, slip a feeler gauge between the ends of the ring **(see illustration)** and compare the measurement to the Specifications.

4 If the gap is larger or smaller than specified, double check to make sure that you have the correct rings before proceeding.

5 If the gap is too small, it must be enlarged or the ring ends may come in contact with each other during engine operation, which can cause serious damage. The end gap can be increased by filing the ring ends very carefully with a fine file **(see illustration)**. When performing this operation, file only from the outside in.

6 Excess end gap is not critical unless it is greater than the limits listed in this Chapter's Specifications. Again, double check to make sure you have the correct rings for your engine.

7 Repeat the procedure for each ring that will be installed in the first cylinder and for each ring in the remaining cylinders. Remember to keep the rings, pistons and cylinders matched up.

8 Once the ring end gaps have been checked and corrected, the rings can be installed on the pistons.

9 The oil control ring (lowest on the piston) is installed first. It is composed of three separate components. Slip the expander into the groove, then install the upper side rail **(see illustrations)**. Do not use a piston ring installation tool on the oil ring side rails as they may be damaged. Instead, place one end of the side rail into the groove

27.9a Installing the oil ring expander - make sure the ends don't overlap

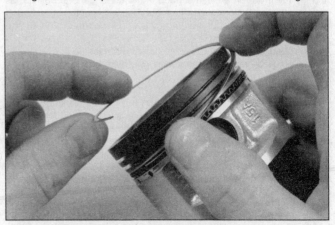

27.9b Installing an oil ring side rail - don't use a ring installation tool to do this

Chapter 2 Engine, clutch and transmission

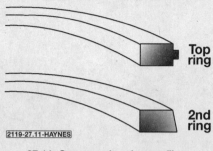

27.11 Compression ring profiles

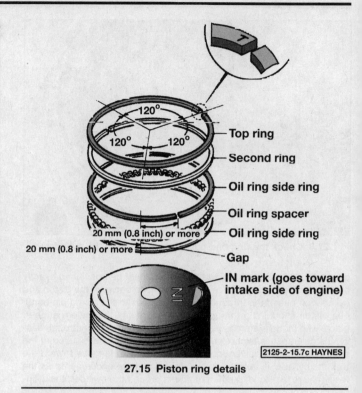

27.15 Piston ring details

between the spacer expander and the ring land. Hold it firmly in place and slide a finger around the piston while pushing the rail into the groove. Next, install the lower side rail in the same manner.

10 After the three oil ring components have been installed, check to make sure that both the up
per and lower side rails can be turned smoothly in the ring groove.

11 Install the second (middle) ring next. It can be distinguished from the top ring by its profile **(see illustration)**. Do not mix the top and middle rings.

12 To avoid breaking the ring, use a piston ring installation tool and make sure that the identification mark is facing up. Fit the ring into the middle groove on the piston. Do not expand the ring any more than is necessary to slide it into place.

13 Finally, install the top ring in the same manner. Make sure the identifying mark is facing up.

14 Repeat the procedure for the remaining pistons and rings. Be very careful not to confuse the top and second rings.

15 Once the rings have been properly installed, stagger the end gaps, including those of the oil ring side rails **(see illustration)**.

28 Main and connecting rod bearings - general note

1 Even though main and connecting rod bearings are generally replaced with new ones during the engine overhaul, the old bearings should be retained for close examination as they may reveal valuable information about the condition of the engine.

2 Bearing failure occurs mainly because of lack of lubrication, the presence of dirt or other foreign particles, overloading the engine and/or corrosion. Regardless of the cause of bearing failure, it must be corrected before the engine is reassembled to prevent it from happening again.

3 When examining the bearings, remove the main bearings from the case halves and the rod bearings from the connecting rods and caps and lay them out on a clean surface in the same general position as their location on the crankshaft journals. This will enable you to match any noted bearing problems with the corresponding side of the crankshaft journal.

4 Dirt and other foreign particles get into the engine in a variety of ways. It may be left in the engine during assembly or it may pass through filters or breathers. It may get into the oil and from there into the bearings. Metal chips from machining operations and normal engine wear are often present. Abrasives are sometimes left in engine components after reconditioning operations such as cylinder honing, especially when parts are not thoroughly cleaned using the proper cleaning methods. Whatever the source, these foreign objects often end up imbedded in the soft bearing material and are easily recognized. Large particles will not imbed in the bearing and will score or gouge the bearing and journal. The best prevention for this cause of bearing failure is to clean all parts thoroughly and keep everything spotlessly clean during engine reassembly. Frequent and regular oil and filter changes are also recommended.

5 Lack of lubrication or lubrication breakdown has a number of interrelated causes. Excessive heat (which thins the oil), overloading (which squeezes the oil from the bearing face) and oil leakage or throw off (from excessive bearing clearances, worn main oil pump or high engine speeds) all contribute to lubrication breakdown. Blocked oil passages will also starve a bearing and destroy it. When lack of lubrication is the cause of bearing failure, the bearing material is wiped or extruded from the steel backing of the bearing. Temperatures may increase to the point where the steel backing and the journal turn blue from overheating.

6 Riding habits can have a definite effect on bearing life. Full throttle low speed operation, or lugging the engine, puts very high loads on bearings, which tend to squeeze out the oil film. These loads cause the bearings to flex, which produces fine cracks in the bearing face (fatigue failure). Eventually the bearing material will loosen in pieces and tear away from the steel backing. Short trip driving leads to corrosion of bearings, as insufficient engine heat is produced to drive off the condensed water and corrosive gases produced. These products collect in the engine oil, forming acid and sludge. As the oil is carried to the engine bearings, the acid attacks and corrodes the bearing material.

7 Incorrect bearing installation during engine assembly will lead to bearing failure as well. Tight fitting bearings which leave insufficient bearing oil clearances result in oil starvation. Dirt or foreign particles trapped behind a bearing insert result in high spots on the bearing which lead to failure.

8 To avoid bearing problems, clean all parts thoroughly before reassembly, double check all bearing clearance measurements and lubricate the new bearings with engine assembly lube or moly-based grease during installation.

29 Connecting rod bearings - removal, inspection and installation

Removal

1 Refer to Section 24 and remove the connecting rod/piston assemblies from the engine.

2 Remove the rod bearing inserts from one rod at a time. Roll the bearing inserts sideways to separate them from the rods and caps

Chapter 2 Engine, clutch and transmission

29.7 Bearing thickness is indicated by a color code on the edge of the bearing

30.4 Unbolt the main bearing caps; each cap has an arrowhead mark next to one of the cap bolts that points to the top of the engine when installed

30.5 Lift the crankshaft out of the bearings and slip it out of the primary chain

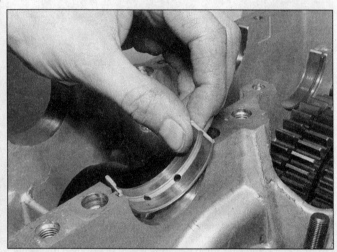

30.6 Push the center of each bearing sideways and roll it out of the saddle or cap

(see illustration 24.4b). Keep them in order so they can be reinstalled in their original locations. Wash the parts in solvent and dry them with compressed air, if available.

Inspection

3 Examine the connecting rod bearing inserts. If they are scored, badly scuffed or appear to have been seized, new bearings must be installed. Always replace the bearings in the connecting rods as a set. If they are badly damaged, check the corresponding crankshaft journal. Evidence of extreme heat, such as discoloration, indicates that lubrication failure has occurred. Be sure to thoroughly check the main oil pump and its pressure relief valve, as well as the scavenging pump and all oil holes and passages, before reassembling the engine.

Clearance check

4 If you don't have a micrometer and a bore gauge, connecting rod bearing clearance can be checked inexpensively with Plastigage, using the same methods used for the main bearings (see Section 30).
5 If you have a micrometer, check the crankpin journal diameter at a number of points around the journal's circumference to determine whether or not the journal is out-of-round. Take the measurement at each end of the journal to determine if the journal is tapered. If any journal is tapered or out-of-round or bearing clearance is beyond the maximum listed in this Chapter's Specifications, replace the crankshaft.

6 Install the bearings and connecting rod cap and tighten the cap bolts to the torque listed in this Chapter's Specifications. Measure the inside diameter of the assembled bearing with a bore gauge. If the clearance is excessive and the crankpin diameter is within the Specifications, select new bearings as described below.

Connecting rod bearing selection

Refer to illustration 29.7

7 Each connecting rod has a number stamped across its parting line, ranging from 1 to 3 (see illustration 24.3). There's a corresponding letter on the crankshaft web next to the connecting rod. Using the letter and number together, refer to this Chapter's Specifications to select the correct bearing color code for each connecting rod. The color codes are stamped on the edge of the bearing (see illustration).
8 Repeat the bearing selection procedure for the remaining connecting rods.

Installation

9 Refer to Section 24 for bearing and connecting rod installation.

30 Crankshaft and main bearings - removal, inspection, main bearing selection and installation

Removal

Refer to illustrations 30.4, 30.5 and 30.6

1 Before removing the crankshaft check the endplay, using a dial indicator mounted in-line with the crankshaft. Honda doesn't provide endplay specifications, but if the endplay is excessive (more than a few thousandths of an inch), the ball bearing on the end of the crankshaft may be worn.
2 Look for main bearing cap number marks. If you don't see any, make your own, numbering from front to rear of the engine.
3 Unbolt the connecting rods from the crankshaft (see Section 24). The right connecting rods and pistons don't need to be removed from the cylinders.
4 Unbolt the main bearing caps (see illustration). Use the bolts as levers to rock the caps from side-to-side to free them from the engine, then lift them out.
5 Lift the crankshaft out and set it on a clean surface (see illustration).
6 The main bearing inserts can be removed from their saddles by pushing their centers to the side, then lifting them out (see illustration). Keep the bearing inserts in order. The main bearing oil clearance should be checked, however, before removing the inserts (see Step 8).

30.13 Lay a strip of Plastigage along the bearing journal, parallel to the crankshaft centerline

30.16 Measure the width of the crushed Plastigage with the scale on the envelope

Inspection

Refer to illustrations 30.13 and 30.16

7   Clean the crankshaft with solvent, using a rifle-cleaning brush to scrub out the oil passages. If available, blow the crank dry with compressed air. Check the main and connecting rod journals for uneven wear, scoring and pits. Rub a copper coin across the journal several times - if a journal picks up copper from the coin, it's too rough. Replace the crankshaft.

8   Check the crankshaft for cracks and other damage. It should be magnafluxed to reveal hidden cracks - a dealer service department or motorcycle machine shop will handle the procedure.

9   Steps 9 though 11 require precision measuring equipment. You can have the measurements done by a dealer or motorcycle repair shop. Measure the main bearing journals with a micrometer. Compare the readings with the values listed in this Chapter's Specifications.

10 Assemble the main caps and bearings and tighten them to the specified torque. Measure the inside diameter of the bearing bore with a bore gauge.

11 Set the crankshaft on V-blocks and check the runout with a dial indicator touching each of the main journals, comparing your findings with this Chapter's Specifications. If the runout exceeds the limit, replace the crank.

12 Wipe the main bearing inserts, saddles and bearing caps clean, using a lint-free cloth.

13 Install the bearing inserts in the saddles and caps. Make sure the tab on the bearing engages with the notch in the rod or cap **(see illustration 30.6)**. Lay a strip of Plastigage (type HPG-1) across each bearing insert (in the saddle, not in the cap), parallel with the journal axis **(see illustration)**.

14 Wipe off the main bearing journals with a lint-free cloth.

15 Lay the crankshaft in the saddles, then install the main bearing caps (with their steel plates). Tighten the rod caps to the torque listed in this Chapter's Specifications, but don't allow the crankshaft to rotate at all.

16 Unscrew the bolts and remove the caps and crankshaft, being very careful not to disturb the Plastigage. Compare the width of the crushed Plastigage to the scale printed in the Plastigage envelope to determine the bearing oil clearance **(see illustration)**.

17 If the clearance is within the range listed in this Chapter's Specifications and the bearings are in perfect condition, they can be reused. If the clearance is beyond the standard range, replace the bearing inserts with new inserts that have the same color code, then check the oil clearance once again. Always replace all of the inserts at the same time.

18 The clearance should now be within the range listed in this Chapter's Specifications.

19 Spin the ball bearing on the end of the crankshaft and check it for roughness, looseness and noise **(see illustration 21.20)**. If problems

30.21 These marks on the front of the engine (arrow) are used for main bearing selection; the numbers 1, 2 and 3 represent the front, center and rear main bearings, while the Roman numerals are the bearing code

are found, remove the snap-ring, washer and bearing. Install a new bearing and washer and secure them with a new snap-ring. Install the snap-ring with its sharp edge away from the bearing and its rounded edge toward the bearing.

Main bearing

Selection

Refer to illustration 30.21

20 The clearance should be within the range listed in this Chapter's Specifications.

21 Use the number marks on the crankshaft and on the case to determine the bearing sizes required. The numbers stamped on the crankshaft next to the main journals are the main journal numbers. These correspond with the numbers on the front of the crankcase **(see illustration)**. Use these numbers and this Chapter's Specifications to determine the correct bearing color code for each journal. The color codes are painted on the edges of the bearings **(see illustration 29.7)**.

Installation

22 Clean the bearing saddles in the case halves, then install the bearing inserts in the case **(see illustration 30.6)**. When installing the bearings, use your hands only - don't tap them into place with a hammer.

23 Lubricate the bearing inserts with engine assembly lube or moly-based grease.

Chapter 2 Engine, clutch and transmission

2-49

31.2a Remove the mainshaft end cap; on installation, position its locating tab in the notch

31.2b Lift the primary chain oiler out of the crankcase

31.2c Lift the mainshaft out of its saddles and slip it out of the primary chain

31.3a The shift forks should look like this

A Left fork
B Center fork
C Right fork
D Mainshaft bearing retainers

24 Install the seal on the end of the crankshaft.
25 Carefully lower the crankshaft into place **(see illustration 30.5)**.
26 Install the main bearing caps in their correct locations, referring to the number marks made during disassembly. Be sure the arrowhead marks on the caps point to the top of the engine **(see illustration 30.4)**.
27 Install the steel plate on top of the center and rear caps. Lubricate the threads and the underside of the bolt heads with clean engine oil, then finger-tighten the bolts.

28 Tighten the bolts in several stages, in a criss-cross pattern, to the torques listed in this Chapter's Specifications. **Note:** *The front cap's torque setting is different from the center and rear caps' setting.*
29 Turn the crankshaft. If should turn easily by hand. If it doesn't, there's a problem; find and fix it before assembling the engine further. You may have forgotten to lubricate the bearing inserts; the bearings may be the wrong size; or a bearing cap may be in the wrong location or installed backwards (with its arrowhead pointing to the bottom of the engine). Any of these can cause bearing damage when the engine is first started, or may prevent it from turning at all.
30 If the crankshaft turns freely, continue with assembly.

31 Transmission shafts, shift drum and forks - removal and installation

Refer to illustrations 31.2a, 31.2b, 31.2c, 31.3a, 31.3b, 31.3c, 31.3d, 31.4a, 31.4b, 31.4c, 31.5, 31.6 and 31.7

Removal

1 Remove the engine and separate the case halves (see Sections 5 and 21). Remove the external shift linkage and shift drum bearing retainer (Section 20).
2 Remove the mainshaft end cap and the primary chain oiler, then lift out the mainshaft **(see illustrations)**. If it's stuck, use a soft-face hammer and gently tap on the bearings on the ends of the shaft to free it. Slip the mainshaft out of the primary chain.
3 Note the position marks (F, C and R for front, center and rear) on the shift forks **(see illustrations)**. Bend back the lockwasher tab and undo the fork shaft bolt **(see illustration)**. Pull out the fork shaft and lift

31.3b The letters on the forks indicate their installed directions and positions; the L and C marks (arrows) face the rear of the engine . . .

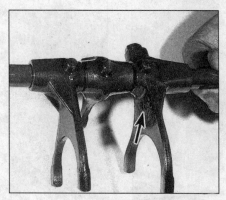

31.3c . . . and the R mark (arrow) faces the front

31.3d Bend back the lockwasher tab and remove the bolt from the fork and shaft

31.4a Remove the countershaft bearing retainer screws . . .

31.4b . . . and pull out the retainer with the bearing . . .

31.4c . . . and slide fifth gear off the countershaft

31.5 On later models, the countershaft rear bearing's retainer is below the mainshaft bearing retainer shown here; expand its ends with snap-ring pliers to free the bearing

the forks away from the gears. It's a good idea to reassemble the forks to the shaft right away so you don't forget how they go.

4   Remove the countershaft bearing retainer screws and pull out the retainer **(see illustration)**. Pull the front countershaft bearing out of the case and pull fifth gear off the countershaft **(see illustrations)**.

5   If you're working on a 1986 or 1987 model, reach down through the mainshaft retainer slot with a pair of snap-ring pliers and expand the ends of the countershaft bearing retaining ring **(see illustration)**.

6   On all models, pull the countershaft forward to clear its rear bearing, then tilt it and lift it out of the case **(see illustration)**.

7   Pull the shift drum forward out of the case **(see illustration)**.

8   Refer to Section 32 for information pertaining to shift drum and fork inspection and Section 33 for information pertaining to the transmission shafts.

31.6 Pull the countershaft forward, then tilt it and lift it out of the case

31.7 Pull the shift drum out of the case

Chapter 2 Engine, clutch and transmission

31.13 Place the lockwasher tabs (arrows) against the flats on the fork; make sure the machined end of the bolt fits into the opposite side of the fork and bend the lockwasher tab against the flat on the bolt

31.14 The assembled transmission shafts and shift forks should look like this

Installation

Refer to illustrations 31.13 and 31.14

9   Install the shift drum in the case **(see illustration 31.7)**.
10 Lower the countershaft into the case and insert its rear end into the rear bearing **(see illustration 31.6)**. If you're working on a 1986 or 1987 model, expand the rear bearing's retainer ring with snap-ring pliers. Push the bearing into its bore and release the retainer ring, making sure it's fully engaged with the case and the bearing.
11 Install the countershaft fifth gear and front bearing. Make sure the bearing retainer oil hole is clear, then install the retainer. Tighten its screws securely.
12 Place the shift forks in their installed positions and push the shaft through them. Be sure the F, C and R marks on the forks face the proper directions **(see illustrations 31.3a, 31.3b and 31.3c)**.
13 Place a new lockwasher over the fork shaft bolt hole and bend its tabs against the fork shaft **(see illustration)**. Install the bolt, making sure its end fits through the shaft and into the fork on the opposite side. Tighten the bolt to the torque listed in this Chapter's Specifications, then bend a lockwasher tab against one of the flats on the bolt.
14 Lay the mainshaft in its bearing journals and engage the center shift fork with its gear groove **(see illustration)**.
15 The remainder of installation is the reverse of removal.
16 Make sure the gears are in the neutral position. When they are, it will be possible to rotate the transmission shafts independently of each other.

32 Shift drum and forks - inspection

Refer to illustrations 32.1, 32.3a and 32.3b

1   Check the edges of the grooves in the shift drum for signs of excessive wear **(see illustration)**. If the grooves are worn, replace the shift drum.
2   Check the pins on the front end of the shift drum for wear and damage. Spin the bearing and check for roughness, looseness or noise. If problems are found, take the bearing off the drum and install a new one.
3   Check the shift forks for distortion and wear, especially at the fork fingers and pins **(see illustrations)**. If they are discolored or severely worn they are probably bent. If damage or wear is evident, check the shift fork groove in the corresponding gear as well. Inspect the shaft bore for excessive wear and replace any defective parts with new ones.
4   Check the shift fork shaft for evidence of wear, galling and other damage. Make sure the shift forks move smoothly on the shaft. If the shaft is worn or bent, replace it with a new one.

32.1 Check the shift drum grooves for wear, especially at the points

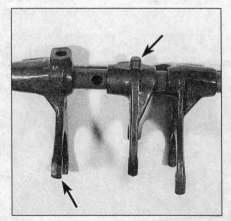

32.3a Check the forks for wear at the fingers and pins (arrows)

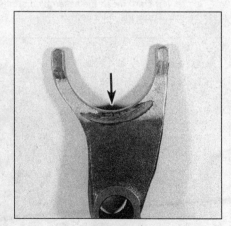

32.3b An arc-shaped burn mark like this means the fork was rubbing against a gear, probably due to bending or worn fork fingers

Chapter 2 Engine, clutch and transmission

33.4a Remove the thrust washer from the mainshaft

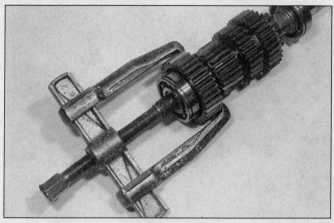

33.4b Use a puller attached to fifth gear to remove the bearing

33.4c Slide off the thrust washer . . .

33.4d . . . fifth gear . . .

33.4e . . . and its splined bushing; on installation, align the bushing oil hole with the oil hole in the shaft

33 Transmission shafts - disassembly, inspection and reassembly

Note: *When disassembling the transmission shafts, place the parts on a long rod or thread a wire through them to keep them in order and facing the proper direction.*

1   Remove the shafts from the case (see Section 31).
2   Before you start, mesh the assembled shafts, noting how they're assembled and how they fit together.

Mainshaft

Disassembly

Refer to illustrations 33.4a through 33.4j

3   Slide the primary driven gear assembly off the mainshaft (Section 34).
4   To disassemble the mainshaft, refer to the accompanying illustrations **(see illustrations)**.

33.4f Remove the splined washer and snap-ring . . .

33.4g . . . and slide off the second-third gear

Chapter 2 Engine, clutch and transmission

33.4h Remove the snap-ring; on installation, the snap-ring gaps should be evenly centered on a gap between the splines, not offset as shown here

33.4i Remove the splined washer . . .

32.4j . . . and slide off fourth gear

33.6 1984 through 1986 models use this permanent fourth gear bushing; 1987 models use a separate bushing

Inspection

Refer to illustrations 33.6 and 33.9

5 Wash all of the components in clean solvent and dry them off. Rotate the bearings, feeling for tightness, rough spots and excessive looseness and listening for noises. If any of these conditions are found, replace the bearing.

6 Check the gear teeth for cracking and other obvious damage. Check the gear bushings and the surface in the inner diameter of each gear for scoring or heat discoloration **(see illustration)**. If the gear or bushing is damaged, replace it. If you have precision measuring equipment, measure the inside diameters of the removable gears and compare the measurements with the values listed in this Chapter's Specifications. Replace worn gears.

7 Inspect the dogs and the dog holes in the gears for excessive wear. Replace worn or damaged gears as a set with their mating gear on the countershaft.

8 Measure the bushing outside diameters at the smooth sections. Use this measurement, together with the gear inside diameter, to calculate gear-to-bushing clearance.

9 Check the mainshaft for damaged splines and for scoring at the bearing mounting surfaces **(see illustration)**. Replace the mainshaft if problems are found.

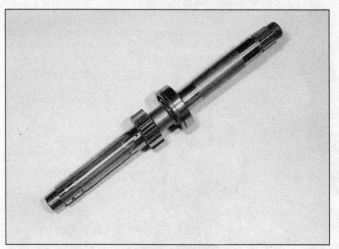

33.9 First gear is integral with the mainshaft; replace the bearing if it's worn or damaged

Reassembly

Refer to illustration 33.11

10 Lubricate the components with engine oil before assembling them.

11 Assembly is the reverse of the disassembly procedure with the following additions:

a) *Align the oil holes in the mainshaft bushings with the holes in the shaft.*

2-54   Chapter 2 Engine, clutch and transmission

33.11 The assembled length of the mainshaft must be correct to align the bearing grooves with the retainers

33.13a Remove the second gear snap-ring; this snap-ring is installed correctly, with its gap centered on a gap in the countershaft splines

33.13b Slide off the bushing and second gear; on installation, the bushing oil hole must align with the hole in the shaft

33.13c At the other end of the shaft, slide off the output gear (1984 through 1986 models)

33.13d Slide off first gear . . .

b) After assembly, make sure the assembled length of the mainshaft is as listed in this Chapter's Specifications **(see illustration)**. This is necessary to align the bearings with their retainers in the case.

33.13e . . . and its bushing; on assembly, the bushing oil hole must align with the hole in the shaft

Countershaft

Disassembly

Refer to illustrations 33.13a through 33.13k

12 If you're working on a 1987 model, place the output gear (the helical-cut gear on the rear end of the countershaft) in a padded vise. Unscrew the locknut, remove the rear bearing and slide the countershaft out of the output gear. Remove the gear from the vise.

13 To disassemble the countershaft, refer to the accompanying illustrations **(see illustrations)**.

Inspection

14 Refer to Steps 5 through 9 above to inspect the countershaft components.

Reassembly

15 Assembly is the reverse of the disassembly procedure, with the following additions:

a) Lubricate the components with engine oil before assembling them.
b) Align the oil holes in each bushing with the corresponding oil hole in the shaft.
c) If you're working on a 1987 model, install the output gear with its RR mark facing the rear of the engine (away from the other gears on the shaft). Use a new locknut and tighten it to the torque listed in this Chapter's Specifications.

Chapter 2 Engine, clutch and transmission

33.13f Slide off the splined washer and remove the snap-ring

33.13g Slide off fourth gear

33.13h Remove the third gear snap-ring; on installation, center the snap-ring gap on a gap between the shaft splines, as shown in illustration 33.13a (NOT aligned with a spline, as shown here)

33.13i Slide off the bushing and third gear . . .

33.13j On installation, the oil hole in the bushing . . .

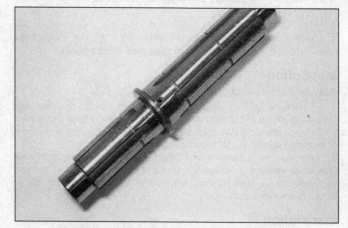

33.13k . . . must align with the oil hole in the shaft

34 Primary chain and gears - removal, inspection and installation

Removal

Refer to illustrations 34.4a and 34.4b

1 Remove the crankshaft (Section 30) and slip the chain off the drive gear on the rear end of the crankshaft.

2 Raise the mainshaft out of its bearing saddles (Section 31), then slip the chain off the driven gear. **Note:** *If you're going to re-use the primary chain, label it so it can be reinstalled in the same direction of rotation.*

3 Slide the driven gear assembly off the mainshaft.

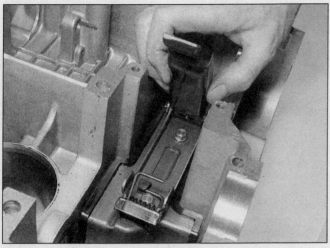

34.4a Unbolt the chain tensioner and lift it out . . .

34.4b . . . and remove the oil catch plate

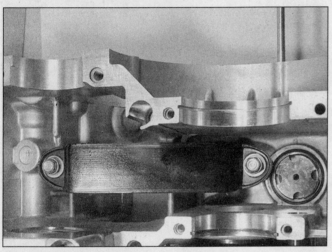

34.5 Replace the primary chain guide if its pad is worn or scored

34.7a Remove the snap-ring and thrust washer

4   Unbolt the primary chain tensioner from the left side of the crankcase and remove the oil catch plate **(see illustrations)**.

Inspection

Refer to illustrations 34.5, 34.7a and 34.7b

5   Check the primary chain guide in the right side of the crankcase **(see illustration)**. If it's scored or worn, unbolt it and install a new one.
6   Check the tensioner components for wear or damage and a bent or distorted spring. Replace damaged or worn parts.
7   Remove the snap-ring and thrust washer from the driven gear **(see illustration)**. Lift out the coupling and inspect the rubber damped segments inside **(see illustration)**. If they're compressed, brittle or deteriorated, replace them.

Installation

8   Installation is the reverse of the removal steps, with the following addition: If you're reusing the primary chain, install it so it will rotate in the same direction as before it was removed.

34.7b . . . and lift out the coupling for access to the rubber segments

35 Initial start-up after overhaul

1   Make sure the engine oil level is correct and the cooling system is full, then remove the spark plugs from the engine. Place the engine kill switch in the Off position and unplug the primary wires from the coils.

2   Turn on the key switch and crank the engine over with the starter several times to build up oil pressure. Reinstall the spark plugs, connect the wires and turn the switch to On.

Chapter 2 Engine, clutch and transmission

3 Make sure there is fuel in the tank, then turn the fuel tap to the On position and operate the choke.
4 Start the engine and allow it to run at a moderately fast idle until it reaches operating temperature.
5 Check carefully for oil leaks and make sure the transmission and controls, especially the brakes, function properly before road testing the machine. Refer to Section 36 for the recommended break-in procedure.

36 Recommended break-in procedure

1 Any rebuilt engine needs time to break in, even if parts have been installed in their original locations. For this reason, treat the machine gently for the first few miles to make sure oil has circulated throughout the engine and any new parts installed have started to seat.
2 Even greater care is necessary if the cylinders have been rebored or a new crankshaft has been installed. In the case of a rebore, the engine will have to be broken in as if the machine were new. This means greater use of the transmission and a restraining hand on the throttle until at least 500 miles have been covered. There's no point in keeping to any set speed limit - the main idea is to keep from lugging the engine and to gradually increase performance until the 500 mile mark is reached. These recommendations can be lessened to an extent when only a new crankshaft is installed. Experience is the best guide, since it's easy to tell when an engine is running freely. The following recommendations, which Honda provides for new motorcycles, can be used as a guide:

  a) *Don't lug the engine (full throttle at low engine speeds).*
  b) *0 to 600 miles (0 to 1000 km): Keep sustained engine speed below 4,000 rpm.*
  c) *600 to 1000 miles (1000 to 1600 km): Don't run the engine for long periods above 5000 rpm, or at all above 5500 rpm. Rev the engine freely through the gears, but use full throttle only for very short periods. Change engine speeds often.*
  d) *Above 1000 miles (1600 km): Full throttle can be used. Don't exceed maximum recommended engine speed (redline).*

3 If a lubrication failure is suspected, stop the engine immediately and try to find the cause. If an engine is run without oil, even for a short period of time, severe damage will occur.

Notes

Chapter 3
Cooling system

Contents

	Section		Section
Coolant level check	See Chapter 1	Cooling system draining, flushing and refilling	See Chapter 1
Coolant reservoir - removal and installation	3	General information	1
Coolant temperature gauge and sender unit - check and replacement	5	Radiator - removal and installation	7
		Radiator cap - check	2
Coolant tubes and thermostat housing - removal and installation	9	Thermostat - removal, check and installation	6
Cooling fan and thermostatic switch - check and replacement	4	Water pump - check, removal, disassembly, inspection and installation	8
Cooling system check	See Chapter 1		

Specifications

General

Coolant type	See Chapter 1
Mixture ratio	See Chapter 1
Cooling system capacity	See Chapter 1
Radiator cap pressure rating	11 to 15 psi

Thermostat rating
Opening temperature	80 to 84 degrees C (176 to 183 degrees F)
Fully open at	95 degrees C (203 degrees F)
Valve travel (when fully open)	Not less than 8 mm (5/16 inch)

Fan thermoswitch continuity
Below 98 to 102 degrees C (208 to 216 degrees F)	No continuity
Above 98 to 102 degrees C (208 to 216 degrees F)	Continuity

Gauge temperature sensor resistance
60 degrees C (140 degrees F)	104 ohms
85 degrees C (185 degrees F)	44 ohms
110 degrees C (230 degrees F)	20 ohms
120 degrees C (248 degrees F)	16 ohms

Torque specifications

Cooling fan thermoswitch	28 Nm (20 ft-lbs)*
Temperature gauge sensor	23 Nm (17 ft-lbs)*

*Use a new O-ring and apply silicone sealant to the threads.

Chapter 3 Cooling sytem

1 General information

The models covered by this manual are equipped with a liquid cooling system which utilizes a water/antifreeze mixture to carry away excess heat produced during the combustion process. The cylinders are surrounded by water jackets, through which the coolant is circulated by the water pump. The coolant passes through hoses and tubes, around the cylinders and to the thermostat. When the engine is warm, the thermostat opens and allows coolant to flow into the radiator, where it is cooled by the passing air, routed through another hose and back to the water pump, where the cycle is repeated. The water pump is mounted to the left front corner of the crankcase and driven by the oil pump shaft.

An electric fan, mounted behind the radiator and automatically controlled by a thermostatic switch, provides a flow of cooling air through the radiator when the motorcycle is not moving.

The coolant temperature sender unit, threaded into the thermostat housing, senses the temperature of the coolant and controls the coolant temperature gauge on the instrument cluster.

The entire system is sealed and pressurized. The pressure is controlled by a valve which is part of the radiator cap. By pressurizing the coolant, the boiling point is raised, which prevents premature boiling of the coolant. An overflow hose, connected between the radiator and reservoir tank, directs coolant to the tank when the radiator cap valve is opened by excessive pressure. The coolant is automatically siphoned back to the radiator as the engine cools.

Many cooling system inspection and service procedures are considered part of routine maintenance and are included in Chapter 1.

Warning 1: *Do not allow antifreeze to come in contact with your skin or painted surfaces of the motorcycle. Rinse off spills immediately with plenty of water. Antifreeze is highly toxic if ingested. Never leave antifreeze lying around in an open container or in puddles on the floor; children and pets are attracted by its sweet smell and may drink it. Check with local authorities about disposing of used antifreeze. Many communities have collection centers which will see that antifreeze is disposed of safely.*

Warning 2: *Do not remove the pressure cap from the thermostat housing when the engine and radiator are hot. Scalding hot coolant and steam may be blown out under pressure, which could cause serious injury. To open the pressure cap, remove the right side panel on the inside of the fairing. When the engine has cooled, lift up the panel and place a thick rag, like a towel, over the radiator cap; slowly rotate the cap counterclockwise to the first stop. This procedure allows any residual pressure to escape. When the steam has stopped escaping, press down on the cap while turning counterclockwise and remove it.*

2 Radiator cap - check

If problems such as overheating and loss of coolant occur, check the entire system as described in Chapter 1. The radiator cap opening pressure should be checked by a dealer service department or service station equipped with the special tester required to do the job. If the cap is defective, replace it with a new one.

3 Coolant reservoir - removal and installation

Refer to illustration 3.4

1 Refer to Chapter 8 and remove the top compartment.
2 Disconnect the siphon hose from the reservoir and catch any escaped coolant. Plug the end of the siphon hose so it doesn't siphon coolant from the system.
3 Remove the reservoir mounting bolt and take it out.
4 Check around the mounting bolt hole for cracks in the plastic, especially if the reservoir has required repeated topping up **(see illustration)**. If cracks are found, replace the reservoir.
5 Installation is the reverse of the removal steps. Position the tabs on the bottom of the reservoir in their grommets.

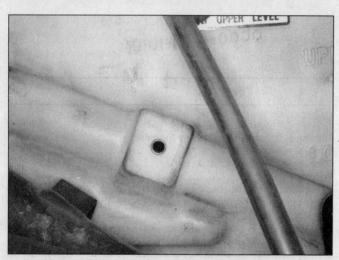

3.4 Cracks around the reservoir bolt hole will allow coolant to seep out

4 Cooling fan and thermostatic switch - check and replacement

Check

Refer to illustrations 4.2, 4.4a and 4.4b

1 If the engine is overheating and the cooling fan isn't coming on, first remove the left rear side cover and check the fan and main fuses. If a fuse is blown, check the fan circuit for a short to ground (see the *Wiring diagrams* at the end of this book). Check that the battery is fully charged.
2 If the fuses and battery are good, follow the wiring harness from the fan motor to the electrical connector and unplug the connector **(see illustration)**. Using two jumper wires, apply battery voltage to the terminals in the fan motor side of the electrical connector. If the fan doesn't work, replace the motor.
3 If the fan does come on, the problem lies in the fan switch or the wiring that connects the components. Remove the jumper wires and reconnect the electrical connector to the fan.

4.2 Follow the harness from the fan to the electrical connector and unplug it

Chapter 3 Cooling system   3-3

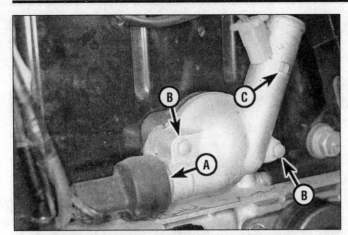

4.4a The fan switch is mounted in the thermostat cover

A Fan switch boot
B Thermostat cover bolts
C Radiator hose stop

4.4b Pull back the boot and unplug the connector to expose the fan switch

4   Remove the fairing lower covers (see Chapter 8). Unplug the connector from the fan thermoswitch in the thermostat housing **(see illustrations)**. Connect the two wires in the connector to each other with a short jumper wire. If the fan comes on, the circuit to the motor is good and the switch is defective.

5   If the switch is good, refer to Chapter 9 and test the ignition switch.

Replacement

Fan motor

Refer to illustration 4.7

Warning: *The engine must be completely cool before beginning this procedure.*

6   Refer to Section 7 and remove the radiator.
7   Remove the screws securing the fan motor bracket to the radiator **(see illustration)**. Separate the fan and bracket from the radiator.
8   Remove three mounting screws and the noise suppression capacitor screw from the fan motor bracket. Take the fan motor out of the bracket together with the capacitor.
9   To separate the fan from the motor, remove the screws.
10 Installation is the reverse of the removal steps.

Thermoswitch

Warning: *The engine must be completely cool before beginning this procedure.*

11 Prepare the new switch by wrapping the new threads with Teflon tape or by coating the threads with RTV sealant.
12 Disconnect its electrical connector and unscrew the switch from the thermostat housing **(see illustrations 4.4a and 4.4b)**.
13 Quickly install the new switch, tightening it to the specified torque.
14 Connect the electrical connector to the switch. Check, and if necessary, add coolant to the system (see Chapter 1).

5 Coolant temperature gauge and sender unit - check and replacement

Check

1   If the engine has been overheating but the coolant temperature gauge hasn't been indicating a hotter than normal condition, begin with a check of the coolant level (see Chapter 1). If it's low, add the recommended type of coolant and be sure to locate the source of the leak.

2   Check the fuses and ignition switch (see Chapter 9) and replace them if necessary. Check that the battery is fully charged.

Temperature gauge test

Refer to illustrations 5.4a and 5.4b

3   Remove the fairing lower covers (see Chapter 8). This will provide access to the coolant temperature sensor, which is mounted in the thermostat housing behind the fan shroud.
4   Locate the temperature sensor **(see illustrations)**. Make a short jumper with a terminal that will plug into the temperature sensor wire when it's disconnected.

4.7 Four hex-head screws secure the fan motor bracket to the radiator; three Phillips screws secure the fan motor to the bracket

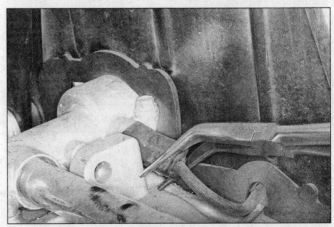

5.4a Pull the connector off the coolant temperature sender; note how the wiring harness is routed through a notch in the radiator shroud

Chapter 3 Cooling sytem

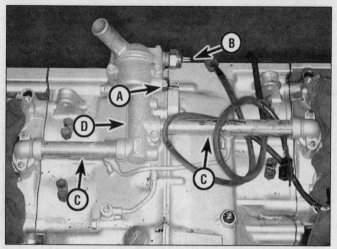

5.4b Coolant tube and thermostat housing details

- A Temperature sender
- B Fan thermoswitch
- C Coolant tubes
- D Thermostat housing

6.4 Take the cover off and remove the thermostat; use a new O-ring on installation

5 **Caution:** *During this step, don't leave the jumper wire connected for more than a few seconds or the temperature gauge will be damaged.* Disconnect the wire from the temperature sensor. Connect the jumper wire between the disconnected wire and ground. Turn the ignition key to the On position and watch the gauge; it should move all the way to the Hot side. Quickly disconnect the jumper wire; the gauge should move all the way to the Cold side.

6 If the gauge passes both of these tests, but doesn't operate correctly under normal riding conditions, the temperature sender unit is probably defective and must be replaced. Before replacing, test the sender in the same way as the fan thermoswitch (see Section 4) and compare the ohmmeter readings to those listed in this Chapter's Specifications.

7 If the gauge didn't respond to the tests properly, either the wire to the gauge is bad or the gauge itself is defective.

Replacement

Sender unit

Warning: *The engine must be completely cool before beginning this procedure.*

8 Prepare the new sender unit by wrapping the threads with Teflon tape or coating them with silicone sealant.

9 Disconnect its electrical connector and unscrew the sender unit from the thermostat housing and quickly install the new unit, tightening it to the specified torque.

10 Connect the electrical connector to the sender unit. Check, and if necessary, add coolant to the system (see Chapter 1).

Temperature gauge

11 Refer to Chapter 9 for the coolant temperature gauge replacement procedure.

6 Thermostat - removal, check and installation

Warning: *The engine must be completely cool before beginning this procedure.*

Removal

Refer to illustration 6.4

1 If the thermostat is functioning properly, the coolant temperature gauge should rise to the normal operating temperature quickly and then stay there, only rising above the normal position occasionally when the engine gets abnormally hot. If the engine does not reach normal operating temperature quickly, or if it overheats, the thermostat should be removed and checked, or replaced with a new one.

2 Refer to Chapter 1 and drain the cooling system. If necessary for access, remove the radiator (see Section 7).

3 Unbolt the thermostat housing cover **(see illustration 4.4a)**.

4 Take off the cover and O-ring and lift out the thermostat **(see illustration)**.

Check

5 Remove any coolant deposits, then visually check the thermostat for corrosion, cracks and other damage. If it was open when it was removed, the thermostat is defective.

6 To check the thermostat operation, submerge it in a container of water along with a thermometer. The thermostat should be suspended so it does not touch the sides of the container. **Warning:** *Antifreeze is poisonous. DO NOT use a cooking pan to test the thermostat!*

7 Gradually heat the water in the container with a hot plate or stove and check the temperature when the thermostat first starts to open.

8 Compare the opening temperature to the values listed in this Chapter's Specifications.

9 Continue heating the water until the valve is fully open.

10 Measure how far the thermostat valve has opened and compare to the value listed in this Chapter's Specifications.

11 If these specifications are not met, or if the thermostat doesn't open while the water is heated, replace it with a new one.

Installation

12 Install the thermostat into the housing.

13 If you're working on a model with a separate O-ring, install a new one in the groove.

14 Place the cover on the housing and install the bolts, tightening them securely.

15 The remainder of installation is the reverse of the removal steps. Fill the cooling system with the recommended coolant (see Chapter 1).

7 Radiator - removal and installation

Refer to illustrations 7.4, 7.5a, 7.5b, 7.6a, 7.6b and 7.7

Warning: *The engine must be completely cool before beginning this procedure.*

1 Place the bike on its centerstand.

2 Drain the cooling system (see Chapter 1).

3 Remove the top compartment. If you're working on an Aspencade or Interstate, remove the lower fairing covers (see Chapter 8).

Chapter 3 Cooling system

7.4 Disconnect the siphon hose from the radiator filler neck

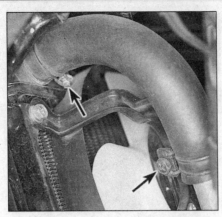

7.5a Loosen the clamp screws (arrows) and remove the upper radiator hose

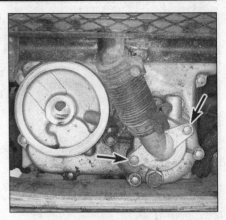

7.5b Loosen the lower hose clamp screws and remove the water pump cover bolts (arrows)

7.6a The radiator is secured by nuts and studs at the bottom and tabs at the top (arrows); the stone shield is secured to the radiator by six bolts

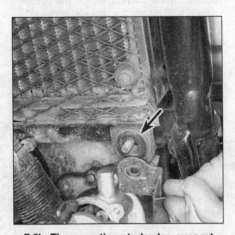

7.6b The mounting studs also support fairing brackets on some models; replace the grommets (arrow) if they're worn or deteriorated

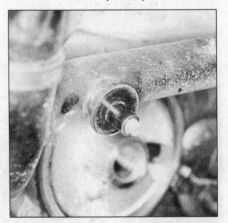

7.7 Check the collars and mounting studs for corrosion or damage

4 Remove the radiator cap and disconnect the siphon hose from the radiator (see illustration).
5 Loosen the clamps at the ends of the upper and lower hoses (see illustrations). Refer to Section 8 and remove the water pump cover from the pump and lower hose. Work the hoses free from the fittings, taking care not to damage the fittings in the process.
6 Remove the mounting nuts from the bottom of the radiator (see illustration). If you're working on an Interstate or Aspencade, remove the lower fairing brackets that are secured by the radiator nuts (see illustration). Pull the radiator forward off the mounting studs and disconnect the fan connector. Lower the radiator out of its upper mounts and remove it from the motorcycle.
7 Inspect the radiator mounting grommets. Replace them if they're cracked or deteriorated. Check the mounting studs for corrosion (see illustration).
8 Installation is the reverse of the removal steps, with the following additions:
   a) Don't forget to connect the fan wires.
   b) Fill the cooling system with the recommended coolant (see Chapter 1).

8 Water pump - check, removal, disassembly, inspection and installation

Warning: *The engine must be completely cool before beginning this procedure.*

Check and removal

Refer to illustrations 8.1, 8.6a, 8.6b, 8.8a, 8.8b and 8.8c

1 Visually check the area around the water pump for coolant leaks. Try to determine if the leak is simply the result of a loose hose clamp or deteriorated hose. Coolant dripping from the telltale hole in the underside of the pump body indicates a leaking mechanical seal; in this case the pump will have to be replaced with a new one (see illustration).

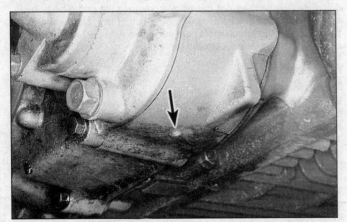

8.1 If coolant is leaking from the telltale hole (arrow), it's time for a new water pump

Chapter 3 Cooling sytem

8.6a Remove the pump housing bolts (arrows) ...

8.6b ... take the housing off the pump body and locate the dowels (arrows)

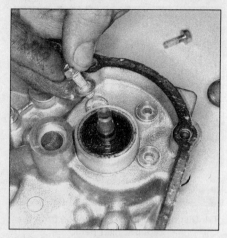

8.8a Remove the three pump body bolts and washers

8.8b Thread a pair of long bolts into two of the bolt holes ...

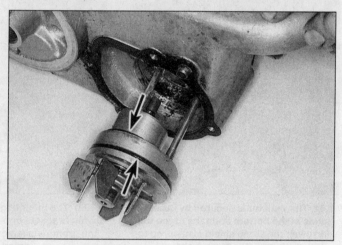

8.8c ... and use the long bolts to push the pump body out of the front case cover; use new O-rings (arrows) on installation

2 Place the bike on its centerstand.
3 If you're working on an Interstate or Aspencade, remove the fairing lower covers (see Chapter 8).
4 Drain the engine oil and coolant following the procedure in Chapter 1.

5 Remove the water pump cover and lower radiator hose **(see illustration 7.5b)**.
6 Remove the pump housing bolts and take off the pump housing **(see illustrations)**. Disconnect the water pump hose from the pump housing.
7 Refer to Chapter 2 and remove the engine front case cover.
8 From inside the front case cover, remove the pump body bolts and washers **(see illustration)**. Thread a pair of long bolts into two of the bolt holes and tap on them gently and evenly to push the pump out of the case cover **(see illustrations)**.

Inspection

Refer to illustration 8.9

9 Check the shaft seal for leaks (indicate by coolant leaking from the telltale hole) **(see illustration)**. Replace the water pump if the seal has been leaking.
10 Try to wiggle the pump impeller back-and-forth and in-and-out. Check the impeller blades for corrosion. If you can feel movement or the impeller blades are heavily corroded, the water pump must be replaced.
11 If the impeller blades are heavily corroded, flush the system thoroughly (it would also be a good idea to check the internal condition of the radiator).
12 Remove the O-rings from their grooves with a pointed tool and install new ones **(see illustration 8.8c)**.
13 Clean away all traces of the old gasket **(see illustration 8.6b)**.

8.9 Stains around the telltale hole and corrosion on the pump body indicate that it's time for a new water pump

Chapter 3 Cooling system

Installation

14 Installation is the reverse of the removal steps, with the following additions:
   a) Align the slot in the water pump shaft with the drive tooth in the oil pump shaft (see illustration 8.8a).
   b) Use a new gasket.
   c) Tighten the mounting bolts securely, but don't overtighten them and strip the threads.

9 Coolant tubes and thermostat housing - removal and installation

Refer to illustration 9.3

Warning: *The engine must be completely cool for this procedure.*

1 Refer to Chapter 1 and drain the cooling system.
2 You'll need to remove the radiator and carburetors for access to the tubes on top of the engine (see Section 7 and Chapter 4).
3 To remove the tubes, undo their mounting bolts and work the tubes free of their bores in the thermostat housing **(see illustration)**. Unbolt the thermostat housing from the engine **(see illustration 5.4b)**.
4 Installation is the reverse of the removal steps, with the following addition: Use new O-rings and lubricate them with multi-purpose grease. Use new gaskets, coated with sealant.

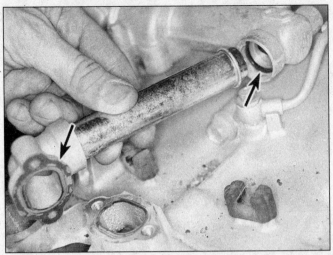

9.3 Use new gaskets and O-rings (arrows) when reinstalling the coolant tubes

Notes

Chapter 4
Fuel and exhaust systems

Contents

	Section
Air filter element - servicing	See Chapter 1
Air filter housing - removal and installation	5
Carburetor overhaul - general information	7
Carburetors - disassembly, cleaning and inspection	10
Carburetors - reassembly and float level adjustment	11
Carburetors - removal and installation	8
Carburetors - separation and reconnection	9
Emission control systems - inspection and component replacement	14
Exhaust system - removal and installation	13
Fuel pump - testing, removal and installation	4
Fuel system - check and filter replacement	See Chapter 1
Fuel tank - cleaning and repair	3
Fuel tank - removal and installation	2
General information	1
Idle fuel/air mixture adjustment	6
Idle speed - check and adjustment	See Chapter 1
Throttle and choke cables - removal, installation and adjustment	12
Throttle operation/grip freeplay - check and adjustment	See Chapter 1

Specifications

Carburetor
Carburetor type .... 32 mm CV (two)
Idle speed .... See Chapter 1
Pilot screw setting
  Sea level to 2000 meters (6500 ft)
    1984
      Except California .... 3-1/2 turns out
      California .... 3 turns out
    1985
      Except California .... 2-1/4 turns out
      California .... 3 turns out
    1986 .... 2 turns out
    1987
      Except California .... 1-3/4 turns out
      California .... 2-1/8 turns out
  Continuous operation above 2000 meters (6500 ft)
    1984 .... 1 turn out
    1985
      Except California .... 3/4 turn out
      California .... 1 turn out
    1986 .... 1/2 turn out
    1987 .... 1 turn out
Float level .... 7.5 mm (9/32 inch)

Fuel pump
Flow rate
  1984 through 1986
    Per minute .... 500 cc (16.9 fl oz)
    In 5 seconds .... 42 cc (1.4 fl oz)
  1987
    Per minute .... 750 cc (25.4 fl oz)
    In 5 seconds .... 62 cc (2.1 fl oz)

4-2　Chapter 4　Fuel and exhaust systems

Torque specifications

Carburetor insulator screws	5 Nm (43 inch-lbs)
Carburetor mounting screws	10 Nm (7 ft-lbs)
Fuel pump mounting bolts	10 Nm (7 ft-lbs)
Throttle linkage pivot screw	5 Nm (43 inch-lbs)
Exhaust pipe mounting nuts	18 Nm (13 ft-lbs)
Muffler clamp bolts	22 Nm (16 ft-lbs)
Muffler mounting bolts	40 Nm (30 ft-lbs)

1 General information

The fuel system consists of the fuel tank, the fuel tap and filter, the carburetors and connecting lines, hoses and control cables and an electric fuel pump.

The carburetors used on these motorcycles are four Mikunis with butterfly-type throttle valves. For cold starting, an enrichment circuit is actuated by a cable and the choke lever mounted on the left handlebar.

The exhaust system is a four-into-two design.

Many of the fuel system service procedures are considered routine maintenance items and for that reason are included in Chapter 1.

2 Fuel tank - removal and installation

Refer to illustrations 2.7, 2.8, 2.9, 2.10 and 2.11

Warning: *Gasoline is extremely flammable, so take extra precautions when you work on any part of the fuel system. Don't smoke or allow open flames or bare light bulbs near the work area, and don't work in a garage where a natural gas-type appliance (such as a water heater or clothes dryer) is present. If you spill any fuel on your skin, rinse it off immediately with soap and water. When you perform any kind of work on the fuel system, wear safety glasses and have a fire extinguisher suitable for class B fires on hand.*

1　The fuel tank is mounted beneath the seat and is held in place at the rear end by a bolt. At the front, cups on each side of the tank fit over rubber mounts on the frame.

2　Disconnect the cable from the negative terminal of the battery.

3　Remove the seat, top compartment and rear fender (see Chapter 8).

4　Remove the rear wheel and shock absorbers. Unbolt the rear master cylinder and tie it in an upright position so brake fluid won't spill

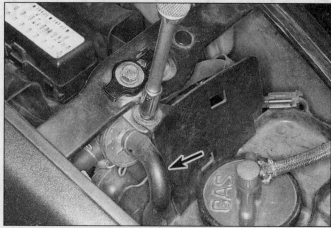

2.7 Disconnect the lower end of the hose (arrow) and remove the splash shield mounting nut

(see Chapters 6 and 7).

5　Remove the battery and battery tray (see Chapter 9).

6　Remove the cap from the fuel tank and disconnect the hose from the left rear corner of the fuel tray.

7　If there's a splash shield at the front of the fuel tray, disconnect the hose that passes through the loop on its left side **(see illustration)**. Remove the shield's mounting nut and lift the shield free of the fuel tray.

8　Remove the fuel filler cap. Free the wiring harness from the clips molded into the leading edge of the fuel tray, then remove the fuel tray **(see illustration)**.

9　Unbolt the crosspiece from the frame **(see illustration)**.

2.8 Work the wiring harness free of the molded retainers (arrows)

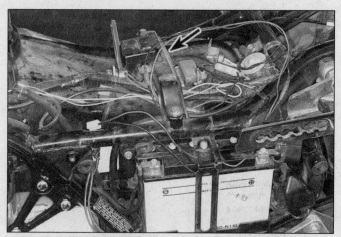

2.9 Unbolt the crosspiece (arrow) and lift it off the frame

Chapter 4 Fuel and exhaust systems

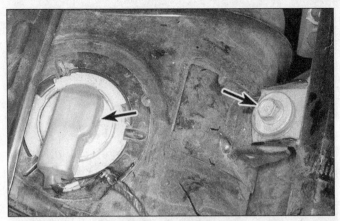

2.10 Disconnect the sender wires (left arrow) and remove the mounting bolt (right arrow)

2.11 Remove two screws and take the fuel tap off the tank; use new O-rings on installation

10 Unplug the electrical connectors for the fuel level sensor (see illustration).
11 Turn the fuel tap to the Off position and unbolt it from the tank (see illustration). Detach the fuel filter bracket from the tank.
12 Remove the mounting bolt and collar and pull the tank rearward out of the frame (see illustration 2.10).
13 Before installing the tank, check the condition of the hoses and rubber mounting dampers - if they're hardened, cracked, or show any other signs of deterioration, replace them.
14 When replacing the tank, reverse the above procedure. Make sure the tank seats properly and does not pinch any control cables or wires. If difficulty is encountered when trying to slide the tank onto the dampers, a small amount of light oil should be used to lubricate them.

3 Fuel tank - cleaning and repair

1 All repairs to the fuel tank should be carried out by a professional who has experience in this critical and potentially dangerous work. Even after cleaning and flushing of the fuel system, explosive fumes can remain and ignite during repair of the tank.
2 If the fuel tank is removed from the vehicle, it should not be placed in an area where sparks or open flames could ignite the fumes coming out of the tank. Be especially careful inside garages where a natural gas-type appliance is located, because the pilot light could cause an explosion.

4 Fuel pump - testing, removal and installation

Testing

Refer to illustration 4.3

1 Look up the specified fuel flow listed in this Chapter's Specifications. Obtain a container marked in fluid ounces or cubic centimeters and place a piece of tape at the five-second level.
2 Make sure the ignition switch is in the off position.
3 Disconnect the outlet line from the fuel pump and connect a length of tubing in its place (see illustration). Place the other end of the tube in the marked container.
4 Follow the wiring harness from the fuel pump to the pump relay (beneath the ignition coils) and unplug it. One of the wires is blue-yellow; the other wires vary in color depending on model and year. Connect a short jumper wire between the other two wires' terminals (not the blue-yellow wire). This bypasses the relay so the pump will run.
5 Turn the ignition switch to the On position for five seconds. The pump will run and fuel will flow into the container. If the fuel reaches the specified level, the pump is operating normally. If the pump runs but there's little or no fuel, the pump is probably defective. If the pump doesn't run at all, check the wiring connections before assuming the pump is at fault.

Removal and installation

Refer to illustration 4.7

6 Disconnect the fuel line at the pump and unplug the electrical connector (see illustration 4.3).
7 Remove the mounting nuts and separate the pump from the mounting bracket. If necessary, unbolt the bracket from the engine (see illustration).
8 Installation is the reverse of the removal steps.

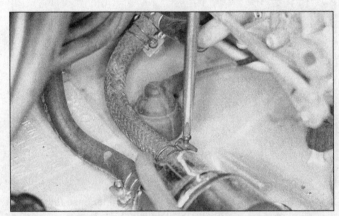

4.3 Undo the fuel pump outlet hose and attach a length of tubing in its place

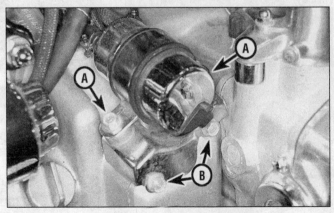

4.7 Fuel pump mounting details

A Mounting nuts (one nut hidden)
B Bracket bolts

4-4 Chapter 4 Fuel and exhaust systems

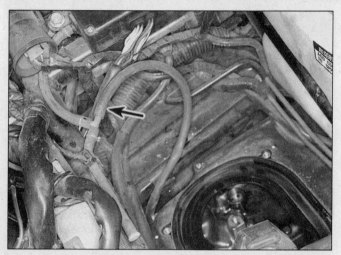

5.3 Disconnect the vacuum line (arrow) at the T-fitting

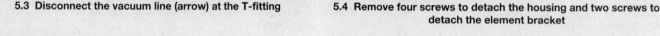

5.4 Remove four screws to detach the housing and two screws to detach the element bracket

5 Air filter housing - removal and installation

Refer to illustrations 5.3, 5.4 and 5.5

1   Remove the top compartment (see Chapter 8).

5.5 Be sure the Front mark on the air cleaner base faces forward on installation

2   Remove the housing cover and the air filter (see Chapter 1).
3   Disconnect the vacuum line at the T-fitting next to the air cleaner **(see illustration)**.
4   Remove the air cleaner housing screws **(see illustration)**. If necessary, remove the element bracket as well.
5   Remove the air cleaner housing **(see illustration)**.
6   Installation is the reverse of the removal steps.

6 Idle fuel/air mixture adjustment

Refer to illustrations 6.3a, 6.3b and 6.3c

1   Due to the increased emphasis on controlling motorcycle exhaust emissions, certain governmental regulations have been formulated which directly affect the carburetion of this machine. The pilot screws are sealed with plugs, and setting them requires a tachometer which can accurately indicate changes of 50 rpm or less.
2   If the engine runs extremely rough at idle or continually stalls, and all of the non-carburetor problems listed in Section 7 have been eliminated, try adjusting the pilot screws as described below.
3   Drill out the pilot screw plugs with a 4 mm (5/32-inch) drill bit **(see illustration)**. **Caution:** *Don't drill into the pilot screw.* Thread a self-tapping screw into the hole and grip it with locking pliers, then pry the locking pliers away from the carburetor to extract the plug **(see illustrations)**.

6.3a Drill a hole in the plug, but be careful not to hit the pilot screw with the drill (carburetor shown inverted)

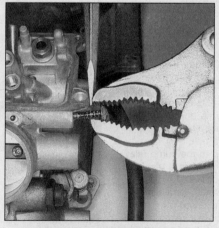

6.3b Grip the screw with locking pliers and pry the pliers away from the carburetor . . .

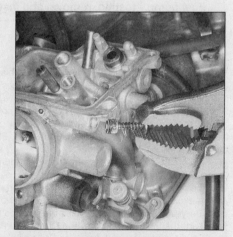

6.3c . . . to pull out the pilot screw plug

Chapter 4 Fuel and exhaust systems

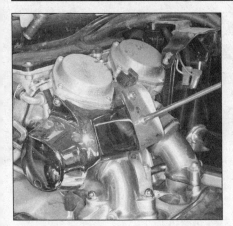

8.5 Remove the carburetor covers

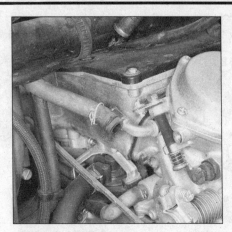

8.7a On California models, disconnect the vent hoses . . .

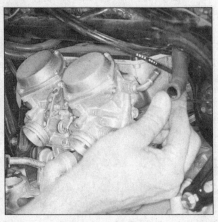

8.7b . . . there's one at each corner of the carburetor assembly

4 Turn the screws clockwise until they seat lightly, then back them out the number of turns listed in this Chapter's Specifications. **Caution:** *Don't bottom the screws hard or their tips will be damaged, resulting in an unstable idle mixture.*

5 Warm the engine to normal operating temperature (stop-and-go riding for about 10 minutes should be enough). Park the bike, shut it off and connect a tune-up tachometer following the tachometer manufacturer's instructions.

6 Start the engine and let it idle. Adjust idle speed, using the procedure and specifications listed in Chapter 1.

7 Turn both of the pilot screws counterclockwise 1/2 turn and note the reading on the tachometer. If it increases by 50 rpm or more, bring it back down by turning the pilot screws (not the throttle stop screw). Turn the screws out evenly, 1/2 turn at a time, until engine speed drops (but don't drop it more than 50 rpm).

8 Readjust idle speed to the Chapter 1 Specifications, using the throttle stop screw.

9 Turn the pilot screw on the no. 1 carburetor clockwise just enough to reduce engine speed by 50 rpm. Turn it counterclockwise exactly one turn. This will cause the idle speed to change, so you'll need to reset it to the Chapter 1 Specifications with the throttle stop screw.

10 Repeat Step 9 on the pilot screws for the no. 2, no. 3 and no. 4 carburetors in order. At this point, the engine should idle smoothly, at the rpm listed in the Chapter 1 Specifications.

11 Tap new plugs into the pilot screw bores, using a 7 mm driver. The plugs should be recessed 1 mm from the top of the bore when fully installed.

7 Carburetor overhaul - general information

1 Poor engine performance, hesitation, hard starting, stalling, flooding and backfiring are all signs that major carburetor maintenance may be required.

2 Keep in mind that many so-called carburetor problems are really not carburetor problems at all, but mechanical problems within the engine or ignition system malfunctions. Try to establish for certain that the carburetors are in need of maintenance before beginning a major overhaul.

3 Check the fuel filter, the fuel lines, the fuel tank cap vent (if equipped), the intake tube clamps, the rubber portions of the intake tubes and the O-rings that seal the metal portions to the cylinder heads, the vacuum hoses, the air filter element, the cylinder compression, the spark plugs, the carburetor synchronization and the fuel pump before assuming that a carburetor overhaul is required.

4 Most carburetor problems are caused by dirt particles, varnish and other deposits which build up in and block the fuel and air passages. Also, in time, gaskets and O-rings shrink or deteriorate and cause fuel and air leaks which lead to poor performance.

5 When a carburetor is overhauled, it is generally disassembled completely and the parts are cleaned thoroughly with a carburetor cleaning solvent and dried with filtered, unlubricated compressed air. The fuel and air passages are also blown through with compressed air to force out any dirt that may have been loosened but not removed by the solvent. Once the cleaning process is complete, the carburetor is reassembled using new gaskets, O-rings and, generally, a new inlet needle valve and seat.

6 Before disassembling the carburetors, make sure you have a carburetor rebuild kit (which will include all necessary O-rings and other parts), some carburetor cleaner, a supply of rags, some means of blowing out the carburetor passages and a clean place to work. It is recommended that only one carburetor be overhauled at a time to avoid mixing up parts. **Caution:** *Don't separate the carburetors from each other unless one of the joints between them is leaking. The carburetors can be overhauled completely without being separated, and reconnecting them properly can be difficult.*

8 Carburetors - removal and installation

Warning: *Gasoline is extremely flammable, so take extra precautions when you work on any part of the fuel system. Don't smoke or allow open flames or bare light bulbs near the work area, and don't work in a garage where a natural gas-type appliance (such as a water heater or clothes dryer) is present. If you spill any fuel on your skin, rinse it off immediately with soap and water. When you perform any kind of work on the fuel system, wear safety glasses and have a class B type fire extinguisher (flammable liquids) on hand.*

Removal

Refer to illustrations 8.5, 8.7a, 8.7b, 8.8a, 8.8b and 8.9

1 Remove the top compartment. If you're working on an Interstate or Aspencade, remove the lower and inner fairing covers (see Chapter 8).

2 If you're working on a 1987 Interstate or Aspencade, detach the panel stay from the fairing bracket on the right side of the bike. If you're working on a 1987 Aspencade, follow the wiring harness from the cruise control's throttle cancel switch to the connector and unplug it. Disconnect the cruise control vacuum line at the check valve.

3 Remove the air filter housing (see Section 5).

4 Follow the fuel pump outlet line to the T-fitting at the carburetors and disconnect it **(see illustration 4.3)**.

5 Remove the carburetor covers **(see illustration)**.

6 Refer to Chapter 1 and disconnect the spark plug wires, then separate the wires from their retainers.

7 If you're working on a California bike, disconnect the vent hoses from the corners of the carburetor assembly **(see illustrations)**. On all

4-6 Chapter 4 Fuel and exhaust systems

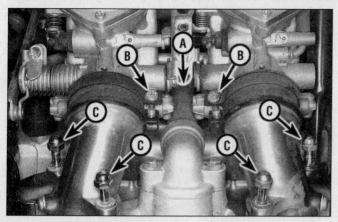

8.8a Carburetor right side mounting details

A Ignition control vacuum hose fitting (hidden)
B Insulator clamp screws
C Intake tube bolts (shown partially removed)

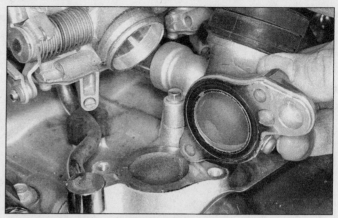

8.8b Pull the intake tubes off the carburetors; on installation, use a new O-ring between the intake tube and cylinder head

models, disconnect the pulse air tubes from the cylinder heads and move them out of the way (see Section 14).

8 On the right-hand side of the bike, disconnect the ignition control vacuum tube **(see illustrations)**. On both sides, loosen the clamp screws on the insulators and unbolt the intake tubes from the cylinder head. **Caution:** *Don't try to separate the insulators from the intake tubes. They're permanently bonded to keep them in alignment.*

9 Pad the left cylinder head cover with rags and lift the carburetor assembly partway out to the left **(see illustration)**. Refer to Section 12 and disconnect the throttle and choke cables.

10 After the carburetors have been removed, stuff clean rags into the openings to prevent the entry of dirt or other objects.

11 Inspect the insulators **(see illustration 8.8a)**. If they're cracked or brittle, replace them, together with the intake tubes.

Installation

12 Loosely install the intake tube on the right side of the carburetor assembly. Don't tighten the intake tube clamps until the assembly is installed.

13 The remainder of installation is the reverse of the removal steps, with the following additions:

a) *Connect the choke cable to the linkage, then connect the cable bracket to the engine.*
b) *Connect the throttle cables to the linkage while the carburetor assembly is partway installed, then install the linkage the rest of the way.*
c) *Check the operation of the throttle and choke cables.*
d) *Adjust the throttle grip freeplay (see Chapter 1).*

8.9 Pull the carburetor assembly partway out, then disconnect the throttle and choke cables

e) *Check and, if necessary, adjust the idle speed and carburetor synchronization (see Chapter 1).*

9 Carburetors - separation and reconnection

Refer to illustrations 9.1a, 9.1b, 9.2, 9.3, 9.4, 9.5a, 9.5b, 9.6a, 9.6b, 9.6c and 9.7

1 Refer to Section 8 and remove the carburetor assembly from the engine. Before you start separating the carburetors, study the assem-

9.1a Carburetors - assembled bottom view

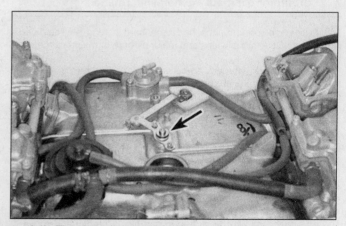

9.1b The choke linkage rods pivot on the bottom of the air chamber (arrow)

Chapter 4 Fuel and exhaust systems

9.2 Be sure the Front mark on the air chamber cover is forward when installed

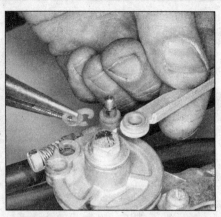

9.3 The throttle rods pivot on nylon bushings; remove the cotter pin, metal washer and nylon washer to detach the rods from the pivot

9.4 Remove the cotter pins and washer to free each choke rod from its pivot; there's a second washer on the other side of the bushing

9.5a The carburetor mounting screws also secure wire screens, two on each side of the air chamber

9.5b Pull each pair of carburetors off the air chamber and locate the dowels

bled views **(see illustrations)**.
2   Remove four screws and lift the cover off the top of the air chamber **(see illustration)**.
3   Remove the throttle rod cotter pins, metal washers, nylon washers and bushings from the pulley on the air chamber **(see illustration)**. Slip the arms off their pivots, then reinstall the bushing, washers and cotter pins so they won't be lost. **Note:** *As an alternative, you can detach the throttle rods from the carburetors.*
4   Remove the cotter pins and washers and push the choke rods out of the bushings at the center pivots **(see illustration)**. As with the throttle rods, you can detach the choke rods at the carburetors instead.
5   Remove the carburetor-to-air chamber screws on one side of the air chamber and take off the wire screens **(see illustration)**. Pull the pair of carburetors off the air chamber **(see illustration)**. Locate the air chamber dowels; they may have come off with the air chamber or stayed in the carburetors.
6   Note how each pair of carburetors fits together. Remove the O-rings that seal the carburetors to the air chamber and the thrust spring that fits between each pair of carburetors **(see illustrations)**.

9.6a Use new O-rings between the carburetors and air chamber on installation

9.6b Remove the thrust spring from between each pair of carburetors

9.6c Assembled synchronizer screws and springs should look like this

4-8 Chapter 4 Fuel and exhaust systems

7   Pull the carburetors straight apart from each other (see illustration). Don't bend or twist them or the connecting tubes may be bent. Separate the carburetors and remove the O-rings from the connecting tubes.

8   Reconnection is the reverse of the separation steps, with the following additions:
  a) Use new O-rings on the connecting tubes and at the air chamber, its fuel tube and the air horn.
  b) Replace any removed cotter pins with new ones.
  c) Make sure the choke and throttle linkages operate smoothly.

10 Carburetors - disassembly, cleaning and inspection

Warning: *Gasoline is extremely flammable, so take extra precautions when you work on any part of the fuel system. Don't smoke or allow open flames or bare light bulbs near the work area, and don't work in a garage where a natural gas-type appliance (such as a water heater or clothes dryer) is present. If you spill any fuel on your skin, rinse it off immediately with soap and water. When you perform any kind of work on the fuel system, wear safety glasses and have a fire extinguisher suitable for class B fires (flammable liquids) on hand.*

Disassembly
Refer to illustrations 10.2a through 10.2g

1   Remove the carburetors from the motorcycle as described in Section 8, then separate them as described in Section 9. Set the assembly on a clean working surface. **Note:** *Work on one carburetor at a time to avoid getting parts mixed up.*

2   Refer to the accompanying illustrations to disassemble the carburetor (see illustrations).

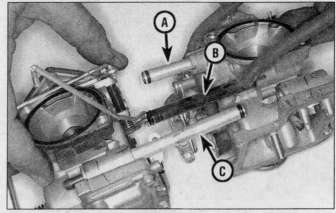

9.7 Pull the carburetors straight apart, without bending or twisting them; use new O-rings on assembly

A Vent tube   B Air tube   C Fuel tube

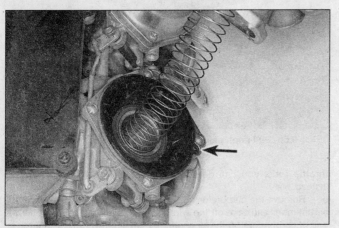

10.2a Remove the cover screws and lift off the cover to remove the spring and diaphragm; on assembly, align the diaphragm tab (arrow) with the notches in carburetor body and cover

10.2b Remove the screws and take off the float chamber cover; on assembly, use a new O-ring and make sure the dowels are in position

10.2c Pull out the float pivot pin and lift the float out, pulling the needle valve with it; unscrew the main jet (A) and slow jet (C) with a screwdriver, and use a wrench to unscrew the main jet holder (B)

10.2d Unscrew the pilot screw all the way and pull it out, together with the spring, washer and O-ring

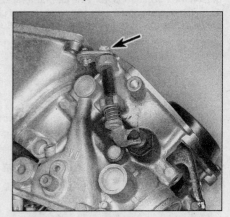

10.2e Remove the nut and lockwasher from the choke lever (arrow), then work the choke lever fork free of the choke valve

Chapter 4 Fuel and exhaust systems

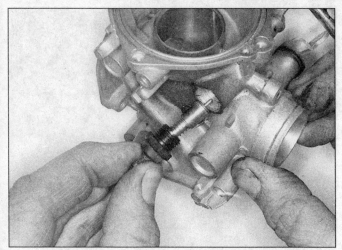

10.2f Unscrew the choke valve from the carburetor body

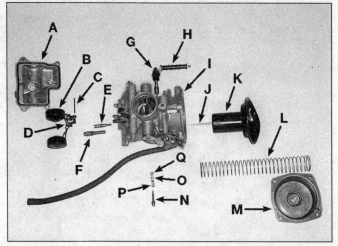

10.2g Carburetor details

A	Float chamber cover and O-ring	I	Carburetor body
B	Floats	J	Jet needle
C	Float pivot pin	K	Piston and diaphragm
D	Needle valve and clip	L	Spring
E	Slow jet	M	Cover
F	Main jet and holder	N	Pilot screw
G	Choke valve	O	Spring
H	Choke lever	P	Washer
		Q	O-ring

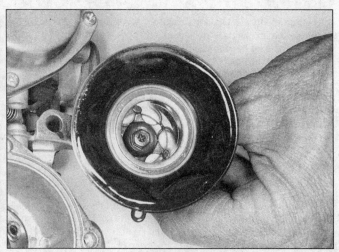

10.10 Turn the needle jet holder with a screwdriver to release the needle jet

Inspection

Refer to illustration 10.10

3 Check the tip of the needle valve. If it has grooves or scratches in it, it must be replaced. Push in on the rod in the other end of the needle valve, then release it - if it doesn't spring back, replace the valve needle.

4 Check the operation of the choke plunger. If it doesn't move smoothly, replace it, along with the return spring. Inspect the needle on the end of the choke plunger and replace it if it's worn.

5 Check the tapered portion of the pilot screw for wear or damage. Replace the pilot screw if necessary.

6 Check the carburetor body, float chamber cover and vacuum chamber cover for cracks, distorted sealing surfaces and other damage. If any defects are found, replace the faulty component, although replacement of the entire carburetor will probably be necessary (check with your parts supplier for the availability of separate components).

7 Check the diaphragm for splits, holes and general deterioration. Holding it up to a light will help to reveal problems of this nature.

8 Insert the throttle piston in the carburetor body and see that it moves up-and-down smoothly. Check the surface of the piston for wear. If it's worn excessively or doesn't move smoothly in the bore, replace the carburetor.

9 Check the jet needle for straightness by rolling it on a flat surface (such as a piece of glass). Replace it if it's bent or if the tip is worn.

10 If you need to replace the jet needle or diaphragm, insert a screwdriver in the jet needle holder and rotate it 1/4 turn to release the needle **(see illustration)**. Lift the holder, spring and jet needle out of the piston.

11 Operate the throttle shaft to make sure the throttle butterfly valve opens and closes smoothly. If it doesn't, replace the carburetor.

12 Check the floats for damage. This will usually be apparent by the presence of fuel inside one of the floats. If the floats are damaged, they must be replaced.

Cleaning

Caution: *Use only a petroleum based solvent for carburetor cleaning. Don't use caustic cleaners.*

13 Submerge the metal components in the solvent for approximately thirty minutes (or longer, if the directions recommend it).

14 After the carburetor has soaked long enough for the cleaner to loosen and dissolve most of the varnish and other deposits, use a brush to remove the stubborn deposits. Rinse it again, then dry it with compressed air. Blow out all of the fuel and air passages in the main body. **Caution:** *Never clean the jets or passages with a piece of wire or a drill bit, as they will be enlarged, causing the fuel and air metering rates to be upset.*

11 Carburetors - reassembly and float level adjustment

Caution: *When installing the jets, be careful not to over-tighten them - they're made of soft material and can strip or shear easily.*

Note: *When reassembling the carburetors, be sure to use the new O-rings, gaskets and other parts supplied in the rebuild kit.*

Reassembly

1 Assembly is the reverse of the disassembly steps, with the following additions.

2 Install the pilot screw (if removed) along with its spring, washer and O-ring, turning it in until it seats lightly. Now, turn the screw out the number of turns listed in this Chapter's Specifications. Refer to Section 6 and adjust the fuel mixture.

Chapter 4 Fuel and exhaust systems

11.5 Hold the carburetor like this so the float hangs down, then measure the distance from the float to the gasket surface; bend the float tang (arrow) to change float level

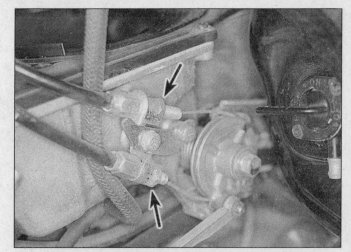

12.2a Loosen the mounting nuts (arrows) and slip the cable ends out of the bracket

3 The diaphragm must be supported in the up position when installing the cover. To do this, open the throttle plate by hand and tie it in the open position with a piece of wire on the throttle linkage. Insert two pieces of rubber or vinyl tubing into the throttle bore, so the piston will rest on the tubing when it's installed. Position the pieces of tubing so the jet needle can pass between them.

4 Install the jet needle and piston, inserting the jet needle between the tubing into the needle jet. Be sure to place the diaphragm tab in its groove **(see illustration 10.2a)**. Align the notch in the diaphragm cover with the diaphragm tab, then install the diaphragm cover and tighten its screws evenly.

Float level adjustment

Refer to illustration 11.5

5 With the float chamber cover removed, make sure the needle valve is fully seated and hold the carburetor so the float hangs down **(see illustration)**. Position the carburetor so the float arm just touches the needle valve, then measure the distance from the float chamber gasket surface to the bottom of the floats. If it differs from the value listed in this Chapter's Specifications, bend the float arm, in very small amounts, to change it.

12.2b Rotate the cable to align it with its pulley slot, then slide the cable end sideways out of the pulley

12 Throttle and choke cables - removal, installation and adjustment

Throttle cables

Refer to illustrations 12.2a, 12.2b and 12.5

1 For access to the carburetor ends of the cables, you'll need to remove the carburetor assembly partway (see Section 8).

2 Loosen the accelerator cable mounting nuts and slip the cables out of their brackets **(see illustration)**. Rotate the cables so they align with the slots in the pulley and slip them out **(see illustration)**.

3 Loosen the cable locknuts at the underside of the throttle switch housing.

4 Remove the handlebar switch mounting screws and separate the halves of the handlebar switch (see Chapter 9).

5 Detach the accelerator and decelerator cables from the throttle grip pulley **(see illustration)**. Remove the cables, noting how they are routed.

6 Take the throttle grip off the handlebar. Clean the handlebar and apply a light coat of multi-purpose grease.

7 Route the cables into place. Make sure they don't interfere with any other components and aren't kinked or bent sharply.

8 Lubricate the ends of the accelerator and decelerator cables with multi-purpose grease and connect them to the throttle pulleys at the carburetors and at the throttle grip.

9 Follow the procedure outlined in Chapter 1, *Throttle operation/grip freeplay - check and adjustment*, to adjust the cables.

10 Turn the handlebars back and forth to make sure the cables don't

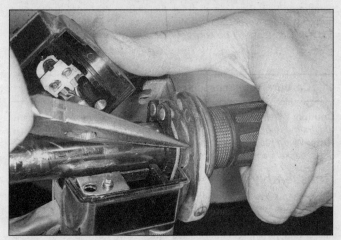

12.5 Use the same technique to detach the cables from the throttle grip pulley

Chapter 4 Fuel and exhaust systems

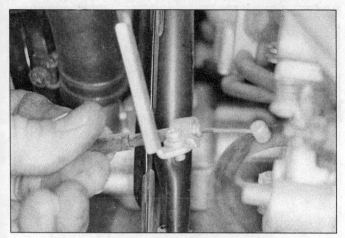

12.13a Remove the bracket screws and detach the choke cable end . . .

12.13b . . . from the linkage lever, which is mounted on the underside of the air chamber (arrow)

cause the steering to bind. With the engine idling, turn the handlebars back and forth and make sure idle speed doesn't change. If it does, find and fix the cause before riding the motorcycle.
11 Install components removed for access.

Choke cables

Refer to illustrations 12.13a and 12.13b
12 As with the throttle cables, you'll need to remove the carburetor assembly partway for access to the carburetor end of the cable (see Section 8).
13 Remove the choke cable bracket screws and take the bracket off the carburetor assembly **(see illustration)**. Rotate the end of the cable to align with the slot in the choke arm and slip the cable out **(see illustration)**.
14 Remove the screws from the underside of the left handlebar switch. Lift off the top half of the switch housing and detach the choke cable from its pulley.
15 Installation is the reverse of the removal steps. The end of the choke cable housing should be flush with the edge of the cable bracket **(see illustration 12.13a)**. Lubricate the ends of the cable with multi-purpose grease.

13 Exhaust system - removal and installation

Refer to illustrations 13.2, 13.3 and 13.4
1 Place the bike on its centerstand.

2 Remove the nuts and retainers and lower the exhaust pipes away from the cylinder head **(see illustration)**.
3 Remove the muffler mounting bolts and remove the exhaust system from the motorcycle **(see illustration)**.
4 Installation is the reverse of the removal steps, with the following addition: Use new gaskets at the cylinder head **(see illustration)**.

13.2 Remove the nuts and retainers and lower the pipes away from the cylinder head

13.3 Remove the muffler mounting bolt (arrow)

13.4 Use new gaskets in the exhaust ports (arrows)

4-12 Chapter 4 Fuel and exhaust systems

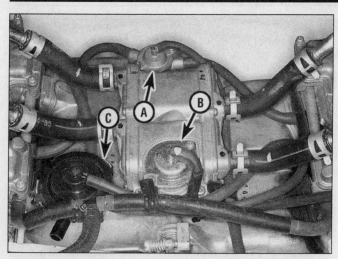

14.1 The secondary air supply system is mounted beneath the carburetor air chamber

A Slow air cutoff valve
B Anti-afterburn valve
C Purge control valve (California models)

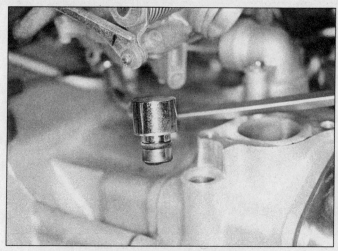

14.3 Pry the air tubes out of the cylinder head; use new O-rings on installation

14 Emission control systems - inspection and component replacement

Secondary air supply system

Refer to illustrations 14.1, 14.3 and 14.5a through 14.5f

1   This system uses exhaust gas pulses to suck fresh air into the exhaust ports, where it mixes with hot combustion gases. The additional oxygen provided by the fresh air allows combustion to continue for a longer time, reducing unburned hydrocarbons in the exhaust. Reed valves allow the flow of air into the ports and prevent exhaust gas from flowing into the system **(see illustration)**. There are four reed valves, one for each cylinder. The anti-afterburn valve and slow air cutoff valve regulate system operation to prevent backfiring.
2   Check the hoses for loose connections, damage and deterioration. Tighten or replace loose or damaged hoses.
3   Access to the components other than air tubes generally requires removal of the carburetors and air chamber (see Section 8). To remove air tubes from the cylinder heads, carefully pry them loose **(see illustration)**. Use a new O-ring, coated with clean engine oil, when you reconnect a tube.
4   To replace the anti-afterburn valve or slow air cutoff valve, remove the mounting screws and disconnect the hose **(see illustration 14.1)**.
5   To replace reed valves, remove the mounting screws and discon-

14.5a Remove the three reed case mounting screws and take the case off the air chamber

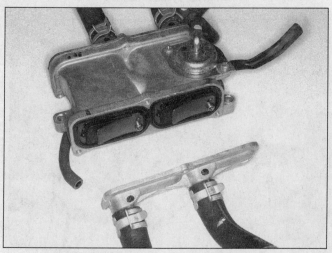

14.5b Remove the screws and reed cover . . .

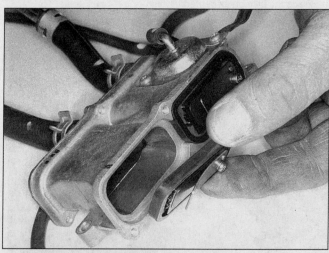

14.5c . . . and take the reeds out of the case

Chapter 4 Fuel and exhaust systems

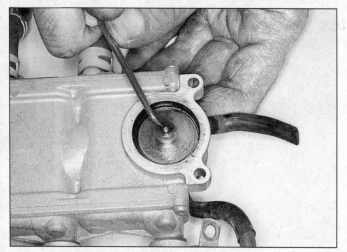

14.5d The anti-afterburn valve plate is secured by a retaining ring

14.5e This O-ring isn't easily accessible, so it's a good idea to replace it with a new one whenever the reed case is removed

nect the hoses **(see illustration)**. Remove the reed case cover screws and take off the covers to expose the reeds **(see illustrations)**.
6   Installation is the reverse of the removal steps.

Evaporation control system (California models)

Refer to illustrations 14.7a and 14.7b

7   The evaporation control system used on California models prevents fuel vapor from escaping into the atmosphere. When the engine isn't running, the vapor is stored in a canister, then routed into the combustion chambers for burning when the engine starts **(see illustration 14.1 and the accompanying illustrations)**.
8   The hoses should be checked periodically for loose connections, damage and deterioration. Tighten or replace the hoses as needed.
9   To remove the canister, disconnect the hoses and remove the mounting bolts.
10 Inspect the rubber mounting bushings and replace them if they're cracked or deteriorated. Bolt the canister to its bracket and reconnect the hoses.

Crankcase breather system

11 The breather system allows air into the crankcase. Its storage tank traps deposits.
12 The storage tank should be removed occasionally and any accumulated deposits cleaned out (see Chapter 1).

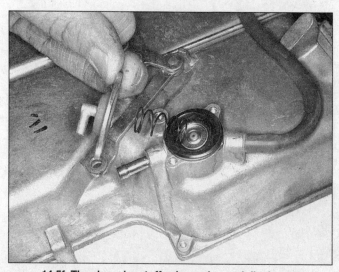

14.5f The slow air cutoff valve spring and diaphragm are beneath this cover

14.7a Disconnect the canister hoses . . .

14.7b . . . and undo the mounting bolts; replace the grommets (arrows) if they're damaged or deteriorated

Notes

Chapter 5
Ignition system

Contents

	Section		Section
Crankshaft timing rotor	See Chapter 2	Ignition system - check	2
General information	1	Pulse generators - check, removal and installation	4
Ignition coils - check, removal and installation	3	Spark plugs - replacement	See Chapter 1
Ignition control unit - check, removal and installation	5		

Specifications

General

Ignition coil primary resistance	2.7 +/- 0.3 ohms at 20-degrees C (68-degrees F)
Ignition coil secondary resistance	
With cap resistors installed	20,100 to 27,900 ohms at 20-degrees C (68-degrees F)
Without cap resistors	16,300 to 21,700 ohms
Spark plug cap resistor resistance	3750 to 6250 ohms
Arcing distance	6 mm (1/4 inch)
Pulse generator resistance	1100 to 1300 ohms at 20-degrees C (68-degrees F)
Pulse generator air gap (1984)	0.40 to 0.90 mm (0.016 to 0.035 inch)
Ignition timing	Not adjustable
Spark plugs	See Chapter 1

Torque specifications

Pulse generator rotor bolt torque (1984)	10 Nm (7 ft-lbs)

1 General information

This motorcycle is equipped with a battery operated, fully transistorized, breakerless ignition system. The system consists of the following components:
- Ignition control unit
- Pulse generators and timing rotor
- Battery and fuse
- Ignition coils
- Spark plugs
- Ignition (main) and engine kill (stop) switches
- Primary and secondary circuit wiring

The transistorized ignition system functions on the same principle as a breaker point DC ignition system with the pulse generators, timing rotor and ignition control unit performing the tasks previously associated with the breaker points and mechanical advance system. As a result, adjustment and maintenance of ignition components is eliminated (with the exception of spark plug replacement).

All models use a pair of pulse generators. On 1984 models, they're mounted at the rear of the engine. On 1985 through 1987 models they're mounted at the front.

The ignition control unit varies ignition timing according to engine rpm when the transmission is in first, second or third gear. When the transmission is shift to fourth or fifth gear, the unit varies ignition timing according to carburetor vacuum.

Because of their nature, the individual ignition system components can be checked but not repaired. If ignition system troubles occur, and the faulty component can be isolated, the only cure for the problem is to replace the part with a new one. Keep in mind that most electrical parts, once purchased, can't be returned. To avoid unnecessary expense, make very sure the faulty component has been positively identified before buying a replacement part.

2.13 A simple spark gap testing fixture can be made from a block of wood, a large alligator clip, two nails, a screw and a piece of wire

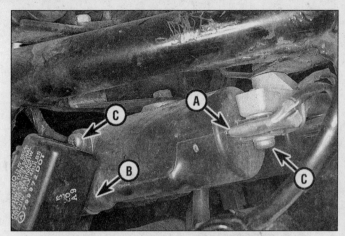

3.3 Ignition coil mounting details (right coil shown)

A Primary terminals
B Secondary terminals
C Mounting screws

2 Ignition system - check

Refer to illustration 2.13

Warning: *Because of the very high voltage generated by the ignition system, extreme care should be taken when these checks are performed.*

1   If the ignition system is the suspected cause of poor engine performance or failure to start, a number of checks can be made to isolate the problem.
2   Make sure the engine kill switch is in the Run position.

Engine will not start

3   Disconnect one of the spark plug wires, connect the wire to a spare spark plug and lay the plug on the engine with the threads contacting the engine. If necessary, hold the spark plug with an insulated tool. Crank the engine over and make sure a well-defined, blue spark occurs between the spark plug electrodes. **Warning:** *Don't remove one of the spark plugs from the engine to perform this check - atomized fuel being pumped out of the open spark plug hole could ignite, causing severe injury!*
4   If no spark occurs, the following checks should be made:
5   Detach the spark plug caps from the plugs and check the resistance of the resistor inside each cap with an ohmmeter. If the resistance is not within the range listed in this Chapter's Specifications, replace the spark plug cap.
6   Connect a voltmeter between the terminals of one ignition coil (positive to black-white, negative to blue-yellow). Turn the ignition switch to the On position and note the voltmeter reading, then crank the engine and note the reading again. If voltage doesn't change by more than one volt, check the primary wiring. Make sure all electrical connectors are clean and tight. Check all wires for shorts, opens and correct installation.
7   Check the battery voltage with a voltmeter and check the specific gravity with a hydrometer (see Chapter 1). If the voltage is less than 12-volts or if the specific gravity is low, recharge the battery.
8   Check the ignition fuse and the fuse connections. If the fuse is blown, replace it with a new one; if the connections are loose or corroded, clean or repair them.
9   Refer to Chapter 9 and check the ignition switch, engine kill switch, neutral switch and sidestand switch.
10 Refer to Section 3 and check the ignition coil primary and secondary resistance.
11 Refer to Section 4 and check the pulse generator resistance.

Engine starts but misfires

12 If the engine starts but misfires, make the following checks before deciding that the ignition system is at fault.

13 The ignition system must be able to produce a spark across a six millimeter (1/4-inch) gap (minimum). A simple test fixture **(see illustration)** can be constructed to make sure the minimum spark gap can be jumped. Make sure the fixture electrodes are positioned six millimeters apart.
14 Connect one of the spark plug wires to the protruding test fixture electrode, then attach the fixture's alligator clip to a good engine ground/earth.
15 Crank the engine over (it will probably start and run on the remaining cylinders) and see if well-defined, blue sparks occur between the test fixture electrodes. If the minimum spark gap test is positive, the ignition coil for that cylinder (and its companion cylinder) is functioning properly. Repeat the check on one of the spark plug wires that is connected to the other coils. If the spark will not jump the gap during either test, or if it is weak (orange colored), refer to Steps 5 through 11 of this Section and perform the component checks described.

3 Ignition coils - check, removal and installation

Check

Refer to illustrations 3.3 and 3.7

1   In order to determine conclusively that the ignition coils are defective, they should be tested by an authorized Honda dealer service department which is equipped with the special electrical tester required for this check.
2   However, the coils can be checked visually (for cracks and other damage) and the primary and secondary coil resistances can be measured with an ohmmeter. If the coils are undamaged, and if the resistances are as specified, they are probably capable of proper operation.
3   To check the primary resistances, remove the top compartment (see Chapter 8) and disconnect the primary wires from the coil being tested **(see illustration)**.
4   Place the ohmmeter selector switch in the Rx1 position. Attach one ohmmeter lead to the black/white terminal in the primary connector, then connect the other ohmmeter lead to the yellow-blue or blue-yellow terminal. Compare the measured resistance to the value listed in this Chapter's Specifications.
5   If the primary resistance isn't as specified, the coil is defective and must be replaced as described below.
6   If the coil primary resistance is as specified, check the coil secondary resistance. Disconnect the spark plug wires from the plugs and connect an ohmmeter between the disconnected wires. Place the ohmmeter selector switch in the Rx100 position and compare the measured resistance to the values listed in this Chapter's Specifications.

Chapter 5 Ignition system

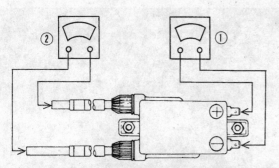

3.7 To test the coil primary resistance, connect the ohmmeter leads between the primary terminals (1); to check secondary resistance, connect the ohmmeter between the spark plug wires, then directly to the spark plug terminals on the coil

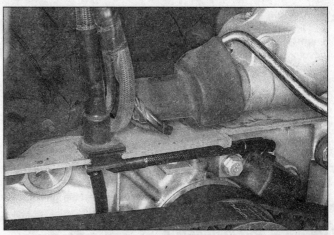

4.2 A U-shaped wiring harness grommet fits into a matching notch in the crankcase

7 If the resistance reading is not within the specified range, unscrew the spark plug wires from the bottom of the coil **(see illustration 3.3)** and connect the ohmmeter leads between the pair of spark plug wire terminals on each coil **(see illustration)**.

8 If the resistances are not as specified, the coil is probably defective and should be replaced with a new one.

Removal and installation

9 To remove the coils, remove the top compartment (Chapter 8) and the air cleaner housing (Chapter 4). Remove the ignition control unit (Section 5) and the relay bracket beneath it. Disconnect the spark plug wires from the plugs and unscrew them from the coils. After labeling them with tape to aid in reinstallation, unplug the coil primary circuit electrical connectors **(see illustration 3.3)**.

10 Support the coils with one hand and remove the coil mounting screws **(see illustration 3.3)**. Lift the coil out.

11 Installation is the reverse of removal. Make sure the primary circuit electrical connectors are attached to the proper terminals and the plug wires to the correct plugs. A black/white wire connects to each coil. The yellow/blue wire connects to the coil for cylinders 1 and 3. The blue-yellow wire connects to the coil for cylinders 2 and 4.

4 Pulse generators - check, removal and installation

Check

Refer to illustration 4.2

1 If you're working on a 1984 model, remove the left side cover (see Chapter 8). Locate the pulse generator connector just forward of the battery (white/yellow/ yellow, blue and white/blue wires). Unplug the connector.

2 If you're working on a 1985 through 1987 model, follow the pulse generator harness from its grommet at the timing belt cover to the connector and unplug it **(see illustration)**.

3 Probe the terminals in the pickup coil connector with an ohmmeter and compare the resistance readings with the value listed in this Chapter's Specifications.

4 If either pulse generator has a resistance reading outside the specified range, replace it.

Removal

1984 models

Refer to illustration 4.6

5 Remove the swingarm (see Chapter 6).

6 Unbolt the pulse generator cover from the rear of the engine. Remove the pulse generator screws **(see illustration)**. Work the wiring harness grommet free of the crankcase and remove the pulse generators.

1985 through 1987 models

Refer to illustration 4.8

7 Remove the timing belt covers and the right timing belt (see Chapter 2).

8 Remove the pulse generator mounting bolts. Work the wiring harness grommet free of the crankcase and remove the pulse generators **(see illustration 4.2 and the accompanying illustration)**.

4.6 The 1984 pulse generators are mounted on the rear of the engine

4.8 Later pulse generators are mounted on the front of the engine (right arrows); the wiring harness retainer (left arrow) is bolted to the crankcase

All models

9 Installation is the reverse of the removal steps. If you're working on a 1984 model, adjust the gap between the pulse generator and timing rotor to the value listed in this Chapter's Specifications and install a new cover gasket.

5 Ignition control unit - check, removal and installation

Check

1 The ignition control unit is checked by process of elimination (when all other possible causes have been checked and eliminated, the unit is at fault). Because the unit is expensive and can't be returned once purchased, consider having a Honda dealer test the ignition system before you buy a new one.

Removal and installation

Refer to illustration 5.3

2 Remove the top compartment (see Chapter 8).
3 Unplug the electrical connectors and disconnect the vacuum line. Remove the mounting bolts and take the unit out **(see illustration)**.
4 Installation is the reverse of the removal steps.

5.3 The ignition control unit is mounted on the forward part of the frame

Chapter 6
Steering, suspension and final drive

Contents

	Section		Section
Final drive unit - removal, inspection and installation	10	Rear shock absorbers - removal, inspection and installation	8
Forks - disassembly, inspection and reassembly	5	Steering head bearings - adjustment and lubrication	6
Forks - oil change	3	Steering head bearings - check	See Chapter 1
Forks - removal and installation	4	Steering head bearings - replacement	7
General information	1	Swingarm - removal and installation	12
Handlebars - removal and installation	2	Swingarm bearings - check	11
On-board air compressor - removal, desiccant replacement and installation	9	Swingarm bearings - replacement	13

Specifications

Fork spring length
   Standard models (single spring)
      Standard .... 541.4 mm (21.31 inches)
      Limit .... 540.3 mm (21.27 inches)
   Interstate and Aspencade (dual springs)
     Short spring
      Standard .... 162.9 mm (6.41 inches)
      Limit .... 162.6 mm (6.40 inches)
     Long spring
      Standard .... 407.6 mm (16.05 inches)
      Limit .... 406.8 mm (16.02 inches)
Fork oil capacity
   Drain and fill .... 323 cc (10.92 fl oz)
   After overhaul .... 345 cc (11.66 fl oz)
Fork oil level .... Not specified
Fork tube runout limit .... 0.2 mm (0.008 inch)

Torque specifications

Handlebar bracket bolts .... 27 Nm (20 ft-lbs) (1)
Front fork caps .... 23 Nm (17 ft-lbs)
Fork damper rod Allen bolt .... 20 Nm (15 ft-lbs) (2)
Upper triple clamp bolts .... 11 Nm (8 ft-lbs)
Lower triple clamp bolts .... 22 Nm (16 ft-lbs) (1)
Steering stem pinch bolt
   1984 through 1986 .... 22 Nm (16 ft-lbs)
   1987 .... 35 Nm (25 ft-lbs)
Steering stem upper nut (above triple clamp) .... 100 Nm (72 ft-lbs)
Steering stem adjusting nut .... 200 to 250 kg/cm (174 to 217 inch-lbs)
Rear shock absorber bolts
   Upper .... 35 Nm (25 ft-lbs)
   Lower (right shock) .... 23 Nm (17 ft-lbs)
   Lower (left shock) .... 70 Nm (51 ft-lbs)

Chapter 6 Steering, suspension and final drive

Air hoses
- To three-way joint .... 18 Nm (13 ft-lbs)
- To four-way joint .... 10 Nm (7 ft-lbs)
- To elbow .... 10 Nm (7 ft-lbs)
- To sensor .... 10 Nm (7 ft-lbs)
- To shock absorbers .... 6 Nm (48 inch-lbs)

Metal air tubes (selector valve to four-way joint) .... 5.5 Nm (48 inch-lbs)
Final drive unit mounting nuts .... 28 Nm (20 ft-lbs) (3)
Swingarm pivot bolts
- Right side .... 100 Nm (72 ft-lbs)
- Left side .... 19 Nm (14 ft-lbs)

Swingarm pivot bolt locknut
- Indicated torque with special tool .... 90 Nm (65 ft-lbs)
- Actual applied torque .... 100 Nm (72 ft-lbs)

1. Apply engine oil to the threads and the underside of the bolt heads.
2. Apply non-permanent thread locking agent to the threads.
3. Tighten after rear axle is tightened.

1 General information

The steering system on these models consists of a one-piece handlebar and a steering stem, which rides in a steering head attached to the front portion of the frame. All models use tapered roller bearings in the steering head.

The front suspension consists of conventional coil spring, hydraulically-damped telescopic forks with anti-dive units. Air pressure in the forks is adjustable.

The rear suspension is consists of twin shock absorbers and a swingarm. The shock absorber air pressure is adjustable on all models. Interstate models have an air fitting so air can be pumped in from an outside source; Aspencade and SE models have an on-board compressor system that allows air pressure to be changed at the touch of a switch.

The final drive uses a shaft and bevel gears to transmit power from the transmission to the rear wheel.

2 Handlebars - removal and installation

Refer to illustrations 2.1 and 2.2

1 Remove two screws and take off the handlebar center cover **(see illustration)**. If you're working on a 1985 or later Aspencade, turn the cover over and disconnect the electrical connector for the keyboard.

2 If the handlebars must be removed for access to other components, such as the forks or the steering head, simply remove the brackets and lift the handlebar off the upper triple clamp **(see illustration)**. It's not necessary to disconnect the cables, wires or hoses, but it is a good idea to support the assembly with a piece of wire or rope, to avoid unnecessary strain on the cables, wires and the brake or clutch hose.

3 If the handlebars are to be removed completely, refer to Chapter 2 for clutch master cylinder removal procedures, Chapter 7 for the brake master cylinder removal procedures, Chapter 4 for the throttle and choke cable removal procedure and Chapter 9 for the switch removal procedure.

2.1 Remove the screws and lift the cover off the handlebars; if the cover includes the keyboard shown here, turn it over and unplug the wiring connector

2.2 Align the punch mark in the handlebar (lower arrow) with the lower rear corner of the left bracket; install the clamps with their punch marks forward (upper arrows)

Chapter 6 Steering, suspension and final drive

3.2 Remove the drain screw and turn the anti-dive adjuster for maximum oil flow

3.3 Loosen the fork cap

3.4 Position the jack beneath this jacking point at the front of the crankcase

4.5a Pry the trim caps out of the fork brace bolts . . .

4.5b . . . then remove the bolts and take the brace off

4   Check the handlebars for cracks and distortion and replace them if any undesirable conditions are found. When installing the handlebars, align the punch mark on the handlebar with the lower inner corner of the bracket **(see illustration 2.2)**. Place the holders on the bracket with their punch marks forward. Tighten the front bolts, then the rear bolts to the torque listed in this Chapter's Specifications. **Caution:** *If there's a gap between the rear of the holders and the bracket, don't try to close it by tightening beyond the specified torque. You'll crack the holders or bracket.*

3 Forks - oil change

Refer to illustrations 3.2, 3.3 and 3.4

1   Relieve all air pressure in the front forks.
2   Place a drain pan beneath the fork and remove the drain screw **(see illustration)**. Turn the anti-dive adjuster to obtain maximum flow; pumping the forks up and down will also help. Once all the oil has drained, reinstall the drain screw.
3   Loosen the fork caps **(see illustration)**.
4   Place a jack under the engine and raise the front wheel off the ground **(see illustration)**.
5   Remove the fork caps and lift out the fork springs.
6   Pour oil of the amount and type recommended in this Chapter's Specifications into the top of the fork. Honda doesn't specify fork oil level for these models.

7   Reinstall the spring and fork cap. Tighten the fork cap to the torque listed in this Chapter's Specifications, then adjust air pressure to the specified amount.

4 Forks - removal and installation

Removal

Refer to illustrations 4.5a, 4.5b and 4.9a through 4.9e

1   Support the bike securely so it can't be knocked over during this procedure. If you're working on an Interstate or Aspencade, remove the top compartment (see Chapter 8).
2   Place a jack under the engine and raise it slightly to lift the front tire off the ground **(see illustration 3.4)**.
3   Remove the brake calipers and front wheel (see Chapter 7).
4   Remove the front fender (see Chapter 8).
5   Remove the fork brace **(see illustrations)**.
6   Remove any wiring harness clamps or straps from the fork tubes and detach the speedometer cable retainer.
7   If the fork will be disassembled after removal, read through the disassembly procedure (see Section 5), paying special attention to the damper rod bolt removal steps. If you don't have the necessary special tool or a substitute for it, you can loosen the damper rod bolt before the fork is disassembled, while the spring tension will keep the damper rod from spinning inside the fork tube.

Chapter 6 Steering, suspension and final drive

4.9a Loosen the upper triple clamp bolt . . .

4.9b . . . and the lower triple clamp bolts

4.9c Remove the stop ring from the fork tube and slide the tube out of the triple clamps

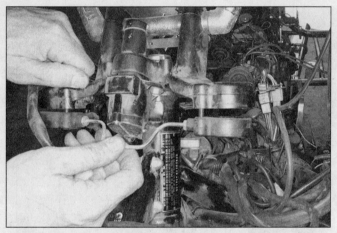

4.9d Remove the screws and lower the air equalizer away from the upper triple clamp

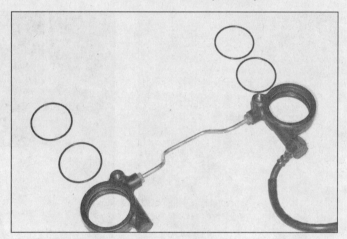

4.9e Use new O-rings and lubricate them with grease

8 Loosen the fork caps.
9 Loosen the fork upper and lower triple clamp bolts **(see illustrations)**. Remove the stop ring from each fork **(see illustration)**, then slide the fork tubes down and remove the forks from the motorcycle. Remove the air equalizer and install new O-rings **(see illustrations)**.

Installation

10 Install the stop ring on each fork leg. Lubricate new equalizer O-rings with grease. Install the air equalizer, but don't tighten it yet. Slide each fork leg into the lower triple clamp.
11 Slide the fork legs up until their stop rings seat, taking care not to nick the equalizer O-rings.
12 Position the fork brace with its F mark toward the front of the bike. Don't tighten the fork brace bolts until the front axle is tightened.
13 The remainder of installation is the reverse of the removal procedure. Tighten all fasteners to the torques listed in this Chapter's Specifications and the Chapter 7 Specifications.
14 Pump the front brake lever several times to bring the pads into contact with the discs.

5 Forks - disassembly, inspection and reassembly

Disassembly

Refer to illustrations 5.2, 5.4, 5.5, 5.6a, 5.6b, 5.7a, 5.7b, 5.8, 5.10a, 5.10b and 5.10c

1 Remove the forks following the procedure in Section 4. Work on one fork leg at a time to avoid mixing up the parts.

5.2 Fork details (dual springs shown)

A Fork cap	H Upper stopper ring
B O-ring	I Spring seat
C Upper (shorter) spring	J Spring
D Spring seat	K Oil lock valve
E Lower (longer) spring	L Lower stopper ring
F Teflon rings	M Rebound spring
G Damper rod	

Chapter 6 Steering, suspension and final drive

5.4 Pry the dust seal from its bore

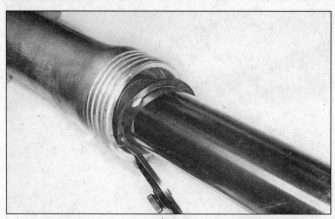

5.5 Remove the retainer from its bore with snap-ring pliers

5.6a Unscrew the damper rod Allen bolt and remove the sealing washer; use a new sealing washer on assembly

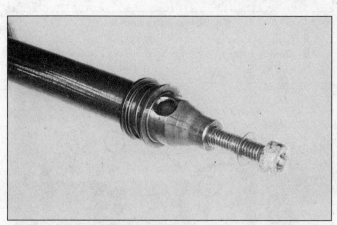

5.6b When the fork is assembled, the damper rod bolt passes through the lower fork tube and threads into the damper rod like this

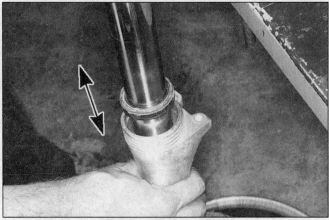

5.7a Yank the tubes apart repeatedly to force out the oil seal . . .

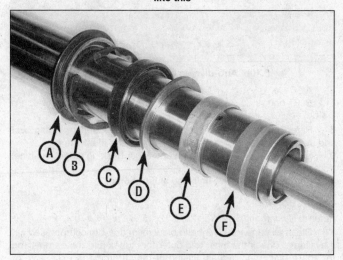

5.7b . . . and bushings

A	Dust seal	D	Back-up ring
B	Retainer	E	Outer tube bushing
C	Oil seal	F	Inner tube bushing

2 **Warning:** *The fork cap is under spring tension. Be sure to point the end of the fork away from yourself while you remove the cap.* Remove the fork cap (it should have been loosened before the forks were removed) **(see illustration 4.9a)**. Remove the spring seat and spring(s) **(see illustration)**. *Note: Some models have two fork springs, with the shorter spring on top of the longer spring.*

3 Invert the fork assembly over a container and extend and compress it several times to drain the oil.

4 Pry the dust seal from the outer tube **(see illustration)**.

5 Remove the retaining ring from its groove in the outer tube **(see illustration)**.

6 Unscrew the Allen bolt at the bottom of the outer tube and remove the copper washer **(see illustrations)**.

7 Hold the outer tube and yank the inner tube away from it, repeatedly (like a slide hammer), until the seal and outer tube guide bushing pop loose **(see illustrations)**.

Chapter 6 Steering, suspension and final drive

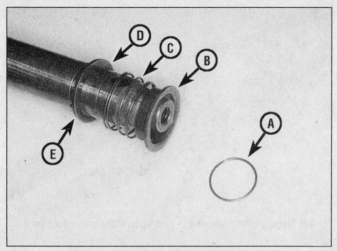

5.8 Oil lock valve details

A Lower stopper ring
B Oil lock valve
C Spring
D Spring seat
E Upper stopper ring (behind spring seat)

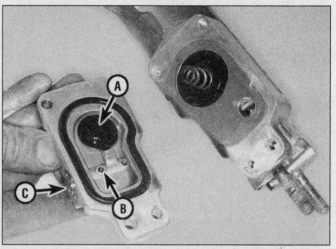

5.10a Undo the Allen bolts and take off the anti-dive case

A Seal
B Set pin
C Orifice

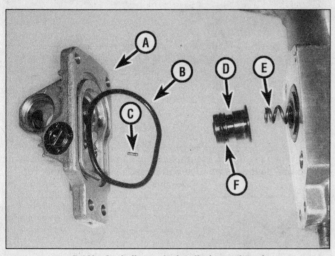

5.10b Anti-dive unit details (one of two)

A Case
B O-ring
C Set pin
D Piston
E Spring
F O-ring

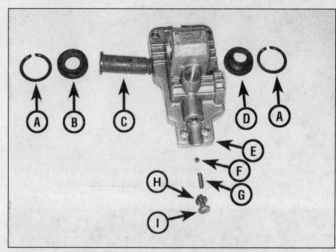

5.10c Anti-dive unit details (two of two)

A Snap-rings
B Seal
C Pivot collar
D Boot
E Anti-dive case
F Steel ball
G Spring
H Washer
I Screw

8   Remove the lower stopper ring, oil lock valve, spring, spring seat and upper stopper ring from the damper rod **(see illustration)**.
9   Slide the oil seal, backup ring and slider bushing (larger bushing) from the inner tube.
10 Remove the anti-dive unit **(see illustrations)**.

Inspection

Refer to illustrations 5.12a, 5.12b, 5.12c, 5.17a and 5.17b

11 Clean all parts in solvent and blow them dry with compressed air, if available. Check the inner and outer fork tubes and the damper rod for score marks, scratches, flaking of the chrome and excessive or abnormal wear. Look for dents in the tubes and replace them if any are found. Check the fork seal seat for nicks, gouges and scratches. If damage is evident, leaks will occur around the seal-to-outer tube junction. Replace worn or defective parts with new ones.
12 A common cause of inner fork tube and seal wear is road dirt, bugs, etc. that stick to the fork tube above the seal. An easily fabricated shield can prevent this **(see illustrations)**.
13 Check the bushings for scoring, scratches or excessive wear. Replace them if they're scored or scratched, or if the Teflon coating has worn away from more than three-quarters of the surface, exposing the copper. If the bushings need to be replaced, pry them apart at the

5.12a Cut a piece of soft, flexible plastic to the width shown . . .

Chapter 6 Steering, suspension and final drive

5.12b ... and attach it to this point on the outer fork tube ...

5.12c ... with a heavy duty tie wrap

5.17a Pull the collar out and remove the O-rings

5.17b Install new O-rings and coat the collar liberally with grease

5.23a Drive the bushing and oil seal into the outer fork seal bore like this

5.23b If you don't have a seal driver, a section of pipe can be used the same way the seal driver would be used - as a slide hammer (be sure to tape the ends of the pipe so it doesn't scratch the fork tube)

slit and take them off the fork tube. Install new ones, prying them just enough so they fit over the tube.

14 Check the inner circumference of the backup ring and replace it if it looks bent or distorted.

15 Have the inner fork tube checked for runout at a dealer service department or other repair shop. **Warning:** *If it is bent, it should not be straightened; replace it with a new one.*

16 Measure the overall length of the fork spring(s) and check for cracks and other damage. Compare the length to the minimum length listed in this Chapter's Specifications. If it's defective or sagged, replace the springs in both forks with new ones. Never replace the spring(s) in only one fork.

17 Slide the caliper mounting bushing out of the fork leg **(see illustration)**. Check the bushing for wear or damage and replace it if necessary. If the bushing is good, install new O-rings and lubricate it with grease, then reinstall it in the fork leg **(see illustration)**.

18 Check the Teflon rings on the damper rod and replace them if they're worn or damaged. Don't remove the rings from the damper rod unless you plan to replace them.

19 Inspect the anti-dive components for wear or damage **(see illustrations 5.17a and 5.17b)**. **Note:** *A swollen anti-dive O-ring can freeze the unit, causing a very harsh ride.*

Reassembly

Refer to illustrations 5.23a and 5.23b

20 Install the rebound spring on the damper rod Install the damper rod in the inner fork tube, then let it slide slowly down until it protrudes from the bottom of the inner fork tube.

21 Install the spring seat, spring, oil lock valve and stopper ring on the damper rod **(see illustrations 5.2 and 5.8)**.

22 Install the inner fork tube in the outer fork tube. Temporarily install the fork spring and cap bolt. Apply non-permanent thread locking agent to the damper rod bolt, then install the bolt and tighten it to the torque listed in this Chapter's Specifications.

23 Slide the slider bushing down the inner tube, then slide the backup ring on behind it. Using a fork seal driver (Honda tool 07947-KA50100 and KF00100 or equivalent) and a used slider bushing placed on top of the slider bushing being installed, drive the bushing into place until it's fully seated **(see illustration)**. If you don't have access to one of these tools, it is highly recommended that you take the assembly to a Honda dealer service department or other motorcycle repair shop to have this done. It is possible, however, to drive the bushing into place using a section of pipe and an old guide bushing **(see illustration)**. Wrap tape around the ends of the pipe to prevent it from scratching the fork tube. Once you've installed the new bushing, remove the old one that was used as a spacer.

24 Lubricate the lips and the outer diameter of the oil seal with the recommended fork oil (see this Chapter's Specifications) and slide it down the inner tube, with the seal lip facing into the outer fork tube. Drive the seal into place with the same tool used to drive in the slider bushing. If you don't have access to these, it is recommended that you take the assembly to a Honda dealer service department or other repair shop to have the seal driven in. If you are very careful, the seal can be driven in with a hammer and a drift punch. Work around the circumference of the seal, tapping gently on the outer edge

6.3a A socket like this one should be used to loosen the steering stem nut, which is very tight

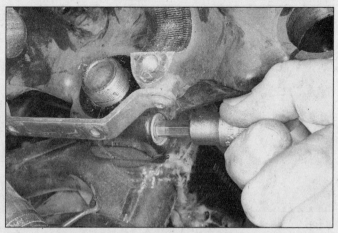

6.3b Loosen the upper triple clamp pinch bolt

6.3c Lift the upper triple clamp off the steering stem; bend back the lockwasher tabs (arrow), unscrew the locknut . . .

6.4a . . . and remove the lockwasher

of the seal until it's seated. Be careful - if you distort the seal, you'll have to disassemble the fork again and end up taking it to a dealer anyway!

25 Install the retainer ring, making sure it's completely seated in its groove.

26 Install the dust seal, making sure it seats completely. The same tool used to drive in the oil seal can be used for the dust seal.

27 Install the anti-dive assembly.

28 Add the recommended type and amount of fork oil.

29 Install the long fork spring, with the closer-wound coils at the bottom. Install the spring seat and upper spring (if equipped).

30 Install the O-ring and fork cap.

31 Install the fork by following the procedure outlined in Section 4. If you won't be installing the fork right away, store it in an upright position.

6 Steering head bearings - adjustment and lubrication

Adjustment

Refer to illustrations 6.3a, 6.3b, 6.3c, 6.4a and 6.4b

1 This procedure is shown with the fairing removed for clarity. It can be done without removing the fairing.

2 Remove the forks (Section 4).

3 Remove the steering stem nut, loosen the pinch bolt and lift off the upper triple clamp **(see illustrations)**.

4 Remove the steering stem locknut, adjusting nut and lockwasher **(see illustrations)**. Clean the threads of the steering stem and adjusting nut, then coat them lightly with grease. Reinstall the adjusting nut without the lockwasher or locknut.

5 Carefully tighten the adjusting nut to the initial torque listed in this Chapter's Specifications, using Honda tool 07916-3710100 **(see illustration 6.4b)**. Turn the steering stem from full left lock to full right lock five times to seat the bearings. Loosen the nut just until it's handtight

6.4b A socket like this one is needed to torque the adjusting nut accurately; if you use an adjustable spanner, make sure there's no looseness or binding in the steering

Chapter 6 Steering, suspension and final drive

7.4a Remove two bolts and a screw (arrow) . . .

7.4b . . . and lower the turn signal self-canceling unit until you can unplug its connector

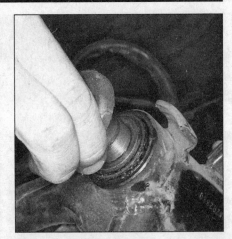

7.6 Lift off the bearing cover

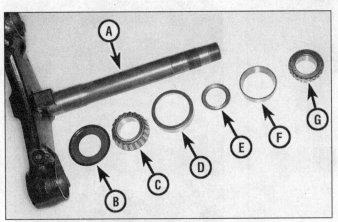

7.7a Steering stem and bearing details

A Steering stem/triple clamp
B Grease seal
C Lower (larger) bearing
D Lower (larger) bearing race
E Upper bearing grease cup
F Upper (smaller) bearing race
G Upper (smaller) bearing

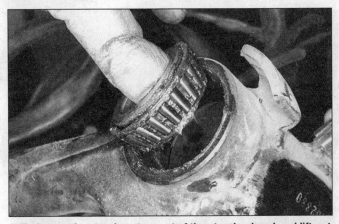

7.7b Lower the steering stem out of the steering head and lift out the upper bearing

(not all the way) and retighten to the final torque listed in this Chapter's Specifications.

6 Once again, turn the steering stem from lock to lock five times, then loosen it until handtight and retighten to the final torque.

7 A third time, turn the steering stem from lock to lock five times. This time, don't loosen the nut; finish by tightening to the final torque.

8 Turn the steering from lock to lock and check for binding. If there is any, remove the bearings for inspection (Section 7).

9 If the steering operates properly, install a new lockwasher with its tabs in the slots of the steering stem nut. Tighten the locknut with fingers only (don't use tools) so its slots align with those of the steering stem nut (don't allow the adjusting nut to turn). **Note:** *The lockwasher tabs are offset. If you can't get the locknut slots to align with the tabs, try removing the locknut and turning the lockwasher over.*

10 Bend two of the lockwasher tabs into locknut slots.

11 Recheck the steering head bearings for play as described in Chapter 1. If necessary, repeat the adjustment procedure. Reinstall all parts previously removed. Tighten the steering stem nut, triple clamp bolts and handlebar bolts to the torques listed in this Chapter's Specifications.

Lubrication

12 Periodic cleaning and repacking of the steering head bearings is recommended by the manufacturer. Refer to Section 7 for steering head bearing lubrication and replacement procedures.

7 Steering head bearings - replacement

Refer to illustrations 7.4a, 7.4b, 7.6, 7.7a, 7.7b, 7.10a, 7.10b, 7.11a, 7.11b, 7.11c, 7.12, 7.14a, 7.14b, 7.17 and 7.18

1 If the steering head bearing adjustment (Section 6) does not remedy excessive play or roughness in the steering head bearings, the entire front end must be disassembled and the bearings and races replaced with new ones.

2 Remove the front wheel (Chapter 7), the front forks (Section 4), the handlebars (Section 2).

3 Remove the front fender. If you're working on an Interstate or Aspencade, remove the instrument cluster cover and the bottom cover from beneath the steering stem (see Chapter 8).

4 Remove the bolts and screw to undo the turn signal self-canceling unit from the bottom of the steering stem **(see illustration)**. Pull the unit down until you can reach its electrical connector, then unplug the connector and remove the unit **(see illustration)**. Once the connector's unplugged, pull the harness out the top of the steering stem.

5 Refer to Section 7 and remove the upper triple clamp, steering stem locknut and steering stem lockwasher.

6 Remove the adjusting nut and bearing cover **(see illustration 6.4b and the accompanying illustration)**.

7 Lower the steering stem and lower triple clamp assembly out of the steering head, then remove the upper bearing **(see illustrations)**. If it's stuck, gently tap on the top of the steering stem with a plastic mallet or a hammer and a wood block.

8 Clean all the parts with solvent and dry them thoroughly, using

Chapter 6 Steering, suspension and final drive

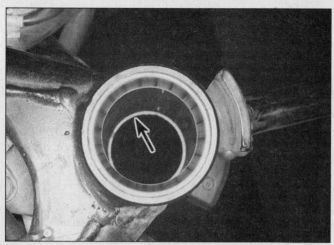

7.10a If the bearing races protrude far enough (arrow) . . .

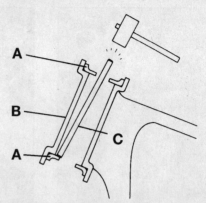

7.10b . . . the races can be driven out with a hammer and drift (drive out the upper race first)

A Outer races   C Drift
B Steering head

7.11a This Honda tool fits into the upper bearing race; tapping the tool upward from below will push the race out

7.11b This tool is inserted into the lower race and expanded to catch its edges . . .

7.11c . . . tapping on the tool from above will push the lower race out (race shown partially removed)

compressed air, if available. If you do use compressed air, don't let the bearings spin as they're dried - it could ruin them. Wipe the old grease out of the frame steering head and bearing races.
9 Examine the races in the steering head for cracks, dents, and pits. If even the slightest amount of wear or damage is evident, the races should be replaced with new ones.
10 The usual method of removing bearing races is to drive them out of the steering head with a hammer and long rod (see illustration). For this method to work, the bearing races must protrude far enough that you can catch the edge of them with the rod (see illustration). A slide hammer with the proper internal-jaw puller will also work.
11 Since these bearing races don't protrude very far into the steering head, special tools may be necessary to remove them. At the top, Honda race remover attachment 07953-MJ1000A fits under the bearing, allowing it to be tapped out from below (see illustration). At the bottom, remover 07946-3710500 can be expanded to grip the race, then tapped out of the steering head together with the race (see illustrations).
12 Since the races are an interference fit in the frame, installation will be easier if the new races are left overnight in a freezer. This will cause them to contract and slip into place in the frame with very little effort. When installing the races, tap them gently into place with a hammer and a bearing driver, punch or a large socket (see illustration). Do not strike the bearing surface or the race will be damaged.
13 Check the bearings for wear. Look for cracks, dents, and pits in the races and flat spots on the bearings. Replace any defective parts with new ones. If a new bearing is required, replace both of them as a set.

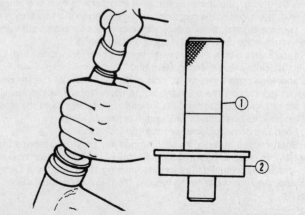

7.12 Drive in the bearing races with a bearing driver or socket the same diameter as the bearing race

1 Bearing driver handle   2 Bearing driver

Chapter 6 Steering, suspension and final drive

7.14a Thread the nut onto the steering stem, then clamp the nut in a vise and tap the bearing off

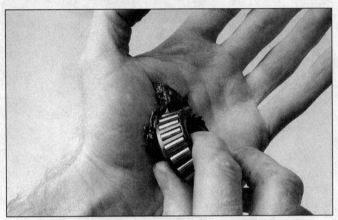

7.17 Work the grease completely into the rollers or balls

14   Don't remove the lower bearing unless it, or the grease seal underneath, must be replaced. To remove the bearing from the steering stem, thread the nut onto the steering stem to protect it, then clamp the nut in a vise so you can drive the bearing toward the nut with a hammer and punch **(see illustration)**. You can also use a bearing splitter and puller setup (these can be rented). Tap the lower bearing on with a hammer and piece of pipe the same diameter as the bearing inner race **(see illustration)**. Don't tap against the rollers or outer race

7.18 The concave side of the grease cup faces upward (toward the threads)

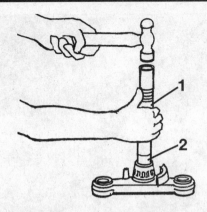

7.14b Drive the grease seal and bearing lower race on with a hollow driver (or an equivalent piece of pipe)

1   Driver
2   Bearing and grease seal

or the bearing will be ruined. As an alternative, take the steering stem to a Honda dealer or motorcycle repair shop for bearing replacement.
15   Check the grease seal under the lower bearing and replace it with a new one if necessary.
16   Inspect the steering stem/lower triple clamp for cracks and other damage. Do not attempt to repair any steering components. Replace them with new parts if defects are found.
17   Pack the bearings with high-quality grease (preferably a moly-based grease) **(see illustration)**. Coat the outer races with grease also.
18   Install the upper bearing grease cup on the steering stem **(see illustration)**. Insert the steering stem/lower triple clamp into the steering head. Install the upper bearing and steering stem nut. Refer to Section 6 and adjust the bearings.
19   The remainder of installation is the reverse of removal.

8   Rear shock absorbers - removal, inspection and installation

Removal

Refer to illustrations 8.4a, 8.4b, 8.5a and 8.5b
1   Place the bike on its centerstand. Remove the seat and side covers (Chapter 8). If you're working on an Interstate or Aspencade, remove the saddlebags and trunk and their bracket. If you're working on a Standard, remove the rear handrail.
2   Support the swingarm so it can't drop.
3   If the bike has an on-board air compressor, follow the air hoses from the shock absorbers to the three-way joint. Place an open-end wrench on the flats of the air hose fitting, then undo the union bolt with another wrench.
4   Remove the shock absorber lower bolt **(see illustrations)**.

8.4a The left lower mounting bolt is threaded next to its head

6-12 Chapter 6 Steering, suspension and final drive

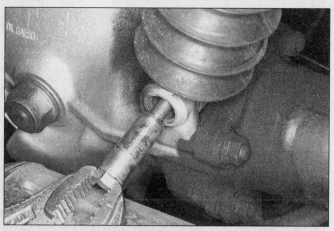

8.4b The right lower mounting bolt is threaded on its end

8.5a The shoulder of the upper nut fits inside the cover

8.5b Remove the washer and slide the shock absorber off the stud

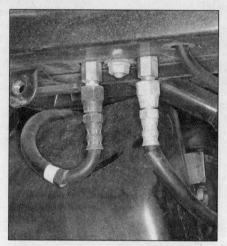

9.2a Note the different colors of the hose fittings . . .

9.2b . . . then hold the fittings with one wrench and undo the hoses with another

5 Remove the shock absorber upper nut, cover and washer **(see illustrations)**. Take the shock absorber out. **Caution:** *If you're going to reuse the shocks, store them upright to prevent fluid loss.*

Inspection

6 Check the shock for signs of oil leaks. The oil seal can be replaced, but this is a job for a Honda dealer or service department or a motorcycle repair shop having the necessary special equipment.

7 Inspect the pivot hardware at the top and bottom of the shock and replace any worn or damaged parts.

Installation

8 Installation is the reverse of the removal procedure, with the following additions:
  a) *Use new O-rings on the air hose fittings. Lubricate them with Pro Honda suspension fluid or equivalent.*
  b) *Install the upper and lower shock absorber bolts and nuts and the air hose union bolt (if equipped), then tighten them to the torque values listed in this Chapter's Specifications.*

9 On-board air compressor - removal, desiccant replacement and installation

Removal

Refer to illustrations 9.2a, 9.2b, 9.3a, 9.3b, 9.4, 9.5a, 9.5b, 9.5c and 9.5d

1 Remove the right fairing pocket and right lower fairing cover (see Chapter 8).

2 Locate the air hose fittings at the four-way joint (they're under the fairing) **(see illustration)**. Place a wrench on each of the air hose fittings and undo the hose with another wrench **(see illustration)**. Remove the nut that secures the four-way joint to the fairing.

3 Remove the cover panel from the switches, then remove the

9.3a Carefully pry the cover loose form the switch panel . . .

Chapter 6 Steering, suspension and final drive

9.3b ... and remove the switch screws (arrows)

9.4 Unscrew the air outlet knob and the air hose hex nut

9.5a Take out the solenoid and sensor assembly ...

9.5b ... and the drier assembly; when installed, the drier assembly fits on the other side of the panel shown. Its rubber retainers (arrows) ...

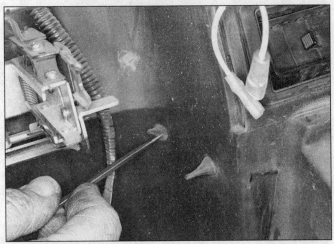

9.5c ... look like this when the drier is installed

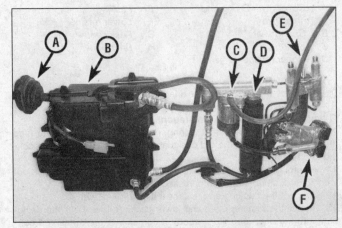

9.5d Compressor system details

- A   Filter
- B   Drier assembly (contains motor)
- C   Solenoid valve
- D   Air pressure sensor
- E   Four-way joint
- F   Selector valve

selector valve screws **(see illustrations)**.

4 Unscrew the air outlet knob **(see illustration)**. Remove the locknut from the air outlet and push it into the fairing.

5 Carefully work the compressor system free of the fairing and lift it out **(see illustrations)**.

6 To test the pump motor, connect it directly to the battery with a pair of jumper wires. If the pump doesn't run, replace it.

Desiccant replacement

Refer to illustrations 9.8, 9.9, 9.10 and 9.13

7 The desiccant should be replaced if it's pink or colorless. New desiccant is a deep blue.

Chapter 6 Steering, suspension and final drive

9.8 Compressor drier (right arrow) and filter (left arrow)

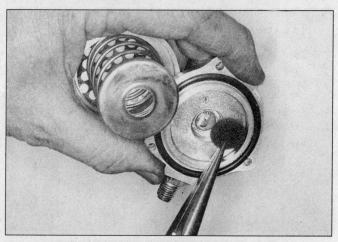

9.9 This small filter fits in a bore in the cover

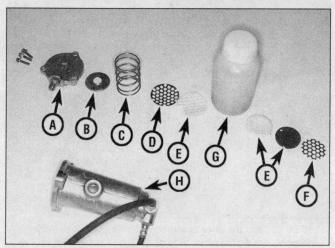

9.10 Drier components

A	Cover (with O-ring and small filter)	E	Packing
B	Spring seat	F	Lower retainer
C	Spring	G	Desiccant
D	Upper retainer	H	Drier body

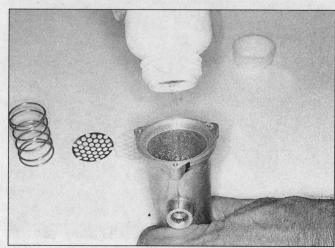

9.13 Pour the desiccant into the drier body (it's pre-measured)

8 Remove the cover from the drier and take it out **(see illustration)**.
9 Remove the cover screws and take the cover off, then remove the O-ring and small filter **(see illustration)**.
10 Remove the spring seat, spring, retainer plate and packing **(see illustration)**. Pour out the old desiccant, then remove the lower packing and retainer plate.
11 Thoroughly dry the inside of the drier and blow its passages out with filtered, unlubricated compressed air.
12 Inspect the packing and replace it if it's dirty or wet.
13 Install the retainer plate and lower packing, then pour the desiccant into the drier **(see illustration)**. It comes in a pre-measured container.
14 Install the upper packing, retainer plate, spring and spring seat. Install the small filter and a new O-ring in the cover, then install the cover on the drier.

Filter element cleaning

15 Locate the filter housing in the air hose **(see illustration 9.8)**. Remove the cover and take out the element. Clean it thoroughly in non-flammable solvent, then let it dry completely. Once the element is dry, saturate it with SAE 80 or 90 gear oil, then squeeze it out. Place the element in the housing and install the cover.

Installation

16 Installation is the reverse of the removal steps, with the following additions:
a) Use new O-rings on the air hose fittings and lubricate them with Pro Honda suspension fluid or equivalent.
b) Tighten the air hose fittings to the torque listed in this Chapter's Specifications.

10 Final drive unit - removal, inspection and installation

Removal

Refer to illustrations 10.2 and 10.4

1 Place the bike on its centerstand and remove the rear wheel (see Chapter 7).
2 Remove the final drive unit mounting nuts and separate the unit from the swingarm **(see illustration)**.
3 To remove the driveshaft from the final drive unit, slip the axle and spacer back into the final drive unit. Grasp the forward end of the driveshaft and wiggle it in a circle while pulling it away form the final drive unit. The stopper ring will provide some resistance, then the driveshaft should pull free of the final drive unit.
4 Remove the snap-ring from the forward end of the driveshaft, then slip the spring seat, spring and oil seal off the driveshaft **(see illustration)**.

Chapter 6 Steering, suspension and final drive

10.2 Remove the four mounting nuts; one nut is hidden behind the swingarm

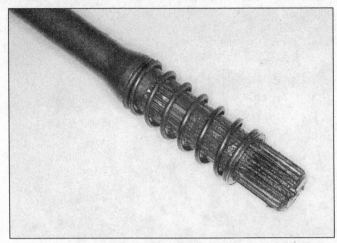

10.4 At the front of the driveshaft, remove the snap-ring and spring seat, then slide the spring off

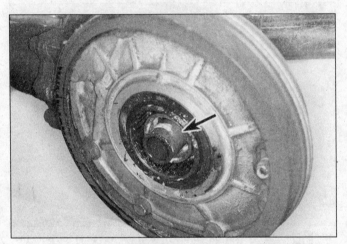

10.5 Check the final drive unit oil seal for leaks; on installation, make sure the spacer (arrow) is in position

10.7 Pry the coupling evenly from the wheel

Inspection

Refer to illustrations 10.5 and 10.7

5   Look into the axle holes and check for obvious signs of wear or damage such as broken gear teeth **(see illustration)**. Also check the seals for signs of leakage. Slip the driveshaft into its splines (if it was removed) and turn the pinion by hand. Final drive unit problems are generally indicated by howling or knocking noises (howling from lack of oil or damaged gear faces; knocking from one or more missing gear teeth).

6   Final drive unit overhaul is a complicated procedure that requires several special tools, for which there are no readily available substitutes. If there's visible wear or damage, or if the rotation is rough or noisy, take it to a Honda dealer for disassembly and further inspection.

7   Check the coupling flange in the rear wheel for wear or damage **(see illustration)**. If necessary, separate the flange from the wheel.

Installation

Refer to illustrations 10.8a and 10.8b

8   Installation is the reverse of the removal steps, with the following additions:

a) Install a new driveshaft oil seal if you removed the driveshaft from the final drive unit. The stopper ring on the rear end of the driveshaft was used for initial assembly at the factory and need not be reinstalled.

b) Lubricate the splines of the coupling and the final drive unit with Honda moly 60 grease or equivalent. Install a new O-ring in the coupling groove **(see illustration)**.

c) Lubricate the inside diameter of the coupling and the flange pins (if the flange was removed from the wheel) with Honda Moly 60 or

10.8a Pry the O-ring out of its groove with a pointed tool and install a new one

10.8b Lubricate the coupling pins if the coupling was removed from the wheel

12.5 Pry out the swingarm pivot caps (there's one on each side of the bike)

12.6a A special tool is needed to fit the slots in the left pivot's locknut

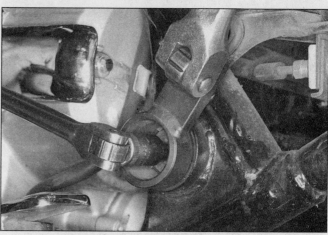

12.6b Place a breaker bar in the hole of the special tool; hold the pivot bolt with an Allen bolt bit while loosening the locknut

equivalent moly-based grease **(see illustration)**.
d) Be sure the spacer is in the final drive unit **(see illustration 10.5)**.
e) Install the final drive unit nuts loosely. Tighten them to the torque listed in this Chapter's Specifications after the rear axle is installed.
f) Check the final drive unit oil level (see Chapter 1).

11 Swingarm bearings - check

1   Remove the rear wheel and detach the brake hose and line from the swingarm (see Chapter 7). Unbolt the rear master cylinder, but leave its hose connected.
2   Remove the shock absorbers (Section 8). Leave the air hoses connected to the right shock and keep them upright. Remove the final drive unit (Section 10).
3   Grasp the rear of the swingarm with one hand and place your other hand at the junction of the swingarm and the frame. Try to move the rear of the swingarm from side to side. Any wear (play) in the bearings should be felt as movement between the swingarm and the frame at the front. The swingarm will actually be felt to move forward and backward at the front (not from side to side). If any play is noted, the bearings should be replaced with new ones (see Section 13).
4   Next, move the swingarm up and down through its full travel. It should move freely, without any binding or rough spots. If it does not move freely, refer to Section 13 for servicing procedures.

12 Swingarm - removal and installation

Note: *Loosening and tightening the pivot bolt locknut on the left side of the swingarm requires a special wrench for which there is no alternative. If you don't have the special Honda tool or an exact equivalent, the locknut must be unscrewed (and later tightened) by a Honda dealer.*

Removal

Refer to illustrations 12.5, 12.6a, 12.6b, 12.7a, 12.7b, 12.8a, 12.8b and 12.8c
1   Remove the exhaust system (see Chapter 4).
2   Remove the rear brake caliper without disconnecting the brake hose and remove the rear wheel (Chapter 7). Detach the rear brake hose from its retainer on the swingarm. Support the caliper so it does not hang by the brake hose.
3   Remove the final drive unit (Section 10).
4   Unbolt the lower end of the left shock absorber from the swingarm (Section 8).
5   Pry the pivot caps out of the swingarm **(see illustration)**.
6   Undo the locknut on the left pivot bolt, using Honda tool KS-HBA-08-469 or equivalent **(see illustrations)**. While you're undoing the locknut, hold the pivot bolt from turning with a 17 mm Allen bolt bit. These are available from tool stores.
7   Unscrew the swingarm pivot bolts **(see illustrations)**.
8   Pull the swingarm back and remove it from the frame, separating

Chapter 6 Steering, suspension and final drive

12.7a Unscrew the left pivot bolt with an Allen bolt bit . . .

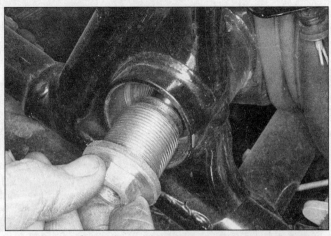

12.7b . . . and unscrew the right pivot bolt with a socket; on installation, grease the pivot bolt tips and make sure they engage the swingarm bearings

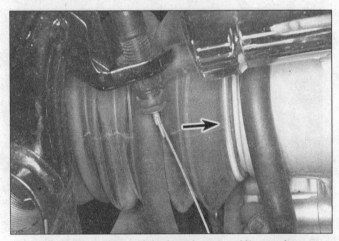

12.8a The universal joint boot is secured by a spring retainer (arrow)

12.8b Pull the universal joint out of the rear engine case and off the output shaft

the universal joint and its boot from the output shaft as you pull **(see illustrations)**. Check the output shaft seal and replace it if it's worn **(see illustration)**.

9 Check the pivot bearings in the swingarm for dryness or deterioration (See Section 13). Lubricate or replace them as necessary.

Installation

Refer to illustration 12.10

10 Lubricate the universal joint splines with moly-based grease. Make sure the universal joint boot is in place, then install the universal joint in the swingarm with its long end toward the engine **(see illustration)**.

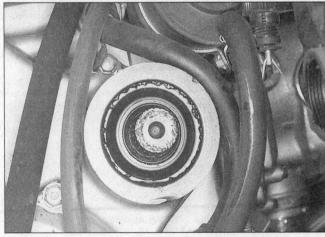

12.8c Replace the output shaft seal if it's worn

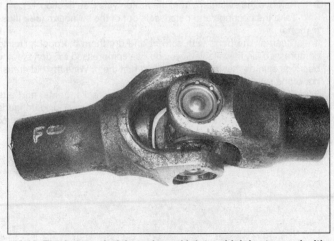

12.10 The long end of the universal joint, which is stamped with an F, goes toward the engine

Chapter 6 Steering, suspension and final drive

13.3a Pry the grease seal out of the swingarm; this seal remover is easy to use, but a screwdriver will also work

13.3b Remove the seal and bearing

11 Place the swingarm in its installed position in the frame, but don't install the universal joint on the output shaft yet. Grease the tips of the pivot bolts and thread them into their holes, making sure the tips fit into the swingarm bearings. Don't tighten the pivot bolts yet.
12 Slide the universal joint forward onto the output shaft.
13 **Note:** *The swingarm pivot bolts and locknut must be tightened in the specified sequence and to the correct torque settings.* Tighten the right pivot bolt to the torque listed in this Chapter's Specifications. Tighten the left pivot bolt after tightening the right pivot bolt. The left pivot bolt's specified torque is much lower than that of the right pivot bolt.
14 Raise and lower the swingarm several times to seat the bearings, then retighten the left pivot bolt to its specified torque.
15 Thread the locknut onto the left pivot bolt as far as you can with fingers. Then place the special wrench on the locknut and install a torque wrench in the special wrench's square hole. Hold the pivot bolt with the 17 mm Allen bolt bit so it won't turn, then tighten the locknut to the torque listed in this Chapter's Specifications. **Note:** *The special wrench increases the torque applied to the nut, so the specified torque is less than the actual applied torque.*
16 The remainder of installation is the reverse of the removal steps.

13 Swingarm bearings - replacement

Refer to illustrations 13.3a, 13.3b and 13.5
1 The swingarm rides in a pair of tapered roller bearings.
2 Remove the swingarm from the motorcycle (see Section 12).
3 Take the bearings and outer seals out of the swingarm **(see illustrations)**.
4 Clean all the parts with solvent and dry them thoroughly, using compressed air, if available. If you do use compressed air, don't let the bearings spin as they're dried - it could ruin them. Wipe the old grease out of the swingarm and bearing races.
5 Examine the races in the swingarm for cracks, dents, and pits **(see illustration)**. If even the slightest amount of wear or damage is evident, the races should be replaced with new ones. If one race (or

13.5 Replace the outer races and bearings as a set if either outer race is worn; don't forget to reinstall the inner grease retainers (arrow)

one bearing) needs to be replaced, replace both of the bearings, as well as their races and seals, as a set.
6 To remove the bearing races, drive them out of the swingarm with a hammer and long rod. A slide hammer with the proper internal-jaw puller will also work. Remove the internal grease retainers as well.
7 Since the races are an interference fit in the swingarm, installation will be easier if the new races are left overnight in a refrigerator. This will cause them to contract and slip into place in the frame with very little effort. When installing the races, tap them gently into place with a hammer and a bearing driver, punch or a large socket. Do not strike the bearing surface or the race will be damaged.
8 Check the bearings for wear. Look for cracks, dents, and pits in the rollers and flat spots on the bearings. Replace any defective parts with new ones. If a new bearing is required, replace both of them, and the bearing races and seals, as a set.

Chapter 7
Brakes, wheels and tires

Contents

	Section		Section
Brake caliper - removal, overhaul and installation	3	Front wheel - removal, inspection and installation	12
Brake check	See Chapter 1	General information	1
Brake discs - inspection, removal and installation	4	Rear brake master cylinder - removal, overhaul	
Brake hoses - inspection and replacement	7	and installation	6
Brake light switches - check and adjustment	See Chapter 1	Rear wheel - removal, inspection and installation	13
Brake pads - replacement	2	Tubeless tires - general information	15
Brake pedal - removal and installation	9	Wheel bearings - replacement	14
Brake system bleeding	8	Wheels - alignment check	11
Front brake master cylinder - removal, overhaul		Wheels - inspection and repair	10
and installation	5	Wheels and tires - general check	See Chapter 1

Specifications

Brakes

Brake lever free-play and pedal position	See Chapter 1
Brake fluid type	See Chapter 1
Front brake disc thickness	
Standard and Interstate models	
Standard	4.5 to 5.2 mm (0.18 to 0.20 inch)
Limit	4.0 mm (0.16 inch)*
Aspencade	
Standard	9.9 to 10.1 mm (0.39 to 0.40 inch)
Limit	9.0 mm (0.35 inch)*
Rear brake disc thickness	
Standard	6.9 to 7.1 mm (0.27 to 0.28 inch)
Limit	6.0 mm (0.24 inch)*

*Refer to marks stamped into the disc (they supersede information printed here)

Disc runout limit	0.3 mm (0.01 inch)
Pad friction material thickness	
Front	
Standard	5.4 to 5.6 mm (0.21 to 0.22 inch)
Limit	See Chapter 1
Rear	
Standard	6.4 to 6.6 mm (0.25 to 0.26 inch)
Limit	See Chapter 1
Front caliper-to-bracket gap	0.7 mm (0.028 inch)

Wheels and tires

Wheel runout limit	
Radial (up-and-down)	2.0 mm (0.08 inch)
Axial (side-to-side)	2.0 mm (0.08 inch)
Axle runout limit	0.2 mm (0.008 inch)
Tire pressures	See Chapter 1
Tire sizes	See Chapter 1

Chapter 7 Brakes, wheels and tires

Torque specifications

Front calipers
    Mounting bolt .... 23 Nm (17 ft-lbs)
        Lower bracket bolt .... 23 Nm (17 ft-lbs)
        Pivot bolt .... 28 Nm (20 ft-lbs)
        Caliper bracket upper mounting bolt to fork leg .... 35 Nm (25 ft-lbs)
        Pad retaining bolt .... Not specified
        Caliper bleed valve .... Not specified
Rear caliper
    Pivot bolt .... 28 Nm (20 ft-lbs)
    Mounting bolt .... 23 Nm (17 ft-lbs)
    Pad pin retainer bolt .... Not specified
Brake disc mounting bolts .... 30 Nm (22 ft-lbs)
Union (banjo fitting) bolts .... 30 Nm (22 ft-lbs)
Metal line flare nuts .... 17 Nm (12 ft-lbs)
Master cylinder mounting bolts
    Front .... 12 Nm (9 ft-lbs)
    Rear .... 27 Nm (20 ft-lbs)
Front axle
    Axle nut .... 60 Nm (44 ft-lbs)
    Axle holder nuts .... 25 Nm (18 ft-lbs)
Rear axle
    Axle nut .... 95 Nm (69 ft-lbs)
    Axle pinch bolt .... 27 Nm (20 ft-lbs)

1 General information

The models covered by this manual are equipped with hydraulic disc brakes on the front and rear. All models use a pair of dual-piston calipers at the front and one dual-piston caliper at the rear. The rear brake and left front brake are operated by the brake pedal; the right front brake is operated by the brake lever on the left handlebar independently of the left front brake.

All models are equipped with cast aluminum wheels, which require very little maintenance and allow tubeless tires to be used.

Caution: *Disc brake components rarely require disassembly. Do not disassemble components unless absolutely necessary. If any hydraulic brake line connection in the system is loosened, the entire system should be disassembled, drained, cleaned and then properly filled and bled upon reassembly. Do not use solvents on internal brake components. Solvents will cause seals to swell and distort. Use only clean brake fluid, brake cleaner or alcohol for cleaning. Use care when working with brake fluid as it can injure your eyes and it will damage painted surfaces and plastic parts.*

2 Brake pads - replacement

Refer to illustrations 2.2a, 2.2b, 2.5a, 2.5b, 2.5c, 2.10 and 2.11

Warning: *The dust created by the brake system may contain asbestos, which is harmful to your health. Never blow it out with compressed air and don't inhale any of it. An approved filtering mask should be worn when working on the brakes.*

Note: *Depending on your braking habits, the pads in one front caliper may wear more quickly than the pads in the other caliper. However, the pads in both calipers should be checked whenever one set is replaced.*

1 Place the bike on its centerstand. If you're replacing the rear pads on an Interstate or Aspencade, remove the left saddlebag (see Chapter 8).
2 Loosen the pad pin retainer bolts **(see illustrations)**.
3 If you're working on a front caliper, remove the caliper mounting bolt and bracket lower bolt **(see illustration 2.2a)**. Loosen the pivot bolt.
4 If you're working on a rear caliper, remove the caliper mounting bolt and pivot bolt **(see illustration 2.2b)**.

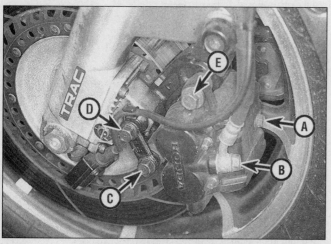

2.2a Front caliper mounting details

A Pad pin retainer bolt
B Brake hose union bolt
C Caliper mounting bolt
D Caliper bracket lower bolt
E Caliper pivot bolt

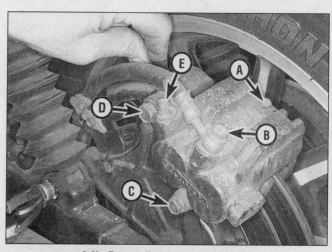

2.2b Rear caliper mounting details

A Pad pin retainer bolt
B Brake hose union bolt
C Caliper mounting bolt
D Caliper bracket bolt
E Bleed valve

Chapter 7 Brakes, wheels and tires

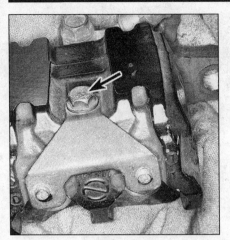

2.5a Undo the retainer bolt (arrow), lift off the retainer and pull out the pins . . .

2.5b . . . take the pads out of the caliper . . .

2.5c . . . and remove the pad spring

5 Pull the caliper off the bracket. Undo the pad pin retainer bolt, lift off the retainer, take the pads out of the caliper and remove the pad spring **(see illustrations)**.

6 Check the condition of the brake discs (see Section 4). If they're in need of machining or replacement, follow the procedure in that Section to remove them. If they are okay, deglaze them with sandpaper or emery cloth, using a swirling motion.

7 Check the rubber pin bushings in the caliper and bracket (Section 3). Replace them if they're deteriorated or damaged.

8 Remove the cap from the master cylinder reservoir (front reservoir for the right caliper and rear reservoir for the rear or left front caliper) and siphon out some fluid. Push the pistons into the caliper as far as possible, while checking the master cylinder reservoirs to make sure they don't overflow. If you can't depress the pistons with thumb pressure, try using a pry bar or C-clamp. If the pistons stick, remove the caliper and overhaul it as described in Section 3.

9 Make sure the pad shims are in place and the steel shield is in place on the bracket (see Section 3). Lubricate the pin bushings with silicone grease and install the caliper on the bracket.

10 Install the pad spring in the caliper, then install the pads **(see illustrations 2.5c and 2.5d)**. Press the pads down against the spring and install the pad pins. Install the retainer over the pins and install its bolt loosely **(see illustration)**. Torque it after the caliper is installed; this will be easier with the caliper bolted in place.

11 Make sure the plate is in place on the front calipers **(see illustration)**. Tighten the caliper bracket and mounting bolts to the torques listed in this Chapter's Specifications. Tighten the pad retainer bolt to the specified torque.

12 Refill the master cylinder reservoir (see Chapter 1). Install the diaphragm and the cap (rear) or cover (front). Operate the brake lever or pedal several times to bring the pads into contact with the disc.

13 Check the operation of the brakes carefully before riding the motorcycle.

14 Refer to Chapter 8 and install the left saddlebag (if removed).

3 Brake caliper - removal, overhaul and installation

Warning: *The dust created by the brake system may contain asbestos, which is harmful to your health. Never blow it out with compressed air and don't inhale any of it. An approved filtering mask should be worn when working on the brakes. Do not, under any circumstances, use petroleum-based solvents to clean brake parts. Use brake cleaner or denatured alcohol only!*

Removal

1 Place the bike on its centerstand.

2 If the brake hydraulic system is in reasonably good condition, it can be used to remove the pistons from the calipers. Leave the fluid hose connected and remove the caliper and pads (see Section 2). Place a drain pan under the caliper to catch the brake fluid that will run out. **Caution:** *Place rags or plastic over nearby painted or plated parts to protect them from brake fluid splashes. Wash off any splashes*

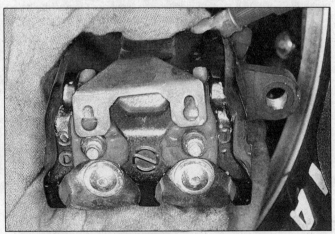

2.10 Slip the larger part of each retainer hole over its pin, then push the retainer down so the smaller part of each hole engages its pin groove

2.11 Be sure this plate (and shim, if equipped) is in position when reinstalling a front caliper

Chapter 7 Brakes, wheels and tires

3.6 Place a piece of wood or some rags in the pad cavity to cushion the pistons

3.7a Remove the dust seals (A) and piston seals (B); inspect the pin bushing (C)

immediately with soap and water to prevent damage to the surfaces. Pump the lever or pedal a few times to force the pistons out of the caliper. If one piston comes out faster than the other one, slip a piece of wood into the pad area to block that piston until the other one is forced out.

3 If the hydraulic system isn't in good enough condition to push out the caliper pistons, you'll need to use compressed air as described below.

4 With a clean rag handy to catch spills, remove the brake hose banjo fitting bolt and separate the hose from the caliper **(see illustration 2.2a or 2.2b)**. Discard the sealing washers. Place the end of the hose in a container and wrap a clean shop rag tightly around the hose fitting to soak up any drips and prevent contamination.

Overhaul

Refer to illustrations 3.6, 3.7a, 3.7b, 3.12a and 3.12b

5 Clean the exterior of the caliper with denatured alcohol or brake system cleaner.

6 If the hydraulic system wasn't in good enough condition to push the pistons out, you'll need to use compressed air. Place a few rags or a piece of wood between the pistons and the caliper frame to act as a cushion, then use compressed air, directed into the fluid inlet, to remove the pistons **(see illustration)**. Use only enough air pressure to ease the pistons out of the bore. If a piston is blown out, even with the cushion in place, it may be damaged. **Warning:** *Never place your fingers in front of the piston in an attempt to catch or protect it when applying compressed air, as serious injury could occur.*

7 Using a wood or plastic tool, remove the dust seals and piston seals **(see illustrations)**. Metal tools may cause bore damage.

3.7b Brake caliper - disassembled view

A	Pin bushings	E	Piston seals
B	Pin	F	Dust seals
C	Pad spring	G	Pistons
D	Caliper body		

8 Clean the pistons and the bores with denatured alcohol, clean brake fluid or brake system cleaner and blow dry them with filtered, unlubricated compressed air. Inspect the surfaces of the pistons for

3.12a A pin bushing as corroded like this one should be replaced

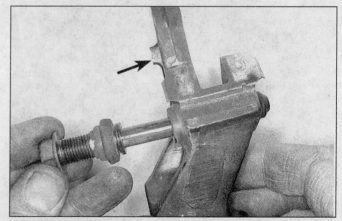

3.12b Check the steel wear shield (arrow) for wear and corrosion

Chapter 7 Brakes, wheels and tires

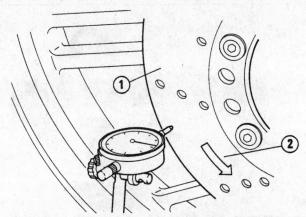

4.3 Set up a dial indicator against the brake disc (1) and turn the disc in its normal direction of rotation (2) to measure runout

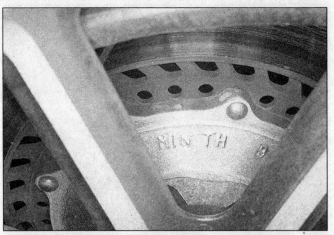

4.4 The minimum thickness is cast into the disc

4.6 Remove the self-locking nuts and take the disc off the wheel; use new nuts on installation

nicks and burrs and loss of plating. Check the caliper bores, too. If surface defects are present, the caliper must be replaced. If the caliper is in bad shape, the master cylinder should also be checked.

9 Lubricate new piston seals with clean brake fluid and install them in their grooves in the caliper bore. Make sure they seat completely and aren't twisted.

10 Lubricate new dust seals with clean brake fluid and install them in their grooves, making sure they seat correctly.

11 Lubricate the pistons with clean brake fluid and install them into the caliper bores. Using your thumbs, push the pistons all the way in, making sure they don't get cocked in the bores.

12 Check the pin bushings, pins, boots and caliper shields for wear, damage and corrosion **(see illustrations)**.

Installation

13 Refer to Section 2 and install the brake pads and caliper.
14 Connect the brake hose to the caliper, using new sealing washers on each side of the fitting. Align the banjo fitting with its tab and tighten the bolt to the torque listed in this Chapter's Specifications.
15 Fill the master cylinder with the recommended brake fluid (see Chapter 1) and bleed the system (see Section 8). Check for leaks.
16 Check the operation of the brakes carefully before riding the motorcycle.

4 Brake discs - inspection, removal and installation

Inspection

Refer to illustrations 4.3 and 4.4

1 Support the bike securely so it can't be knocked over during this procedure, with the wheel to be checked off the ground.
2 Visually inspect the surface of the disc(s) for score marks and other damage. Light scratches are normal after use and won't affect brake operation, but deep grooves and heavy score marks will reduce braking efficiency and accelerate pad wear. If the discs are badly grooved they must be machined or replaced.
3 To check disc runout, mount a dial indicator to a fork leg or the swingarm, with the plunger on the indicator touching the surface of the disc about 1/2-inch from the outer edge **(see illustration)**. Slowly turn the wheel and watch the indicator needle, comparing your reading with the limit listed in this Chapter's Specifications. If the runout is greater than allowed, check the hub bearings for play (see Section 10). If the bearings are worn, replace them and repeat this check. If the disc runout is still excessive, it will have to be replaced.
4 The disc must not be machined or allowed to wear down to a thickness less than the minimum allowable thickness, stamped on the disc and listed in this Chapter's Specifications **(see illustration)**. The thickness of the disc can be checked with a micrometer. If the thickness of the disc is less than the minimum allowable, it must be replaced.

Removal

Refer to illustration 4.6

5 Remove the wheel (see Section 12 for front wheel removal or Section 13 for rear wheel removal). **Caution:** *Don't lay the wheel down and allow it to rest on one of the discs - the disc could become warped.* Set the wheel on wood blocks so the disc doesn't support the weight of the wheel.
6 Mark the relationship of the disc to the wheel, so it can be installed in the same position. Look for L and R marks on the left and right front discs. If you don't see them, make your own. Remove the nuts that retain the disc to the wheel **(see illustration)**. Loosen the bolts a little at a time, in a criss-cross pattern, to avoid distorting the disc. Once all the bolts are loose, take the disc off.

Installation

7 Position the disc on the wheel, aligning the previously applied matchmarks (if you're reinstalling the original disc). If you're installing a front disc, make sure the disc with the L mark goes on the left side of the bike and the disc with the R mark goes on the right side. If there aren't any marks, refer to the groove pattern in the braking surface. Each disc is installed with the concave side of its center facing away from the wheel and the grooves positioned so their outer ends are in forward relative to the inner ends.
8 Install the nuts, tightening them a little at a time, in a criss-cross

Chapter 7 Brakes, wheels and tires

5.7 Remove the Allen bolts (arrows) to separate the clamp from the master cylinder; on installation, the UP mark on the clamp must be upright

5.8 Remove the baffle plate from the bottom of the reservoir

pattern, until the torque listed in this Chapter's Specifications is reached. Thoroughly clean off all grease from the brake disc(s) using acetone or brake system cleaner.
9   Install the wheel.
10 Operate the brake lever or pedal several times to bring the pads into contact with the disc. Check the operation of the brakes carefully before riding the motorcycle.

5 Front brake master cylinder - removal, overhaul and installation

1   If the master cylinder is leaking fluid, or if the lever does not produce a firm feel when the brake is applied, and bleeding the brakes does not help, master cylinder overhaul is recommended. Before disassembling the master cylinder, read through the entire procedure and make sure that you have the correct rebuild kit. Also, you will need some new, clean brake fluid of the recommended type, some clean rags and internal snap-ring pliers. **Note:** *To prevent damage to the paint from spilled brake fluid, always cover plastic or plated parts when working on the master cylinder.*
2   **Caution:** *Disassembly, overhaul and reassembly of the brake master cylinder must be done in a spotlessly clean work area to avoid contamination and possible failure of the brake hydraulic system components.*

Removal
Refer to illustration 5.7
3   Loosen but do not remove the screws holding the reservoir cover in place.
4   Disconnect the electrical connectors from the brake light switch and the cruise cancel switch if equipped (see Chapter 9).
5   Remove the banjo fitting bolt and separate the brake hose from the master cylinder. Wrap the end of the hose in a clean rag and suspend the hose in an upright position or bend it down carefully and place the open end in a clean container. The objective is to prevent excessive loss of brake fluid, fluid spills and system contamination.
6   Remove the locknut from the underside of the lever pivot bolt, then unscrew the bolt.
7   Remove the master cylinder mounting bolts **(see illustration)** and separate the master cylinder from the handlebar.

Overhaul
Refer to illustrations 5.8, 5.9 and 5.10
8   Detach the cover and the rubber diaphragm, then drain the brake fluid into a suitable container. Remove the plate from the bottom of reservoir (if equipped) **(see illustration)**, then wipe any remaining fluid out of the reservoir with a clean rag.
9   Carefully remove the rubber dust boot from the end of the piston **(see illustration)**.
10 Using snap-ring pliers, remove the snap-ring **(see illustration)**

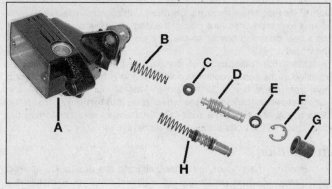

5.9 Front master cylinder details

A Cylinder body	F Snap-ring
B Spring	G Boot
C Primary cup	H Assembled piston, cups
D Piston	and spring
E Secondary cup	

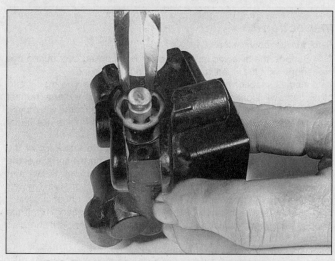

5.10 Remove the snap-ring from the cylinder bore

Chapter 7 Brakes, wheels and tires

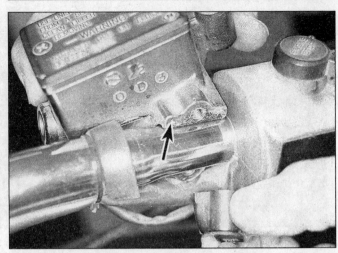

5.15 Align the punch mark on the handlebar (arrow) with the split between the clamp and master cylinder

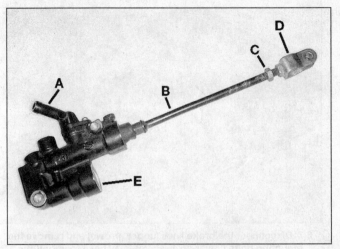

6.5 Rear master cylinder - assembled view

A Fluid feed hose fitting
B Pushrod
C Locknut
D Clevis
E Pressure differential valve (do not disassemble)

and slide out the piston assembly and the spring. Lay the parts out in the proper order to prevent confusion during reassembly.

11 Clean all of the parts with brake system cleaner (available at auto parts stores), isopropyl alcohol or clean brake fluid. **Caution:** *Do not, under any circumstances, use a petroleum-based solvent to clean brake parts. If compressed air is available, use it to dry the parts thoroughly (make sure it's filtered and unlubricated). Check the master cylinder bore for corrosion, scratches, nicks and score marks. If damage is evident, the master cylinder must be replaced with a new one. If the master cylinder is in poor condition, then the calipers should be checked as well.*

12 The piston assembly and spring are included in the rebuild kit. Use all of the new parts, regardless of the apparent condition of the old ones.

13 Before reassembling the master cylinder, soak the piston and the rubber cup seals in clean brake fluid for ten or fifteen minutes. Lubricate the master cylinder bore with clean brake fluid, then carefully insert the piston and related parts in the reverse order of disassembly. Make sure the lips on the cup seals do not turn inside out when they are slipped into the bore.

14 Push the piston into the bore against the spring pressure, then install the snap-ring (make sure the snap-ring is properly seated in the groove). Install the rubber dust boot (make sure the lip is seated properly in the piston groove).

Installation

Refer to illustration 5.15

15 Attach the master cylinder to the handlebar, aligning the split in the clamp with the punch mark in the handlebar **(see illustration)** and tighten the bolts to the torque listed in this Chapter's Specifications.

16 Connect the brake hose to the master cylinder, using new sealing washers. Tighten the banjo fitting bolt to the torque listed in this Chapter's Specifications. Refer to Section 8 and bleed the air from the system.

6 Rear brake master cylinder - removal, overhaul and installation

1 If the master cylinder is leaking fluid, or if the pedal does not produce a firm feel when the brake is applied, and bleeding the brakes does not help, master cylinder overhaul is recommended. Before disassembling the master cylinder, read through the entire procedure and make sure that you have the correct rebuild kit. Also, you will need some new, clean brake fluid of the recommended type, some clean rags and internal snap-ring pliers.

2 **Caution:** *Disassembly, overhaul and reassembly of the brake master cylinder must be done in a spotlessly clean work area to avoid contamination and possible failure of the brake hydraulic system components.*

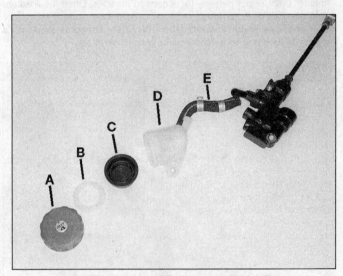

6.6 Rear master cylinder reservoir details

A Cap
B Retainer
C Diaphragm
D Reservoir
E Fluid feed hose

Removal

Refer to illustrations 6.5, 6.6, 6.7 and 6.8

3 Place the bike on its centerstand. If you're working on an Aspencade, remove the right passenger footrest (see Chapter 8).

4 Connect a piece of tubing to the bleed valve and pump out the brake fluid (see Section 8).

5 Remove the cotter pin from the clevis pin on the master cylinder pushrod **(see illustration)**. Remove the clevis pin.

6 Have a container and some rags ready to catch spilling brake fluid. Disconnect the reservoir hose from the master cylinder **(see illustration)**. Direct the end of the hose into the container, unscrew the cap on the master cylinder reservoir and allow the fluid to drain.

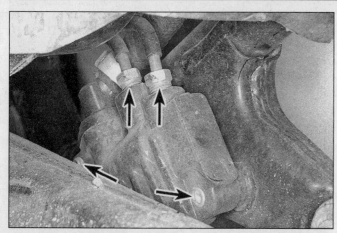

6.7 Disconnect the brake lines (upper arrows) and remove the mounting bolts (lower arrows); you may have to unbolt the cylinder and pull it out partway for access to the brake lines

6.8 The rear reservoir is secured by a single bolt

7 Undo the master cylinder brake lines with a flare nut wrench **(see illustration)**. You may have to remove the mounting bolts and lift the master cylinder out partway for access to the lines. Once the lines are undone and the bolts removed, lift the cylinder body out.

8 If the reservoir is cracked or otherwise damaged, remove its mounting bolt and take it off the bike **(see illustration)**.

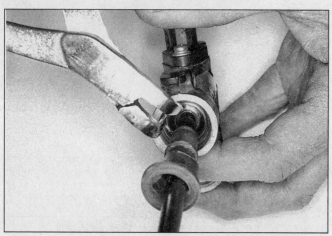

6.10 Remove the snap-ring from the cylinder bore

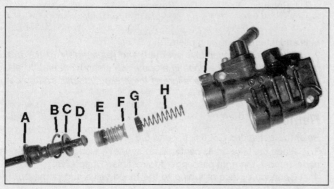

6.11 Rear master cylinder details

A	Boot	F	Piston
B	Snap-ring	G	Primary cup
C	Washer	H	Spring
D	Pushrod	I	Cylinder body
E	Secondary cup		

Overhaul

Refer to illustrations 6.10 and 6.11

9 Don't try to disassemble the pressure control valve built into the rear master cylinder.

10 Pull the boot away from the end of the master cylinder. Depress the pushrod and, using snap-ring pliers, remove the snap-ring **(see illustration)**.

11 Slide out the piston assembly, separate cup and spring. Lay the parts out in the proper order to prevent confusion during reassembly **(see illustration)**.

12 Clean all of the parts with brake system cleaner (available at auto parts stores), isopropyl alcohol or clean brake fluid. **Caution:** *Do not, under any circumstances, use a petroleum-based solvent to clean brake parts.* If compressed air is available, use it to dry the parts thoroughly (make sure it's filtered and unlubricated). Check the master cylinder bore for corrosion, scratches, nicks and score marks. If damage is evident, the master cylinder must be replaced with a new one. If the master cylinder is in poor condition, then the caliper should be checked as well.

13 A new piston, separate cup and spring are included in the rebuild kit. Use them regardless of the condition of the old ones.

14 Before reassembling the master cylinder, soak the piston and the rubber cup seals in clean brake fluid for ten or fifteen minutes. Lubricate the master cylinder bore with clean brake fluid, then carefully insert the parts in the reverse order of disassembly. The flat side of the separate cup faces out of the bore (toward the piston). Make sure the lips on the cup seals do not turn inside out when they are slipped into the bore.

15 Depress the pushrod, then install the snap-ring (make sure the snap-ring is properly seated in the groove). Install the rubber dust boot (make sure the lip is seated properly in the groove).

Installation

16 Place the master cylinder in its installed position. Thread the flare nuts into their fittings with fingers, then tighten them with a flare nut wrench.

17 Bolt the master cylinder to the frame and tighten its bolts to the torque listed in this Chapter's Specifications.

18 Install the reservoir if it was removed. Connect the reservoir hose to the master cylinder inlet fitting and install the hose clamp.

19 Connect the clevis to the brake pedal and secure the clevis pin with a new cotter pin.

20 Fill the fluid reservoir with the specified fluid (see Chapter 1) and bleed the system following the procedure in Section 8.

21 Check the position of the brake pedal (see Chapter 1) and adjust it if necessary. Check the operation of the brakes carefully before riding the motorcycle.

22 If you're working on an Aspencade, install the right passenger footrest.

Chapter 7 Brakes, wheels and tires

7.2a There's a flare nut (arrows) at each end of the metal brake that supplies the left front caliper

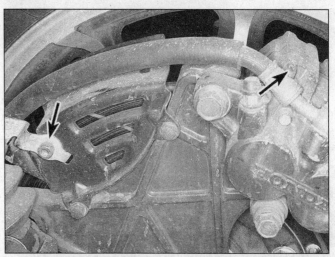

7.2b The rear caliper brake hose is secured by a retainer (left arrow); position the neck of the metal fitting in its stop (arrow)

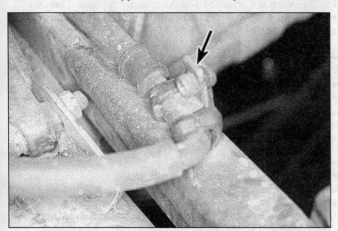

7.2c This retainer secures the rear brake hose to the swingarm

7 Brake hoses - inspection and replacement

Inspection

Refer to illustrations 7.2a, 7.2b and 7.2c
1   Periodically check the condition of the brake hoses.
2   Twist and flex the rubber hoses **(see illustrations)** while looking for cracks, bulges and seeping fluid. Check extra carefully around the areas where the hoses connect with metal fittings, as these are common areas for hose failure.
3   Inspect the metal fittings connected to brake hoses. If the fittings are rusted, cracked or scratched on a sealing surface, replace them.

Replacement

4   Most brake hoses have banjo fittings on each end of the hose. Cover the surrounding area with plenty of rags and unscrew the union bolts on either end of the hose. Detach the hose from any clips that may be present and remove the hose.
5   Position the new hose, making sure it isn't twisted or otherwise strained, between the two components. Make sure the metal tube portion of the banjo fitting is positioned next to the stop on the component it's connected to, if equipped **(see illustration 7.2b)**. Install the union bolts, using new sealing washers on both sides of the fittings, and tighten them to the torque listed in this Chapter's Specifications.
6   Flush the old brake fluid from the system, refill the system with the recommended fluid (see Chapter 1) and bleed the air from the system (see Section 8). Check the operation of the brakes carefully before riding the motorcycle.

8 Brake system bleeding

1   Bleeding the brake is simply the process of removing all the air bubbles from the brake fluid reservoirs, the lines and the brake calipers. Bleeding is necessary whenever a brake system hydraulic connection is loosened, when a component or hose is replaced, or when the master cylinder or caliper is overhauled. Leaks in the system may also allow air to enter, but leaking brake fluid will reveal their presence and warn you of the need for repair.
2   To bleed the brakes, you will need some new, clean brake fluid of the recommended type (see Chapter 1), a length of clear vinyl or plastic tubing, a small container partially filled with clean brake fluid, some rags and a wrench to fit the brake caliper bleeder valves.
3   Cover the fuel tank and other painted components to prevent damage in the event that brake fluid is spilled.
4   Remove the reservoir cap or cover and slowly pump the brake lever or pedal a few times, until no air bubbles can be seen floating up from the holes at the bottom of the reservoir. Doing this bleeds the air from the master cylinder end of the line. Reinstall the reservoir cap or cover.
5   Pull back the rubber cover and slip a box wrench over the caliper bleed valve **(see illustration 2.2b)**. Attach one end of the clear vinyl or plastic tubing to the bleeder valve and submerge the other end in the brake fluid in the container.
6   Remove the reservoir cap or cover and check the fluid level. Do not allow the fluid level to drop below the lower mark during the bleeding process.
7   Carefully pump the brake lever or pedal three or four times and hold it while opening the caliper bleeder valve. When the valve is opened, brake fluid will flow out of the caliper into the clear tubing and the lever will move toward the handlebar or the pedal will move down.
8   Retighten the bleeder valve, then release the brake lever or pedal gradually. Repeat the process until no air bubbles are visible in the brake fluid leaving the caliper and the lever or pedal is firm when applied. **Note:** *The brake pedal operates two calipers, the rear and the left front. Bleed the left front caliper first, then the rear caliper.* Remember to add fluid to the reservoir as the level drops. Use only new, clean brake fluid of the recommended type. Never reuse the fluid lost during bleeding.
9   Replace the reservoir cover, wipe up any spilled brake fluid and check the entire system for leaks. **Note:** *If bleeding is difficult, it may be necessary to let the brake fluid in the system stabilize for a few hours (it may be aerated). Repeat the bleeding procedure when the tiny bubbles in the system have settled out.*

9.1 Unhook the switch spring (A); note the arrangement of the return spring (B) and remove the pedal pinch bolt (C)

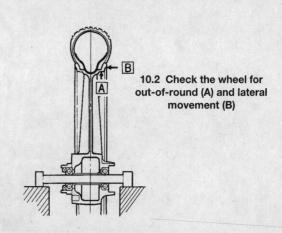

10.2 Check the wheel for out-of-round (A) and lateral movement (B)

9 Brake pedal - removal and installation

Refer to illustration 9.1

1 Note the position of the brake pedal return spring **(see illustration)**. Look for alignment marks on the pedal and its shaft and make your own if you can't see any.
2 Refer to Section 6 and detach the master cylinder from the pedal.
3 Remove the pedal pinch bolt and take the pedal off.
4 Disconnect the lower end of the brake light switch spring from the pedal arm, then remove the pedal arm from its bracket.
5 Installation is the reverse of the removal steps, with the following additions:
   a) *Lubricate the pedal shaft with multi-purpose grease.*
   b) *Align the punch marks on pedal and shaft. Tighten the pedal bolt to the torque listed in this Chapter's Specifications.*
   c) *Check brake pedal adjustment* (see Chapter 1).

10 Wheels - inspection and repair

Refer to illustration 10.2

1 Support the motorcycle securely upright, then clean the wheels thoroughly to remove mud and dirt that may interfere with the inspection procedure or mask defects. Make a general check of the wheels and tires as described in Chapter 1.
2 Raise the wheel to be checked off the ground, then attach a dial indicator to the fork slider or the swingarm and position the stem against the side of the rim. Spin the wheel slowly and check the side-to-side (axial) runout of the rim, then compare your readings with the value listed in this Chapter's Specifications **(see illustration)**. In order to accurately check radial runout with the dial indicator, the wheel would have to be removed from the machine and the tire removed from the wheel. With the axle clamped in a vise, the wheel can be rotated to check the runout.
3 An easier, though slightly less accurate, method is to attach a stiff wire pointer to the fork or the swingarm and position the end a fraction of an inch from the wheel (where the wheel and tire join). If the wheel is true, the distance from the pointer to the rim will be constant as the wheel is rotated. **Note:** *If wheel runout is excessive, refer to the appropriate Section in this Chapter and check the wheel bearings very carefully before replacing the wheel.*
4 The wheels should also be visually inspected for cracks, flat spots on the rim and other damage. Since tubeless tires are involved, look very closely for dents in the area where the tire bead contacts the rim. Dents in this area may prevent complete sealing of the tire against the rim, which leads to deflation of the tire over a period of time.
5 If damage is evident, or if runout in either direction is excessive, the wheel will have to be replaced with a new one. Never attempt to repair a damaged cast aluminum wheel.

11 Wheels - alignment check

1 Misalignment of the wheels, which may be due to a cocked rear wheel or a bent frame or triple clamps, can cause strange and possibly serious handling problems. If the frame or triple clamps are at fault, repair by a frame specialist or replacement with new parts are the only alternatives.
2 To check the alignment you will need an assistant, a length of string or a perfectly straight piece of wood and a ruler graduated in 1/64 inch increments. A plumb bob or other suitable weight will also be required.
3 Support the motorcycle in a level position, then measure the width of both tires at their widest points. Subtract the smaller measurement from the larger measurement, then divide the difference by two. The result is the amount of offset that should exist between the front and rear tires on both sides.
4 If a string is used, have your assistant hold one end of it about half way between the floor and the rear axle, touching the rear sidewall of the tire.
5 Run the other end of the string forward and pull it tight so that it is roughly parallel to the floor. Slowly bring the string into contact with the front sidewall of the rear tire, then turn the front wheel until it is parallel with the string. Measure the distance from the front tire sidewall to the string.
6 Repeat the procedure on the other side of the motorcycle. The distance from the front tire sidewall to the string should be equal on both sides.
7 As was previously pointed out, a perfectly straight length of wood may be substituted for the string. The procedure is the same.
8 If the distance between the string and tire is greater on one side, or if the rear wheel appears to be cocked, refer to Chapter 6, Swingarm bearings - check, and make sure the swingarm is tight.
9 If the front-to-back alignment is correct, the wheels still may be out of alignment vertically.
10 Using the plumb bob, or other suitable weight, and a length of string, check the rear wheel to make sure it is vertical. To do this, hold the string against the tire upper sidewall and allow the weight to settle just off the floor. When the string touches both the upper and lower tire sidewalls and is perfectly straight, the wheel is vertical. If it is not, place thin spacers under one leg of the centerstand.
11 Once the rear wheel is vertical, check the front wheel in the same manner. If both wheels are not perfectly vertical, the frame and/or major suspension components are bent.

Chapter 7 Brakes, wheels and tires

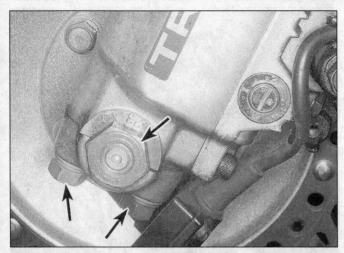

12.4a Remove the left axle holder nuts (lower arrows); the hex head of the axle nut (upper arrow) fits just outside the axle holder and fork

12.4b The right end of the axle fits flush with the axle holder and fork; on installation, the arrow mark on each axle holder (arrow) faces forward

12.5a Hold the axle with one wrench . . .

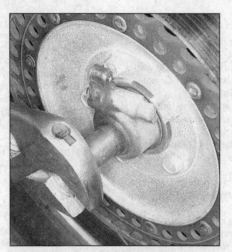

12.5b . . . and remove the axle nut with another

12.6 Take the speedometer drive unit off the axle

12 Front wheel - removal, inspection and installation

Removal

Refer to illustrations 12.4a, 12.4b, 12.5a, 12.5b, 12.6 and 12.7

1 Place the bike on its centerstand. Raise the front wheel off the ground by placing a floor jack with a wood block on the jack head, under the engine (see illustration 3.4 in Chapter 6).
2 Disconnect the speedometer cable or speed sensor from the drive unit (see Chapter 9).
3 Remove the brake calipers, leaving the brake hoses connected (see Section 2). Tie the caliper to a support such as the handlebars with a piece of wire so it doesn't hang by the brake hose. **Note:** *Slip a piece of wood between the brake pads so the pads won't be squeezed together if the brake lever is accidentally pulled.*
4 Undo the axle holders and lower the wheel away from the forks, complete with the axle and speedometer drive unit (see illustrations).
5 Hold the axle with one wrench and unscrew the axle nut with another (see illustrations).
6 Take the speedometer drive unit off the axle and pull the axle out of the wheel (see illustration).
7 Remove the collar from the right side (see illustration). Set the wheel aside. **Caution:** *Don't lay the wheel down and allow it to rest on one of the discs - the disc could become warped. Set the wheel on wood blocks so the disc doesn't support the weight of the wheel.* **Note:** *Don't operate the front brake lever with the wheel removed.*

12.7 Remove the spacer from the right side of the wheel

7-12   Chapter 7   Brakes, wheels and tires

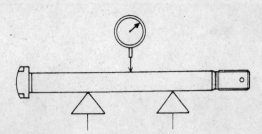

12.8 Check the axle for runout using a dial indicator and V-blocks

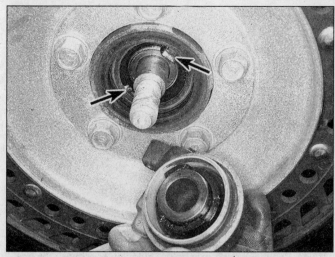

12.12a On installation, make sure the speedometer coupling lugs (arrows) engage the notches in the drive unit

Inspection

Refer to illustration 12.8

8   Set the axle in a pair of V-blocks, rotate it and check run out with a dial indicator **(see illustration)**. If the axle is corroded, remove the corrosion with fine emery cloth.
9   Check the condition of the wheel bearings (see Section 14).

Installation

Refer to illustrations 12.12a and 12.12b

10   Coat the lip of the grease seal on the right side with multi-purpose grease, then install the collar.
11   Install the front axle, then install the axle nut. Hold the axle with a wrench and tighten the axle nut to the torque listed in this Chapter's Specifications **(see illustrations 12.5a and 12.5b)**.
12   Place the ends of the axle under the lower ends of the forks, then lower the jack beneath the engine until the forks drop onto the axle. Make sure the lugs in the speedometer coupling line up with the notches in the speedometer drive unit **(see illustration)**. Make sure the cast boss on the speedometer gear housing rests against the back of the tab on the left fork leg **(see illustration)**.
13   Install the axle holders on the bottoms of the forks with their arrow marks facing the front of the bike **(see illustration 12.4b)**. Install the holder nuts, but don't tighten them yet.
14   Install the brake calipers and tighten their bolts to the torque listed in this Chapter's Specifications (see Section 2).
15   Tighten the axle holder front nuts, then the rear nuts to the torque listed in this Chapter's Specifications.
16   Measure the gap between the right brake disc (both sides) and the caliper bracket. If the gap is less then listed in this Chapter's Specifications, loosen the axle holder nuts and reposition the fork leg (inward or outward) until the gap is as specified. Tighten the axle holder nuts to the specified torque, then spin the wheel, apply the right front brake several times and recheck the clearance between the brake disc and bracket. Don't operate the motorcycle until the gap is correct or the brake disc may be damaged.
17   Reconnect the speedometer cable (see Chapter 9).
18   Apply the front brake, pump the forks up and down several times and check for binding and proper brake operation.

13 Rear wheel - removal, inspection and installation

Removal

Refer to illustrations 13.3, 13.5, 13.6a, 13.6b and 13.8

1   Place the bike on its centerstand.
2   If you're working on an Interstate or Aspencade, remove the left saddlebag, rear fender and rear bumper (see Chapter 8).
3   Remove the axle nut **(see illustration)**.
4   Remove the shock absorber lower mounting bolts (see Chapter 6).
5   Loosen the axle pinch bolt **(see illustration)**.

12.12b Place the speedometer drive unit's boss (arrow) against the rear side of the tab on the fork leg; this keeps the drive unit from spinning with the wheel

13.3 Unscrew the axle nut

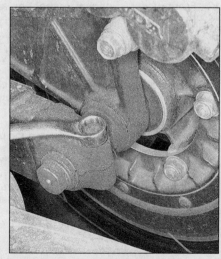

13.5 Loosen the axle pinch bolt . . .

Chapter 7 Brakes, wheels and tires

13.6a ... pull the axle out (inserting a rod or screwdriver in the removal hole (arrow) will give you something to pull on) ...

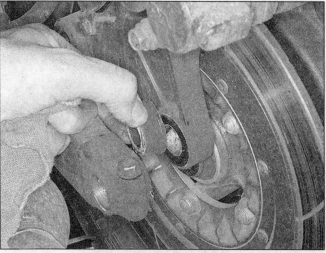

13.6b ... and remove the collar

13.8 Remove a second collar from the left side of the wheel

13.12 The wheel must be replaced if these dampers are worn enough to allow lash in the driveline

6 Carefully jack up the wheel far enough so the axle can be removed past the left muffler. Slip a screwdriver or punch into the axle hole, pull the axle out and remove the collar **(see illustrations)**.

7 Lift the brake caliper and bracket out of the way and tie them up so the caliper doesn't hang by the brake hose. **Note:** *Slip a piece of wood between the pads of the removed caliper so the pads won't be squeezed together if the brake lever is accidentally pulled.*

8 Remove the collar from the left side of the wheel **(see illustration)**.

9 Lower the wheel and remove it from the swingarm. **Caution:** *Don't lay the wheel down and allow it to rest on the disc or the sprocket - they could become warped. Set the wheel on wood blocks so the disc or the sprocket doesn't support the weight of the wheel. Do not operate the brake pedal with the wheel removed.*

Inspection

Refer to illustration 13.12

10 Refer to Section 12 and inspect the axle.

11 Check the condition of the wheel bearings (see Section 14).

12 Pull the coupling out of the wheel (see Chapter 6). Check the rubber damper bushings and their collars for damage and for wear where the coupling pins pass through them **(see illustration)**. Replace the entire wheel if problems are found.

Installation

13 Lubricate the splines of the driven flange with Honda Moly 60 grease or equivalent.

14 The remainder of installation is the reverse of the removal steps. Tighten all fasteners to the torques listed in this Chapter's Specifications and the Chapter 6 Specifications.

15 Check the operation of the brakes carefully before riding the motorcycle.

14 Wheel bearings - replacement

Refer to illustrations 14.4, 14.5a, 14.5b, 14.5c and 14.8

1 Support the bike securely so it can't be knocked over during this procedure and remove the wheel. See Section 12 (front wheel) or 13 (rear wheel).

2 Set the wheel on blocks so as not to allow the weight of the wheel to rest on the brake disc.

3 If you're working on a front wheel, pry the grease seal out of the left side and remove the speedometer drive coupling **(see illustration 12.12a)**. Turn the wheel over and pry the grease seal out of the other side.

Chapter 7 Brakes, wheels and tires

14.4 Pry out the grease seal

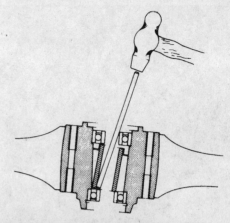

14.5a If there's enough room to tilt a metal rod so it will catch the bearing inner races, drive the bearings from the hub with a metal rod and hammer

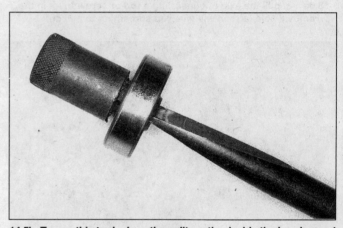

14.5b To use this tool, place the split portion inside the bearing and pass the wedged rod through the hub into the split; tapping on the end of the rod will spread the split portion, locking it to the bearing, so the split portion and bearing can be driven out together

4 If you're working on a rear wheel, pry the grease seal out of the left side **(see illustration)**.

5 A common method of removing wheel bearings is to insert a metal rod (preferably a brass drift punch) inserted through the center of one hub bearing and tap evenly around the inner race of the opposite bearing to drive it from the hub **(see illustration)**. The bearing spacer will also come out. On these motorcycles, it's generally not possible to tilt the rod enough to catch the opposite bearing's inner race. In this case, use a bearing remover tool consisting of a shaft and remover head **(see illustration)**. The head fits inside the bearing, then the wedge end of the shaft is tapped into the groove in the head to expand the head and lock it inside the bearing. Tapping on the shaft from this point will force the bearing out of the hub **(see illustration)**.

6 Lay the wheel on its other side and remove the remaining bearing using the same technique. **Note:** *The bearings must be replaced with new ones whenever they're removed, as they're almost certain to be damaged during removal.*

7 If you're installing bearings that aren't sealed on both sides, pack the new bearings with grease from the open side. Rotate the bearing to work the grease in between the bearing balls.

8 Thoroughly clean the hub area of the wheel. Install the bearing into the recess in the hub, with the sealed side facing out. Using a bearing driver or a socket large enough to contact the outer race of the bearing, drive it in until it's completely seated **(see illustration)**.

9 Turn the wheel over and install the bearing spacer and bearing,

driving the bearing into place as described in Step 8. Install the speedometer drive on the left side of the front wheel **(see illustration 12.12a and 12.12b)**.

10 Coat new grease seals with grease, then install them (on both

14.5c Pass the wedge end of the rod through the hub into the split portion

14.8 Drive in the new bearings and seals with a driver like this one or with a socket the same size as the bearing outer races

TIRE CHANGING SEQUENCE - TUBELESS TIRES

Deflate tire. After releasing beads, push tire bead into well of rim at point opposite valve. Insert lever next to valve and work bead over edge of rim.

Use two levers to work bead over edge of rim. Note use of rim protectors.

When first bead is clear, remove tire as shown.

Before installing, ensure that tire is suitable for wheel. Take note of any sidewall markings such as direction of rotation arrows.

Work first bead over the rim flange.

Use a tire lever to work the second bead over rim flange.

sides of the front wheel and on the left side of the rear wheel). It should be possible to push the seals in with even finger pressure, but if necessary use a seal driver, large socket or a flat piece of wood to drive the seals into place.

11 Clean off all grease from the brake disc(s) using acetone or brake system cleaner.

12 Refer to Section 12 or 13 and install the wheel.

15 Tubeless tires - general information

1 Tubeless tires are used as standard equipment on this motorcycle. They are generally safer than tube-type tires but if problems do occur they require special repair techniques.

2 The force required to break the seal between the rim and the bead of the tire is substantial, and is usually beyond the capabilities of an individual working with normal tire irons.

3 Also, repair of the punctured tire and replacement on the wheel rim requires special tools, skills and experience that the average do-it-yourselfer lacks.

4 For these reasons, if a puncture or flat occurs with a tubeless tire, the wheel should be removed from the motorcycle and taken to a dealer service department or a motorcycle repair shop for repair or replacement of the tire. The accompanying illustrations can be used to replace a tubeless tire in an emergency.

Chapter 8
Fairing and bodywork

Contents

	Section		Section
Engine guards - removal and installation	7	Mirrors - removal and installation	9
Fairing - removal and installation	11	Rear fender - removal and installation	15
Fairing lower, front and inner covers - removal and installation	6	Saddlebags - removal and installation	12
		Seat - removal and installation	2
Fairing pockets and top compartment - removal and installation	3	Side covers - removal and installation	8
		Sidestand and centerstand - maintenance	16
Footrests - removal and installation	4	Trunk - removal and installation	13
Frame - inspection and repair	17	Trunk and saddlebag bracket - removal and installation	14
Front fender - removal and installation	5	Windshield - removal and installation	10
General information	1		

1 General information

Refer to illustration 1.2

This Chapter covers the procedures necessary to remove and install the fairing and other body parts. Since many service and repair operations on these motorcycles require removal of the fairing and/or other body parts, the procedures are grouped here and referred to from other Chapters.

In the event of damage to the fairing or other body part, it is usually necessary to remove the broken component and replace it with a new (or used) one. The material that the fairings are composed of doesn't lend itself to conventional repair techniques. There are, however, some shops that specialize in "plastic welding," so it would be advantageous to check around first before throwing the damaged part away. When you order new body parts, refer to the color label inside the top compartment **(see illustration)** to make sure the new parts match the bike.

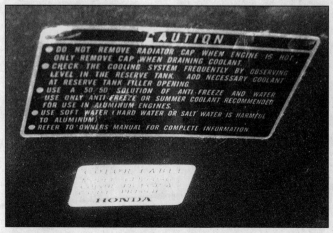

1.2 Refer to the color label inside the top compartment when you order body parts

Chapter 8 Fairing and bodywork

2.2 Remove the seat mounting bolts . . .

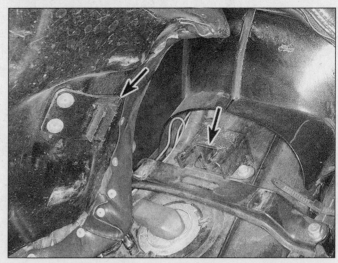

2.3 . . . and pull the seat rearward to disengage its hook from the bracket (arrows)

2 Seat - removal and installation

Refer to illustrations 2.2 and 2.3

1 If you're working on an Interstate or Aspencade, refer to Section 12 and remove the lids from the saddlebags.
2 Remove the Allen bolt on each side of the seat **(see illustration)**.
3 Lift up the back of the seat and pull it rearward to disengage the hook at the front from the fuel tank **(see illustration)**.
4 Installation is the reverse of the removal steps.

3 Fairing pockets and top compartment - removal and installation

Refer to illustrations 3.1a through 3.1e, 3.2a and 3.2b

1 Remove the fairing pocket covers from the left and right sides of the bike **(see illustrations)**.
2 Remove the top compartment bolts (two at the front and two at the rear **(see illustrations)**. Lift the top compartment off.
3 Installation is the reverse of the removal steps.

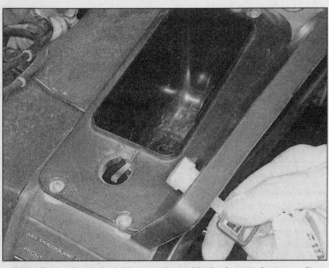

3.1a Open the right fairing pocket with the key and remove its mounting screws

3.1b Remove the right inner trim cover

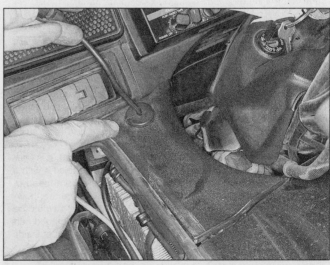

3.1c Pull the left inner fairing cover out past the accessory cable (if equipped)

Chapter 8 Fairing and bodywork 8-3

3.1d The accessory cable grommet fits on the frame like this

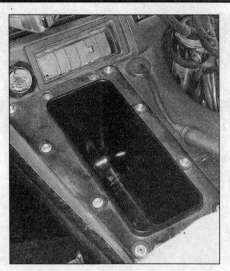

3.1e Remove the mounting screws

3.2a Remove the top compartment mounting bolts at the rear . . .

4 Footrests - removal and installation

Refer to illustration 4.2

1 To remove a front footrest, either unbolt its bracket from the frame or remove the clip and slide out the pivot pin.
2 To remove a rear footrest, remove its clip and pivot pin. To remove the bracket, undo the Allen bolts **(see illustration)**.
3 Installation is the reverse of the removal steps.

5 Front fender - removal and installation

Refer to illustration 5.2

1 Remove the fork brace (Chapter 6).
2 Remove the mounting bolts from inside the fender **(see illustration)**. Take the fender out from between the forks.
3 Installation is the reverse of the removal steps.

3.2b . . . and at the front

4.2 Remove the clip and pivot pin (arrow) to detach the footrest; remove the Allen bolts to detach the bracket

5.2 The front fender is bolted to the fork legs from the inside

6.1a Remove one screw at each upper corner and one at each lower corner (arrow) . . .

6.1b . . . one lower screw and one upper screw (arrow) on each side

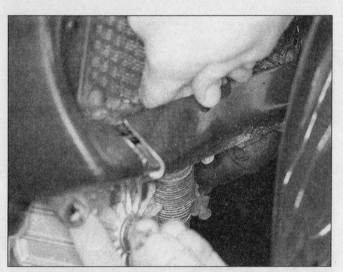

6.2a Separate the front covers from the lower cover . . .

6.2b . . . and lift the front covers off the bike

6.3 Remove the inner cover on each side

6 Fairing lower, front and inner covers - removal and installation

Refer to illustrations 6.1a, 6.1b, 6.2a, 6.2b and 6.3

1 On each side of the bike, remove the screws and collars that attach the lower cover to the bike **(see illustrations)**. If you're working on a 1987 Aspencade, remove four screws that attach the lower cowl below the front cover.

2 Separate the bottom ends of the lower covers from each side of the front cover **(see illustration)**. Take the front cover off, then remove the lower covers **(see illustration)**.

3 Remove the screws that attach the inner cover on each side of the fairing **(see illustration)**.

4 Installation is the reverse of the removal steps.

7 Engine guards - removal and installation

Refer to illustration 7.3

1 Place the bike on its centerstand.
2 Remove the lower fairing cover (Section 6).

Chapter 8 Fairing and bodywork

7.3 The engine guards are held to the frame by a pair of clamps (arrows); under the bike, they're attached to each other

8.1 The side cover posts fit into rubber grommets (arrows)

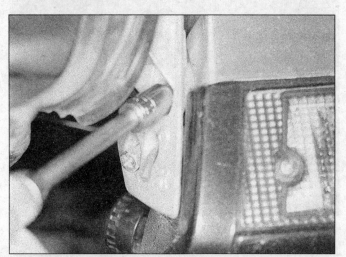

9.1 Pull back the mirror cover and remove the screws . . .

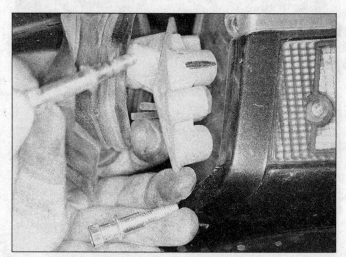

9.2 . . . The screws are different lengths; on installation, install the top screw first

3 Unbolt the front of the engine guard from the frame (see illustration). Working beneath the bike, unbolt the engine guards from each other and take the guard out.
4 Installation is the reverse of the removal steps.

8 Side covers - removal and installation

Refer to illustration 8.1
1 Reach behind the cover and slowly pull the posts out of the rubber grommets on the frame, then take the cover off (see illustration).
2 Installation is the reverse of the removal steps.

9 Mirrors - removal and installation

Refer to illustrations 9.1 and 9.2
1 Pull the mirror cover tabs free of the fairing and pull back the cover to expose the screws (see illustration).
2 Undo the mirror screws and take the mirror off the bike (see illustration).
3 Installation is the reverse of the removal steps. The upper mirror screw is more difficult to align than the lower one, so start it first.

10 Windshield - removal and installation

Refer to illustrations 10.2, 10.3a and 10.3b
1 Remove the mirrors (see Section 9). This detaches the outer ends of the windshield trim.
2 Free the trim from the bracket on the fairing, then lift it up and off (see illustration).

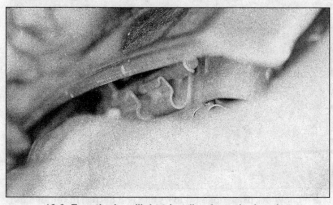

10.2 Free the headlight trim clips from the bracket

10.3a Remove the windshield screws . . .

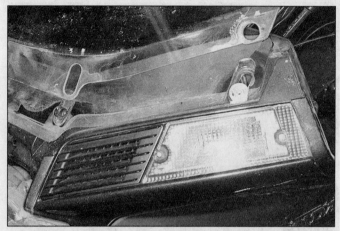

10.3b . . . and take the windshield off

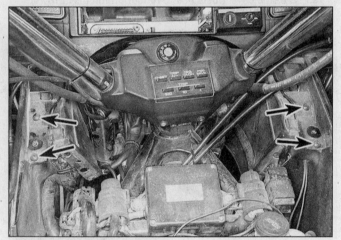

11.2a Remove the screws to detach the harness retainer on each side of the bike (arrows)

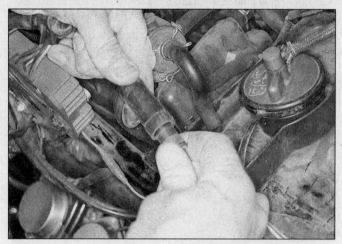

11.2b Unplug the antenna cable

3 Remove the windshield screws and lift the windshield off the bike **(see illustrations)**.
4 Installation is the reverse of removal.

11.3 Follow the drain hose (A) to its clip and detach it; remove the fairing-to-bracket nuts (B)

11 Fairing - removal and installation

Refer to illustrations 11.2a, 11.2b, 11.3, 11.4, 11.7 and 11.8

1 Remove the seat (Section 2). Remove the fairing pockets and the top compartment (Section 3). Remove the fairing lower and inner covers (Section 6).
2 Inside the fairing, remove the screws that secure the main harness connector to the fairing on each side **(see illustration)**. Disconnect the fairing electrical connector from the left main harness connector. If you're working on an Aspencade, locate the antenna cable under the left connector and unplug it **(see illustration)**.
3 Under the right side of the fairing, disconnect the onboard compressor hoses (if equipped) (see Chapter 6). Follow the drain hose down to its retainer next to the radiator and detach it **(see illustration)**.
4 Remove the bottom cover from under the front of the fairing **(see illustration)**.
5 Disconnect the horn wires. On each side of the bike, remove the nuts that secure the fairing bracket to the fairing **(see illustration 11.3)**.
6 Disconnect any remaining electrical connectors and vacuum lines that connect the fairing to the bike. Look carefully for wires leading to non-stock accessories that may have been added.
7 Lift the fairing off the frame **(see illustration)**. **Note:** *The fairing is bulky. There will be less chance of scratching it if you have an assistant to help lift.*
8 To remove the fairing bracket, undo an Allen bolt on each side and two center bolts **(see illustration)**.
9 Installation is the reverse of removal. Tighten all fasteners securely, but don't overtighten them and crack the fairing.

Chapter 8 Fairing and bodywork 8-7

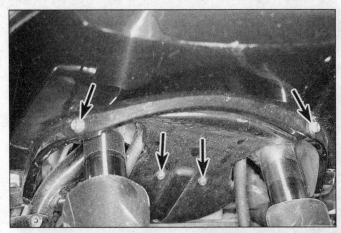

11.4 Remove the bottom cover screws and fairing front bolts (arrows)

11.7 Lift the fairing off the bike; this will be easier with an assistant

11.8 The fairing bracket is secured by an Allen bolt on each side (left arrow) and two bolts and cap nuts in the center (right arrows)

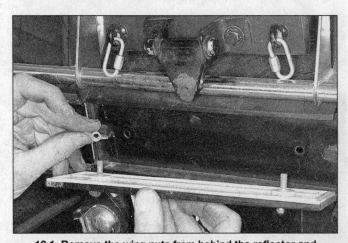

12.1 Remove the wing nuts from behind the reflector and take it off

12 Saddlebags - removal and installation

Refer to illustrations 12.1, 12.2, 12.3 and 12.4

1   Reach behind the rear reflector and undo the wing nut on each side **(see illustration)**. Take the reflector off.
2   Uncover the saddlebag rear screw to detach it from the fender **(see illustration)**.
3   Inside the saddlebag, remove two mounting bolts from the inner side and two from the bottom **(see illustration)**.

12.2 Remove the rear saddlebag screws

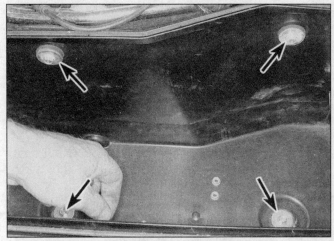

12.3 Remove the mounting bolts from the bottom and side of the saddlebag

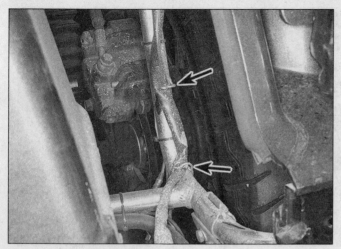

12.4 Lift the saddlebag part way off, detach the harness clips (arrows) and unplug the connector

4 Pull the saddlebag part way off. Free the saddle bag electrical wires from the clips on the saddlebag bracket **(see illustration)**. Follow the wiring harness to the electrical connector, unplug it and lift the saddlebag off the bike.
5 Installation is the reverse of the removal steps.

14.2 Unbolt the antenna bracket from the trunk bracket

14.5 The rear bumper is secured at each end by a clamp

13.2 Remove four mounting bolts from the trunk floor

13 Trunk - removal and installation

Removal

Refer to illustration 13.2
1 If you're working on an Aspencade, remove the seat (see Section 2). Locate the electrical connector for the brake lights and unplug it.
2 Inside the trunk, remove the four mounting bolts from the trunk floor **(see illustration)**. Lift the trunk off the bike.

Installation

3 Installation is the reverse of the removal steps.

14 Trunk and saddlebag bracket - removal and installation

Refer to illustrations 14.2, 14.5 and 14.7
1 Remove the saddlebags and trunk (Sections 12 and 13).
2 If you're working on an Aspencade, remove the antenna bracket **(see illustration)**.

14.7 The upper bolt passes through the bracket into the fender bolt on each side

Chapter 8 Fairing and bodywork

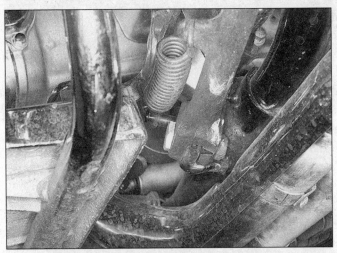

16.1a Unhook the spring and remove the pivot bolt to remove the sidestand

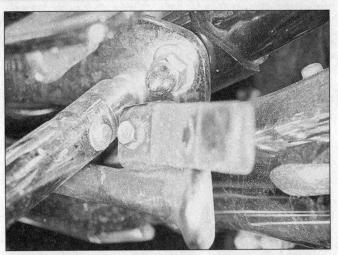

16.1b The sidestand rubber tip can be replaced separately if it's worn

3 If you're working on an Aspencade, remove the seat (Section 2) and the passenger footrests (Section 4). One of the footrest bolts also secures the lower front of the bracket on these models. On all other models, remove the bracket bolt at the lower front.
4 Unbolt the rear section of the fender at the top where it meets the center or front section.
5 Remove the clamps that secure the rear bumper to the lower portion of the bracket **(see illustration)**. Take the rear bumper (the bar that connects the two sides of the saddlebag bracket) out.
6 Remove the shock absorber upper nut (see Chapter 6).
7 Remove the mounting bolt on each side of the upper center **(see illustration)**. Lift the bracket off the motorcycle.
8 Installation is the reverse of the removal steps.

15 Rear fender - removal and installation

1 The rear fender on 1984 Standard models is made in two pieces; on all others it's made in three pieces.

1984 Standard models

2 Remove the seat (Section 2), the side covers (Section 8) and the handrail.
3 Detach the shock absorber air hoses and wiring harnesses form the clips on the fender.
4 Take off the rear fender section, then the front.

Interstate and Aspencade models

5 Remove the trunk and saddlebags (Sections 12 and 13).
6 To remove the rear portion of the fender, unbolt it at the top where it meets the center section and take it off the bike. Take off the fender and license plate bracket.
7 To remove the center portion of the fender, undo the mounting bolts **(see illustration 14.7)**.
8 Move any wires or air hoses aside and detach the front portion of the fender from the frame.
9 Installation is the reverse of the removal steps.

16 Sidestand and centerstand - maintenance

Refer to illustrations 16.1a, 16.1b and 16.1c

1 The sidestand and centerstand are attached to the frame. An extension spring anchored to the bracket ensures that the stand is held in the retracted position **(see illustrations)**.

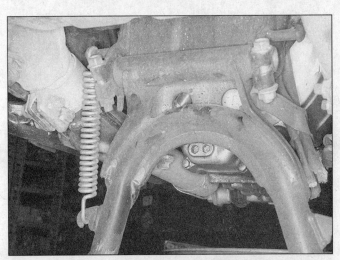

16.1c Unhook the centerstand spring and undo the clamp at each end of the pivot shaft to remove it

2 Make sure the pivot bolt(s) is tight and the extension spring is in good condition and not overstretched. An accident is almost certain to occur if the stand extends while the machine is in motion.

17 Frame - inspection and repair

1 The frame should not require attention unless accident damage has occurred. In most cases, frame replacement is the only satisfactory remedy for such damage. A few frame specialists have the jigs and other equipment necessary for straightening the frame to the required standard of accuracy, but even then there is no simple way of assessing to what extent the frame may have been overstressed.
2 After the machine has accumulated a lot of miles, the frame should be examined closely for signs of cracking or splitting at the welded joints. Corrosion can also cause weakness at these joints. Loose engine mount bolts can cause ovaling or fracturing of the mounting tabs. Minor damage can often be repaired by welding, depending on the extent and nature of the damage.
3 Remember that a frame which is out of alignment will cause handling problems. If misalignment is suspected as the result of an accident, it will be necessary to strip the machine completely so the frame can be thoroughly checked.

Chapter 8 Fairing and bodywork

Notes

Chapter 9
Electrical system

Contents

Section		Section	
Alternator drive unit and starter drive chain - removal, inspection and installation	31	Headlight bulb - replacement	7
		Horn - check and replacement	18
Alternator rotor and starter clutch - removal and installation	30	Ignition main (key) switch - check and replacement	16
Alternator stator - check	29	Instrument and warning light bulbs - replacement	23
Battery - inspection and maintenance	3	Instrument cluster - removal and installation	21
Battery - removal, charging and installation	4	Lighting system - check	6
Battery electrolyte level/specific gravity - check	See Chapter 1	Meters and gauges - check	22
Brake light switches - check and replacement	11	Oil pressure switch - removal, check and installation	15
Charging system - leakage and output test	27	Radio and speakers - removal, check and installation	32
Charging system testing - general information and precautions	26	Regulator/rectifier - check and replacement	28
Clutch switch - check and replacement	14	Speed sensor (Aspencade) - removal, check and installation	20
Electrical troubleshooting	2	Speedometer cable (Standard and Interstate) removal and installation	19
Fuses - check and replacement	5		
Gear position switch (gearshift sensor) - check, removal and installation	17	Starter motor - removal and installation	25
		Starter relay - check and replacement	24
General information	1	Turn signal circuit - check	10
Handlebar switches - check	12	Turn signals and taillight bulbs - replacement	9
Handlebar switches - removal and installation	13	Wiring diagrams	33
Headlight aim - check and adjustment	8		

Specifications

Battery
Capacity/type	12 volts, 20 amp-hours
Specific gravity	See Chapter 1

Charging system
Leakage	0.5 mA maximum
Output	
950 rpm	Minus 1 to zero amps, above 12 volts
3000 rpm	Zero to 3 amps, 14 to 15 volts
5000 rpm	Zero to 8 amps, 14 to 15 volts
Alternator backlash	
Standard	0.05 mm (0.002 inch)
Limit	0.010 to 0.100 mm (0.0004 to 0.0040 inch)

Torque specifications
Oil pressure switch	12 Nm (9 ft-lbs) (1)
Alternator cover bolts	12 Nm (9 ft-lbs)
Alternator drive unit bolts	12 Nm (9 ft-lbs)
Alternator nut	85 Nm (61 ft-lbs) (2)

1. Coat the threads with sealant.
2. Coat the threads of the shaft with non-permanent thread locking agent. Coat the threads and seating surfaces of the nut with engine oil.

1 General information

The machines covered by this manual are equipped with a 12-volt electrical system.

The charging system uses a three-phase alternator with an integrated circuit regulator/rectifier. The regulator maintains the charging system output within the specified range to prevent overcharging. The rectifier converts the AC (alternating current) output of the alternator to DC (direct current) to power the lights and other components and to charge the battery. The alternator is mounted at the left rear corner of the engine inside the rear engine cover.

An electric starter mounted to the back of the engine is standard equipment. The starting system includes the motor, the battery, the relay and the various wires and switches. If the engine kill switch and the ignition switch are both in the On position, the starting circuit allows the starter motor to operate only if the transmission is in Neutral (gear position switch indicating Neutral) or the clutch lever is pulled to the handlebar (clutch switch on) and the sidestand is up (sidestand switch on).

Note: *Keep in mind that electrical parts, once purchased, can't be returned. To avoid unnecessary expense, make very sure the faulty component has been positively identified before buying a replacement part.*

2 Electrical troubleshooting

A typical electrical circuit consists of an electrical component, the switches, relays, etc. related to that component and the wiring and connectors that hook the component to both the battery and the frame. To aid in locating a problem in any electrical circuit, refer to the wiring diagrams at the end of this Chapter.

Before tackling any troublesome electrical circuit, first study the appropriate diagrams thoroughly to get a complete picture of what makes up that individual circuit. Trouble spots, for instance, can often be narrowed down by noting if other components related to that circuit are operating properly or not. If several components or circuits fail at one time, chances are the fault lies in the fuse or ground connection, as several circuits often are routed through the same fuse and ground connections.

Electrical problems often stem from simple causes, such as loose or corroded connections or a blown fuse. Prior to any electrical troubleshooting, always visually check the condition of the fuse, wires and connections in the problem circuit. Intermittent failures can be especially frustrating, since you can't always duplicate the failure when it's convenient to test. In such situations, a good practice is to clean all connections in the affected circuit, whether or not they appear to be good. All of the connections and wires should also be wiggled to check for looseness which can cause intermittent failure. Unplug the electrical connectors in the circuit completely, then clean the terminals and reconnect them securely.

If testing instruments are going to be utilized, use the diagrams to plan where you will make the necessary connections in order to accurately pinpoint the trouble spot.

The basic tools needed for electrical troubleshooting include a test light or voltmeter, a continuity tester (which includes a bulb, battery and set of test leads) and a jumper wire, preferably with a circuit breaker incorporated, which can be used to bypass electrical components. Specific checks described later in this Chapter may also require an ohmmeter.

Voltage checks should be performed if a circuit is not functioning properly. Connect one lead of a test light or voltmeter to either the negative battery terminal or a known good ground. Connect the other lead to a connector in the circuit being tested, preferably nearest to the battery or fuse. If the bulb lights, voltage is reaching that point, which means the part of the circuit between that connector and the battery is problem-free. Continue checking the remainder of the circuit in the same manner. When you reach a point where no voltage is present, the problem lies between there and the last good test point. Most of the time the problem is due to a loose connection. Keep in mind that some

3.4 Undo the negative cable first, then the positive cable; the plastic cover on the positive terminal prevents accidental contact with metal - to remove the battery, unscrew the bracket bolt (arrow) and pivot the holder down

circuits only receive voltage when the ignition key is in the On position.

One method of finding short circuits is to remove the fuse and connect a test light or voltmeter in its place to the fuse terminals. There should be no load in the circuit (it should be switched off). Move the wiring harness from side-to-side while watching the test light. If the bulb lights, there is a short to ground somewhere in that area, probably where insulation has rubbed off a wire. The same test can be performed on other components in the circuit, including the switch.

A ground check should be done to see if a component is grounded properly. Disconnect the battery and connect one lead of a self-powered test light (continuity tester) to a known good ground. Connect the other lead to the wire or ground connection being tested. If the bulb lights, the ground is good. If the bulb does not light, the ground is not good.

A continuity check is performed to see if a circuit, section of circuit or individual component is capable of passing electricity through it. Disconnect the battery and connect one lead of a self-powered test light (continuity tester) to one end of the circuit being tested and the other lead to the other end of the circuit. If the bulb lights, there is continuity, which means the circuit is passing electricity through it properly. Switches can be checked in the same way.

Remember that all electrical circuits are designed to conduct electricity from the battery, through the wires, switches, relays, etc. to the electrical component (light bulb, motor, etc.). From there it is directed to the frame (ground) where it is passed back to the battery. Electrical problems are basically an interruption in the flow of electricity from the battery or back to it.

3 Battery - inspection and maintenance

Refer to illustration 3.4

1   Most battery damage is caused by heat, vibration, and/or low electrolyte levels, so keep the battery securely mounted, check the electrolyte level frequently and make sure the charging system is functioning properly.

2   Refer to Chapter 1 for electrolyte level and specific gravity checking procedures.

3   Check around the base inside of the battery for sediment, which is the result of sulfation caused by low electrolyte levels. These deposits will cause internal short circuits, which can quickly discharge the battery. Look for cracks in the case and replace the battery if either of these conditions is found.

4   Check the battery terminals and cable ends for tightness and corrosion. If corrosion is evident, remove the cables from the battery **(see illustration)** and clean the terminals and cable ends with a wire brush

Chapter 9 Electrical system

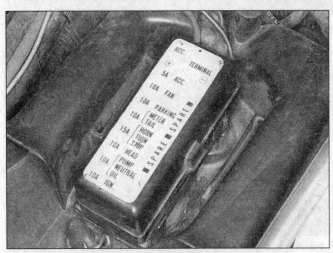

5.1a The accessory fuses are beneath a cover inside the top compartment . . .

5.1b . . . spare fuses are stored in the fuse block

or knife and emery paper. Reconnect the cables and apply a thin coat of petroleum jelly to the connections to slow further corrosion.

5 The battery case should be kept clean to prevent current leakage, which can discharge the battery over a period of time (especially when it sits unused). Wash the outside of the case with a solution of baking soda and water. Do not get any baking soda solution in the battery cells. Rinse the battery thoroughly, then dry it.

6 If acid has been spilled on the frame or battery box, neutralize it with the baking soda and water solution, dry it thoroughly, then touch up any damaged paint. Make sure the battery vent tube (if equipped) is directed away from the frame and is not kinked or pinched.

7 If the motorcycle sits unused for long periods of time, disconnect the cables from the battery terminals. Refer to Section 4 and charge the battery approximately once every month.

4 Battery - removal, charging and installation

1 If the motorcycle sits idle for extended periods or if the charging system malfunctions, the battery can be charged from an external source.

2 To properly charge the battery, you will need a charger of the correct rating, a hydrometer, a clean rag and a syringe for adding distilled water to the battery cells.

3 The maximum charging rate for any battery is 1/10 of the rated amp/hour capacity. As an example, the maximum charging rate for a 12 amp/hour battery would be 1.2 amps and the maximum charging rate for a 14 amp/hour battery would be 1.4 amps. If the battery is charged at a higher rate, it could be damaged.

4 Do not allow the battery to be subjected to a so-called quick charge (high rate of charge over a short period of time) unless you are prepared to buy a new battery.

5 When charging the battery, always remove it from the machine (see illustration 3.4) and be sure to check the electrolyte level before hooking up the charger. Add distilled water to any cells that are low.

6 Loosen the cell caps, hook up the battery charger leads (red to positive, black to negative), cover the top of the battery with a clean rag, then, and only then, plug in the battery charger. Warning: Remember, the gas escaping from a charging battery is explosive, so keep open flames and sparks well away from the area. Also, the electrolyte is extremely corrosive and will damage anything it comes in contact with.

7 Allow the battery to charge until the specific gravity is as specified (refer to Chapter 1 for specific gravity checking procedures). The charger must be unplugged and disconnected from the battery when making specific gravity checks. If the battery overheats or gases excessively, the charging rate is too high. Either disconnect the charger or lower the charging rate to prevent damage to the battery.

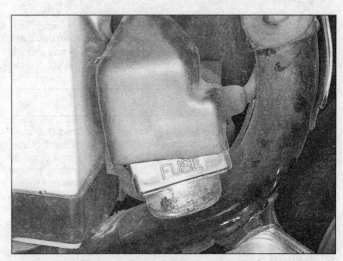

5.1c The main fuse is located next to the battery

8 It's time for a new battery if:
a) *One or more of the cells is significantly lower in specific gravity than the others after a long slow charge;*
b) *The battery as a whole doesn't seem to want to take a charge;*
c) *Battery voltage won't increase;*
d) *The electrolyte doesn't bubble;*
e) *The plates are white (indicating sulfation) or debris has accumulated in the bottom of a cell;*
f) *The plates or insulators are warped or buckled.*

9 When the battery is fully charged, unplug the charger first, then disconnect the leads from the battery. Install the cell caps and wipe any electrolyte off the outside of the battery case.

5 Fuses - check and replacement

Refer to illustrations 5.1a, 5.1b and 5.1c

1 These motorcycles have a fuse block containing accessory fuses and spares **(see illustrations)**. Fuse ratings and functions are printed on the cover. The fuse block is located under the tool tray in the top compartment. On 1987 Aspencade models, several relays are mounted on the fuse block. There's also a main fuse next to the battery **(see illustration)**. The cooling fan circuit is protected by an inline fuse in the fan wiring harness.

2 If you have a test light, the accessory fuses can be checked without removing them. Turn the ignition key to the On position, connect one end of the test light to a good ground, then probe each terminal on top of the fuse. If the fuse is good, there will be voltage available at both terminals. If the fuse is blown, there will only be voltage present at one of the terminals.

3 A blown main fuse can be identified by a break in the element.

4 The accessory and main fuses can also be tested with an ohmmeter or self-powered test light. Remove the fuse and connect the tester to the ends of the fuse. If the ohmmeter shows continuity or the test lamp lights, the fuse is good. If the ohmmeter shows infinite resistance or the test lamp stays out, the fuse is blown.

5 The accessory fuses can be removed and checked visually. If you can't pull the fuse out with your fingertips, use a pair of needle-nose pliers. A blown fuse is easily identified by a break in the element.

6 If a fuse blows, be sure to check the wiring harnesses very carefully for evidence of a short circuit. Look for bare wires and chafed, melted or burned insulation. If a fuse is replaced before the cause is located, the new fuse will blow immediately.

7 Never, under any circumstances, use a higher rated fuse or bridge the fuse block terminals, as damage to the electrical system, including fire, could result.

8 Occasionally a fuse will blow or cause an open circuit for no obvious reason. Corrosion of the fuse ends and fuse block terminals may occur and cause poor fuse contact. If this happens, remove the corrosion with a wire brush or emery paper, then spray the fuse end and terminals with electrical contact cleaner.

6 Lighting system - check

1 The battery provides power for operation of the headlight, position light, taillight, brake light, license plate light, instrument cluster lights and optional accessory lights. If none of the lights operate, always check battery voltage before proceeding. Low battery voltage indicates either a faulty battery, low battery electrolyte level or a defective charging system. Refer to Chapter 1 for battery checks and Sections 27 through 29 for charging system tests. Also, check the condition of the fuses and relays and replace any that are blown or not working correctly.

Headlight

2 If the headlight is out when the engine is running, check the fuse first with the key On (see Section 5), then unplug the electrical connector for the headlight and use jumper wires to connect the bulb directly to the battery terminals. If the light comes on, the problem lies in the wiring or one of the switches or relays in the circuit. Refer to Section 13 for the switch testing procedures, and also the wiring diagrams at the end of this Chapter.

Taillight/license plate light

3 If the taillight fails to work, check the bulbs and the bulb terminals first, then check for battery voltage at the taillight electrical connector. If voltage is present, check the ground circuit for an open or poor connection.

4 If no voltage is indicated, check the fuse and the wiring between the taillight and the ignition switch, then check the switch.

Brake light

5 See Section 11 for the brake light switch checking procedure.

Neutral indicator light

6 If the neutral light fails to operate when the transmission is in Neutral, check the fuse and the bulb (see Section 23 for bulb removal procedures). If the bulb and fuse are in good condition, check for battery voltage at the connector attached to the gearshift sensor. Remove the fairing lower cover from the right side of the bike; follow the wiring harness from the grommet at the top of the front engine cover to the connector. If battery voltage is present, refer to Section 18 for the gearshift sensor check and replacement procedures.

7 If no voltage is indicated, check the wiring between the switch and the bulb for open circuits and poor connections.

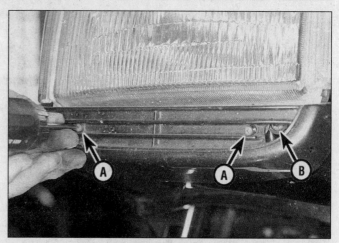

7.3 Remove the screw at each end (A) and take off the front trim piece; the horizontal adjuster screw (B) is behind the trim piece

7 Headlight bulb - replacement

Warning: *If the bulb has just burned out, allow it to cool. It will be hot enough to burn your fingers.*

1984 Standard models

1 Remove three screws from the front surface of the headlight trim ring and pull the headlight out.

Interstate and Aspencade models

Refer to illustrations 7.3, 7.4a, 7.4b, 7.5a, 7.5b, 7.6, 7.8a, 7.8b, 7.8c, 7.8d, 7.9a and 7.9b

2 Remove the mirrors and the trim panel below the windshield (see Chapter 8).

3 Remove the trim piece from below the headlight assembly **(see illustration)**.

4 Remove the headlight assembly mounting bolts and take the assembly off **(see illustrations)**.

5 Unplug the electrical connector from the headlight **(see illustration)**. Note the position of any Top markings for reinstallation and remove the rubber dust cover from the headlight assembly **(see illustration)**.

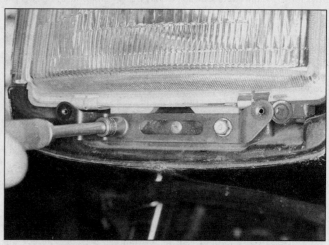

7.4a Remove the lower screw on each side . . .

Chapter 9 Electrical system

7.4b ... and the upper screw on each side ...

7.5a ... then pull the assembly forward and unplug its electrical connectors

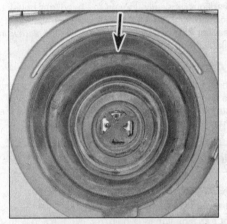

7.5b Note the location of the Top mark (arrow), then pull on the tab to free the dust cover from the housing

7.6 Unhook the clip from the housing, then pull the bulb out; don't touch the glass on the new bulb with bare fingers

7.8a Undo the screw and pull off the vertical aiming knob ...

6 Lift up the retaining clip and swing it out of the way, then remove the bulb (see illustration).
7 When installing the new bulb, reverse the removal procedure. Be sure not to touch the bulb with your fingers - oil from your skin will cause the bulb to overheat and fail prematurely. If you do touch the bulb, wipe it off with a clean rag dampened with rubbing alcohol.
8 To remove the aiming knob and cables, undo the screw, pull off the knob and remove the nut and washers (see illustrations). Detach the cables from the headlight housing and remove them from the bike (see illustration).
9 To replace a position light bulb, pull its socket from the headlight housing (see illustrations). Pull the bulb out, push in a new one and reinstall the socket.

7.8b ... unscrew the nut ...

7.8c ... and remove the metal and rubber washers

7.8d Undo the screws and detach the aiming cables from the housing

7.9a The position light bulb is at the end of the headlight housing (arrow) . . .

7.9b . . . pull the socket out of the housing, then pull the bulb out of the socket

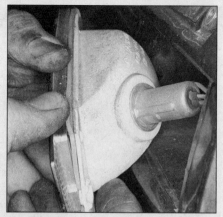

9.1 Take the lens and gasket off the housing for access to the bulb

8 Headlight aim - check and adjustment

1 An improperly adjusted headlight may cause problems for oncoming traffic or provide poor, unsafe illumination of the road ahead. Before adjusting the headlight, be sure to consult with local traffic laws and regulations.
2 The headlight beam can be adjusted both vertically and horizontally. Before performing the adjustment, make sure the fuel tank is at least half full, and have an assistant sit on the seat.

1984 Standard models

1 To adjust the headlight vertically, loosen the headlight housing bolts and rotate the housing. Tighten the bolts after adjustment.
2 To adjust the headlight horizontally, turn the adjusting screw in the right side of the headlight rim.

Interstate and Aspencade models

3 Vertical adjustments can be made with the aiming knob above the left fairing pocket (see illustration 7.8a).
4 Horizontal adjustments can be made with the screw behind the trim piece below the headlight assembly (see illustration 7.3).

9 Turn signals and taillight bulbs - replacement

Front turn signal/marker bulbs

Refer to illustrations 9.1 and 9.3

1 To replace a front turn signal/marker bulb, remove the screw that holds the lens/lamp housing to the fairing (see illustration).
2 Take off the lens and gasket.
3 Push the bulb in and turn it counterclockwise to remove it (see illustration). Check the socket terminals for corrosion and clean them if necessary. Line up the pins on the new bulb with the slots in the socket, push in and turn the bulb clockwise until it locks in place. Note: The pins on some bulbs are offset so it can only be installed one way. It is a good idea to use a paper towel or dry cloth when handling the new bulb to prevent injury if the bulb should break and to increase bulb life.
4 Position the lens and gasket on the housing and install the screws. Be careful not to overtighten them or the lens will crack.

Rear lights (1984 Standard model)

5 To replace either turn signal bulb or the tail/brake/license plate light, remove the lens screws and take off the lens.
6 Refer to Step 3 above to remove the old bulb and install the new one.
7 Clean the inside of the lens with soap and water, dry it and install it on the bike. Don't overtighten the screws or the lens may crack.

Saddlebag-mounted brake and taillights (Interstate and Aspencade)

Refer to illustration 9.8

8 Remove the bulb housing nuts from inside the saddlebag. Lower the bulb housing for access to the sockets (see illustration). Twist the socket of the burned-out bulb counterclockwise and remove it from the housing.
9 Refer to Step 3 above to remove the old bulb and install the new one.
10 Reinstall the bulb housing in the saddlebag and install the nuts.

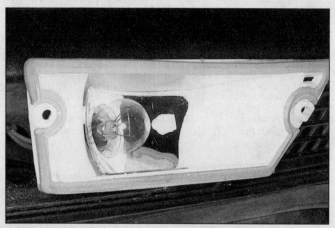

9.3 Pull the bulb out of the socket and push in a new one

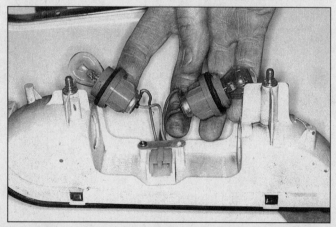

9.8 Twist the sockets counterclockwise and remove them from the housing; press the bulbs in and turn counterclockwise to remove them from the socket

Chapter 9 Electrical system

9.11 Aspencade rear brake lights are accessible from below

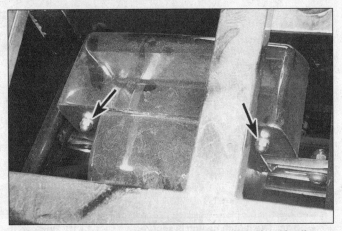

9.13 Remove the nuts (arrows) and take off the housing for access to the license plate bulb

Rear brake lights (Aspencade)

Refer to illustration 9.11

11 Remove the three screws and the lower cover from beneath the trunk. This provides access to the bulb sockets (see illustration).
12 Twist the socket of the burned-out bulb counterclockwise and remove it from the housing. Refer to Step 3 above to remove the old bulb and install the new one. Install the lower cover beneath the trunk.

License plate light (Interstate and Aspencade)

Refer to illustration 9.13

13 Remove the housing nuts and take off the housing (see illustration).
14 Refer to Step 3 above to replace the bulb, then install the housing.

10 Turn signal circuit - check

Refer to illustration 10.3

1 The battery provides power for operation of the signal lights, so if they do not operate, always check the battery voltage and specific gravity first. Low battery voltage indicates either a faulty battery, low electrolyte level or a defective charging system. Refer to Chapter 1 for battery checks and Sections 28 and 29 for charging system tests.
2 Most turn signal problems are the result of a burned out bulb or corroded socket. This is especially true when the turn signals function properly in one direction, but fail to flash in the other direction. Check the bulbs and the sockets (see Section 9).
3 Check the fuses (see Section 5). The turn signal relay can be tested by switching the hazard relay into its position (see illustration).
4 If the fuses and relays are okay, check the wiring in the turn signal circuit (see the wiring diagrams at the end of this Chapter). Make sure the connectors are clean and tight.

11 Brake light switches - check and replacement

Circuit check

Refer to illustration 11.2

1 Before checking any electrical circuit, check the fuses (see Section 5).
2 Using a test light connected to a good ground, check for voltage at the brake light switch (see illustration 6.6 in Chapter 1 and the accompanying illustration). Connect the voltmeter probe into the back of the power wire's terminal without unplugging the connector. If there's no voltage present, check the wire between the switch and the fuse box (see the wiring diagrams at the end of this Chapter).
3 If voltage is available, touch the probe to the other terminal of the switch, then pull the brake lever or depress the brake pedal - if the test light doesn't light up, replace the switch.
4 If the test light does light, check the wiring between the switch and the brake lights (see the wiring diagrams at the end of this Chapter).

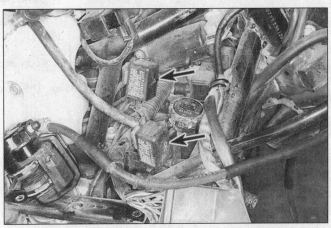

10.3 The turn signal and hazard relays (arrows) are interchangeable

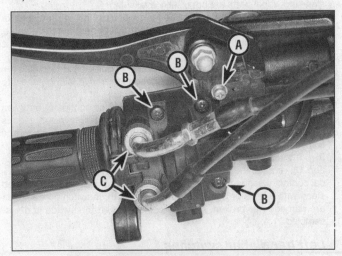

11.2 The front brake light switch is mounted next to the master cylinder

A Brake light switch
B Handlebar switch screws
C Throttle cable locknuts

13.1a The clutch switch is secured by this screw

13.1b Remove the screws from below and separate the upper and lower halves to expose the switches

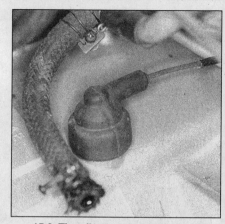

15.2 The oil pressure switch is on top of the engine

Switch replacement

Front brake lever switch

5 Remove the mounting screw and unplug the electrical connector from the switch (see illustration 11.2).
6 Installation is the reverse of the removal procedure. The brake lever switch isn't adjustable.

Rear brake pedal switch

7 Unplug the electrical connector in the switch harness.
8 Unhook the switch spring (see illustration 6.6 in Chapter 1).
9 Turn the plastic nut (not the switch body) until the switch separates from its mounting bracket.
10 Install the switch by reversing the removal procedure, then adjust the switch by following the procedure described in Chapter 1.

12 Handlebar switches - check

1 Generally speaking, the switches are reliable and trouble-free. Most troubles, when they do occur, are caused by dirty or corroded contacts, but wear and breakage of internal parts is a possibility that should not be overlooked. If breakage does occur, the entire switch and related wiring harness will have to be replaced with a new one, since individual parts are not usually available.
2 The switches can be checked for continuity with an ohmmeter or a continuity test light. Always disconnect the battery negative cable, which will prevent the possibility of a short circuit, before making the checks.
3 Trace the wiring harness of the switch in question and unplug the electrical connectors (you'll probably need to remove fairing panels to do this; see Chapter 8).
4 Using the ohmmeter or test light, check for continuity between the terminals of the switch harness with the switches in the various positions. Continuity should exist between the terminals connected by a solid line when the switch is in the indicated position.
5 If the continuity check indicates a problem exists, refer to Section 13, remove the switch and spray the switch contacts with electrical contact cleaner. If they are accessible, the contacts can be scraped clean with a knife or polished with crocus cloth. If switch components are damaged or broken, it will be obvious when the switch is disassembled.

Left handlebar switches

Headlight dimmer switch

6 Lo position - continuity between blue-white and white.
7 Hi position - continuity between blue-white and blue.
8 Middle (N) position - no continuity.

Horn switch

9 Free position - no continuity.
10 Pushed - Continuity between white-green and light green.

Turn signal switch

11 Right turn position - continuity between gray and light blue; brown-white and white; orange and white.
12 Left turn position - continuity between gray and orange; brown-white and white; light blue and white.
13 Middle position - continuity between gray and orange; brown and white; light blue and white.

Right handlebar switches

Brake light switch

14 Lever pulled - continuity.
15 Lever released - no continuity.

13 Handlebar switches - removal and installation

Refer to illustrations 13.1a and 13.1b

1 The handlebar switches are composed of two halves that clamp around the bars. They are easily removed for cleaning or inspection by taking out the clamp screws and pulling the switch halves away from the handlebars (see illustration 11.2 and the accompanying illustrations).
2 To completely remove the switches, the electrical connectors in the wiring harness should be unplugged.
3 When installing the switches, make sure the wiring harnesses are properly routed to avoid pinching or stretching the wires.

14 Clutch switch - check and replacement

Check

1 Disconnect the electrical connector from the clutch switch (see illustration 13.1a).
2 Connect an ohmmeter between the terminals in the clutch switch. With the clutch lever pulled in, the ohmmeter should show continuity (little or no resistance). With the lever out, the ohmmeter should show infinite resistance.
3 If the switch doesn't check out as described, replace it.

Replacement

4 If you haven't already done so, unplug the wiring connector. Remove the mounting screw and take the switch off (see illustration 13.1a).
5 Installation is the reverse of removal.

Chapter 9 Electrical system

16.9 Remove the switch cover . . .

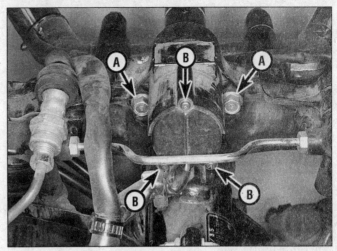

16.10 . . . and the switch mounting bolts

A   Switch mounting bolts   B   Contact base screws

15 Oil pressure switch - removal, check and installation

Refer to illustration 15.2

Check

1 The oil pressure switch is mounted on top of the engine next to the fuel pump.
2 Pull the rubber boot off the switch and disconnect the wire **(see illustration)**.

Light doesn't come on

3 Connect a voltmeter between the switch wire and ground. With the ignition switch in the on position, the voltmeter should indicate battery voltage.
4 If there isn't any voltage, check the oil pressure warning light bulb in the instrument cluster (Section 25). If the bulb is good, check the switch wiring for a break or poor connection.
5 If there is voltage, replace the switch with a new one as described below.

Light stays on

6 Unscrew the switch from the engine and screw a mechanical oil pressure gauge into the switch hole.
7 Run the engine. If the gauge shows oil pressure, replace the switch. If there's still no oil pressure, check the oil level (see Chapter 1). Refer to Chapter 2 and check for clogged oil passages and pickups. Also check the oil pumps for wear or damage.

Replacement

8 Unscrew the switch from the engine and clean the threads in the engine case.
9 Coat the threads of the new switch with sealant, but don't get any sealant on the last 1/8-inch of threads (those that go farthest into the engine). Thread the switch into the engine and tighten it to the torque listed in this Chapter's Specifications.
10 Refer to Chapter 1 and check the oil level.

16 Ignition main (key) switch - check and replacement

Check

1 Follow the wiring harness from the switch to the electrical connector and unplug it.
2 Using an ohmmeter, check the continuity between the terminal pairs indicated in the following steps. Test the switch side of the connector, not the wiring harness side.

3 Lock or off position - no continuity.
4 Acc position - continuity between red and light green-black.
5 On position - continuity between red, black, light green-blue and blue-orange; also continuity between brown-white and brown.
6 P position - Continuity between red, light green-black and brown.
7 If the switch fails any of the tests, replace it.

Replacement

Refer to illustrations 16.9, 16.10 and 16.11

8 If you're working on a 1984 Standard model, remove the headlight housing.
9 If you're working on an Interstate or Aspencade, remove the handlebars and the upper triple clamp (see Chapter 6). Remove the switch cover **(see illustration)**.
10 Remove the switch mounting bolts **(see illustration)**.
11 Free the switch harness from the retainer and unplug the switch electrical connector **(see illustration)**.
12 To separate the contact base from the switch, bend open the wiring harness clamp at the switch. Push the lugs out of the slots on the switch or remove the base screws and take the contact base off.
13 Reverse the removal procedure to install the contact base.
14 The remainder of installation is the reverse of the removal procedure.

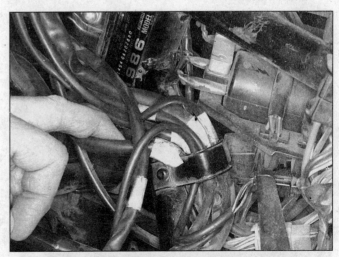

16.11 Free the harness from the retainer and unplug the electrical connector

17 Gear position switch (gearshift sensor) - check, removal and installation

Check

1 Remove the bottom cover from the fairing (see Chapter 8). Unplug the switch connector (it's the black six-pin connector under the instrument cluster).
2 Turn the ignition switch to the On position.
3 Connect a length wire to a convenient ground (nearby bare metal). Move the other end of the wire to each of the connector pins in turn (the cluster side of the connector, not the harness side). The gear position indicator should light up as follows:
   a) First gear - yellow wire
   b) Neutral - light green-red wire
   c) Second gear - blue-yellow wire
   d) Third gear - white-blue wire
   e) Fourth gear - red-white wire
   f) Green-orange wire

Replacement

4 The switch is mounted inside the front engine cover. Refer to Chapter 2 for removal and installation procedures.

18 Horn - check and replacement

18.1 Disconnect the wires and remove the bracket bolt to detach the horn

Check

Refer to illustration 18.1

1 Unplug the electrical connectors from the horn **(see illustration)**. Using two jumper wires, apply battery voltage directly to the terminals on the horn. If the horn sounds, check the switch (see Section 13) and the wiring between the switch and the horn (see the wiring diagrams at the end of this Chapter).
2 If the horn doesn't sound, replace it.

Replacement

3 Unbolt the horn bracket from the frame **(see illustration 18.1)** and detach the electrical connectors.
4 Unbolt the horn from the bracket and transfer the bracket to the new horn.
5 Installation is the reverse of removal.

19 Speedometer cable (Standard and Interstate) removal and installation

1 If you're working on a Standard model, refer to Section 7 and remove the headlight bulb. Remove the headlight case bolt on each side and take the case off.
2 Unscrew the knurled speedometer cable nut from the underside of the speedometer.
3 Remove the attaching screw from the speedometer drive unit at the front wheel.
4 Free the cable from its retainers and take it off the bike.

Installation

5 Installation is the reverse of the removal procedure, with the following additions:
   a) Be sure the speedometer cable is routed so it doesn't cause the steering to bind or interfere with other components.
   b) Be sure the squared-off ends of the cable fit into their spindles in the speedometer and drive gear.
   c) If you're working on a Standard model, check the headlight aim (Section 8).

20 Speed sensor (Aspencade) - removal, check and installation

Removal

Refer to illustrations 20.1a and 20.1b

1 Note how the speed sensor harness is routed at the front brake caliper, then remove its mounting screw **(see illustrations)**.

20.1a Note the routing of the cable over the anti-dive bracket (arrow) . . .

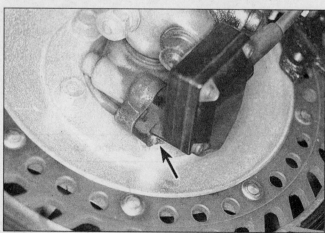

20.1b . . . and remove the screw (arrow) to separate the cable or speed sensor from the drive unit (speed sensor shown)

Chapter 9 Electrical system

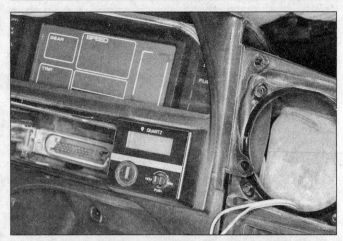

21.7a Remove the mounting screws at each end of the cluster trim cover . . .

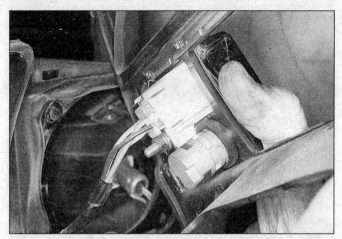

21.7b . . . and lift it off; follow the wiring harness from the clock to its connector and unplug it

2 If you're planning to check the sensor, leave the harness connected to the instrument cluster for the time being. If not, unplug he connector. Free the harness from its retainers and take it off.

Check

3 Insert the probes of a voltmeter into the back of the black-brown and black-yellow terminals in the connector (the connector should be connected).

21.9a Remove the lower mounting nut . . .

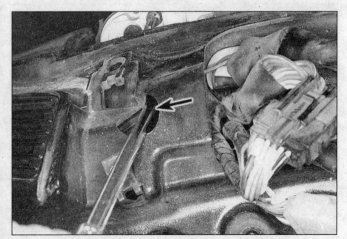

21.9b . . . and the upper nuts (arrow) to free the cluster, then lift it up and unplug the electrical connectors

4 Turn the ignition key to the On position.
5 Insert a screwdriver into the slot in the drive unit and rotate it slowly one full turn. The voltmeter should swing from zero to about 5 volts eight times.
6 If the sensor doesn't perform as described, check the wiring and connector. If they're okay, replace the sensor.

Installation

7 Installation is the reverse of the removal steps.

21 Instrument cluster - removal and installation

Standard models

1 Refer to Section 7 and remove the headlight bulb. Disconnect the cluster electrical connectors inside the headlight case. Remove the headlight case bolt on each side and take the case off.
2 Refer to Section 19 and disconnect the speedometer cable.
3 Remove two mounting nuts from the underside of the cluster and lift it off.
4 Installation is the reverse of the removal steps.

Interstate and Aspencade

Refer to illustrations 21.7a, 21.7b, 21.9a and 21.9b

5 Remove the windshield (see Chapter 8).
6 Remove the radio and speakers (Section 32).
7 Remove the cluster trim cover, together with the clock **(see illustrations)**.
8 Follow the wiring harnesses for the cluster to the electrical connectors and unplug them.
9 Remove the cluster mounting nuts **(see illustrations)**.
10 If you're working on an Interstate, disconnect the speedometer cable from the speedometer.
11 Lift the cluster and bracket out of the fairing.
12 Installation is the reverse of the removal steps.

22 Meters and gauges - check

Coolant temperature gauge

1 Refer to Chapter 4 for coolant temperature gauge checking procedures.

Tachometer and speedometer

2 Special instruments are required to properly check the operation of these meters. Take the instrument cluster to a Honda dealer service department or other qualified repair shop for diagnosis.

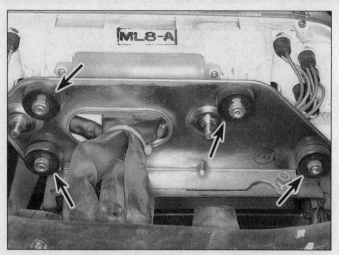

23.1 Remove the mounting nuts and bushings (arrows) and separate the cluster from the bracket

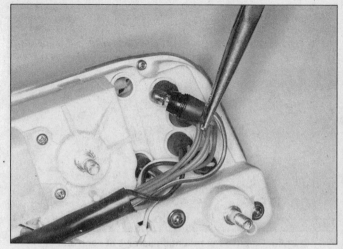

23.2 Pull the bulb socket out of the cluster, then pull the bulb out of the socket

23 Instrument and warning light bulbs - replacement

Refer to illustrations 23.1 and 23.2

1 Remove the instrument cluster (see Section 21). If necessary for access to a particular bulb, remove the mounting nuts and take the bracket off the back of the cluster **(see illustration)**.
2 To replace a bulb, pull the appropriate rubber socket out of the back of the instrument cluster housing **(see illustration)**, then pull the bulb out of the socket. If the socket contacts are dirty or corroded, they should be scraped clean and sprayed with electrical contact cleaner before new bulbs are installed.
3 Carefully push the new bulb into position, then push the socket into the cluster housing.
4 Reinstall the instrument cluster.

24 Starter relay - check and replacement

1 Make sure the battery is fully charged and the relay wiring connections are clean and tight.
2 Remove the left side cover (see Chapter 8).
3 Locate the starter relay behind to the battery **(see illustration 5.1c)**. Turn the ignition switch to the on position, then press the starter button. The relay should click as the wire is connected and disconnected.
4 If the relay doesn't click, disconnect the wires and remove it from its mount. Connect an ohmmeter to the two threaded posts on the relay. The ohmmeter should indicate no continuity (infinite resistance).
5 Connect the motorcycle's battery to the two flat terminals. The ohmmeter should now indicate continuity (little or no resistance).
6 If the relay doesn't test correctly, remove it.

25 Starter motor - removal and installation

Refer to illustrations 25.2, 25.3 and 25.5

Removal

1 Remove two bolts and take the sheet cover off the starter motor.
2 Pull back the rubber cover, remove the nut retaining the starter cable to the starter and disconnect the cable **(see illustration)**.
3 Remove the starter mounting bolts **(see illustration)**.
4 Lift the front end of the starter up a little bit and slide the starter forward out of the engine case. Rotate the front of the starter outward, then pull it away from the bike.
5 Check the condition of the O-ring on the end of the starter and replace it if necessary **(see illustration)**. Also check the starter pinion gear and the driven gear inside the engine for chipped or worn teeth.

Installation

6 Apply a little engine oil to the O-ring and install the starter by reversing the removal procedure.

25.2 Pull back the cover, remove the nut and disconnect the cable from the starter

25.3 Remove the mounting bolts (arrows)

Chapter 9 Electrical system   9-13

25.5 Pull the starter out of the engine and remove its O-ring

26 Charging system testing - general information and precautions

1 If the performance of the charging system is suspect, the system as a whole should be checked first, followed by testing of the individual alternator components (the brushes, slip rings and coils). **Note:** *Before beginning the checks, make sure the battery is fully charged and that all system connections are clean and tight.*

2 Checking the output of the charging system and the performance of the various components within the charging system requires the use of special electrical test equipment. A voltmeter and ammeter or a multimeter are the absolute minimum tools required. In addition, an ohmmeter is generally required for checking the remainder of the system.

3 When making the checks, follow the procedures carefully to prevent incorrect connections or short circuits, as irreparable damage to electrical system components may result if short circuits occur. Because of the special tools and expertise required, it is recommended that the job of checking the charging system be left to a dealer service department or a reputable motorcycle repair shop. **Caution:** *Never disconnect the battery cables from the battery while the engine is running. If the battery is disconnected, the alternator will be damaged.*

27 Charging system - leakage and output test

1 If a charging system problem is suspected, perform the following checks. Start by removing the left rear side cover for access to the battery (see Chapter 8).

Leakage test

Refer to illustration 27.3

2 Turn the ignition switch off and disconnect the cable from the battery negative terminal.

3 Set the multimeter to the mA (milliamps) function and connect its negative probe to the battery negative terminal, and the positive probe to the disconnected negative cable **(see illustration)**. **Caution:** *Don't connect the ammeter between the battery terminals or the ammeter will be ruined.* Compare the reading to the value listed in this Chapter's Specifications.

4 If the reading is too high there is probably a short circuit in the wiring. Thoroughly check the wiring between the various components (see the wiring diagrams at the end of the book).

5 If the reading is satisfactory, disconnect the meter and connect the negative cable to the battery, tightening it securely. Check the alternator output as described below.

Output test

6 Warm the engine to normal operating temperature, then shut it off.

7 Remove the main fuse **(see illustration 5.1c)**. Connect an ammeter between the fuse holder terminals. **Note:** *The ammeter should be able to measure current flow in both directions.*

8 Connect the positive terminal of a voltmeter to the battery positive terminal and the voltmeter's negative terminal to the battery negative terminal (leave the battery cables connected to the battery).

9 Start the engine and let it idle. If the cooling fan is running, wait until it shuts off. Compare the ammeter and voltmeter readings to the values listed in this Chapter's Specifications. If they're not within the specified ranges, perform the tests in Section 28. **Note:** *If the voltmeter reading is above the specified range, the regulator/rectifier is probably defective.*

28 Regulator/rectifier - check and replacement

Refer to illustration 28.3

1 The regulator/rectifier is located inside the left side of the fairing.

2 Remove the seat and top compartment (see Chapter 8).

3 Follow the wiring harness from the regulator/rectifier to its connector and unplug it **(see illustration)**.

4 Connect an ohmmeter between the terminals in the regulator side of the connector (not the wiring harness side). Note the readings:

a) *Positive to each of three yellows in turn, negative to green - 5 to 40 ohms*
b) *Positive to red-white, negative to each of three yellows in turn - 5 to 40 ohms*
c) *Positive to green, negative to each of three yellows in turn - no continuity (at least 6000 ohms)*
d) *Positive to each of three yellows in turn, negative to red-white - no continuity (at least 6000 ohms)*

5 If the regulator doesn't test correctly, unbolt it and install a new one.

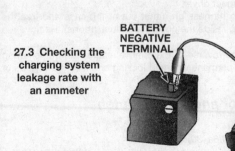

27.3 Checking the charging system leakage rate with an ammeter

28.3 Unplug the regulator/rectifier connector at the bracket (arrow)

9-14 Chapter 9 Electrical system

29.2 The stator wires are often soldered, as shown here; if so, you'll have to cut them

30.3 Remove the screws and plate (you'll need an impact driver) to free the stator from the housing

30.4a Push the grommet out of the housing with a socket

30.4b Free the harness from the clip

30.6a The holder tool fits into this hole in the alternator rotor; its lower end fits into a crankcase hole

29 Alternator stator - check

Stator check

Refer to illustration 29.2

1 Remove the left side cover (see Chapter 8).
2 Locate the three stator wires and disconnect them **(see illustration)**. **Note:** *A common repair on these motorcycles involved replacing the stator and permanently connecting the wires, eliminating the connector. If this has been done, you'll need to cut the wires.*
3 Connect an ohmmeter between pairs of wires in turn (on the alternator side, not the harness side), so that all three wires are connected in pairs to each other. In each case, there should be continuity (little or no resistance).
4 Connect the ohmmeter between each stator wire (the alternator side) and ground. There should be no continuity (infinite resistance).
5 If the stator doesn't test correctly, refer to Section 30 and replace it.

30 Alternator rotor and starter clutch - removal and installation

1 Remove the engine from the frame and remove the rear engine cover from the crankcase (see Chapter 2).

Alternator stator

Refer to illustrations 30.3, 30.4a and 30.4b

2 The stator is mounted in the rear engine cover.
3 Remove the stator screws and plate **(see illustration)**. You'll probably need an impact driver.
4 Push the wiring harness grommet out of the case and free the harness from the clip inside the cover **(see illustrations)**. Remove the stator.
5 Installation is the reverse of the removal steps with the following addition: Apply non-permanent thread locking agent to the threads of the stator screws.

Alternator rotor and starter clutch

Removal

Refer to illustrations 30.6a, 30.6b and 30.7

6 Hold the rotor from turning with Honda tool 07925-3710100 or equivalent **(see illustration)**. Unscrew the rotor nut and remove the washer **(see illustration)**. The bolt on the end of the alternator drive

30.6b Undo the nut and washer to remove the rotor; the bolt need not be removed

Chapter 9 Electrical system

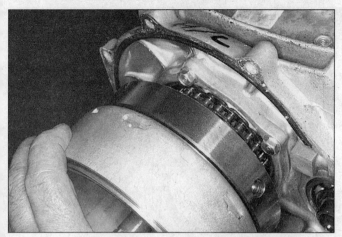

30.7 Pull the rotor and starter clutch off the shaft

30.9a Slip the sprocket into the starter clutch . . .

30.9b . . . and try to turn it both ways; it should turn in one direction only

shaft need not be removed; it's used to turn the engine during installation of the engine in the motorcycle.

7   Pull the rotor off the shaft together with the starter clutch, which is mounted on the back of the rotor **(see illustration)**.

Inspection

Refer to illustrations 30.9a, 309b and 30.10

8   The alternator rotor doesn't rub against anything as it rotates, so it shouldn't be worn or damaged. If it is, replace it. The rotor should also be replaced if the magnets are weak.

9   Try to rotate the starter clutch on its sprocket **(see illustrations)**. If the sprocket is still on the engine, slip the starter clutch over it. The starter clutch should turn one way only. If it turns both ways or neither way, check for worn or damaged parts (see below).

10 Remove the rollers, springs and pins from the starter clutch **(see illustration)**. If any of the parts are worn or damaged, replace them. Check the friction surface on the driven sprocket; if it's worn or damaged, replace it.

Installation

Refer to illustration 30.11

11 Installation is the reverse of the removal steps. Use non-permanent thread locking agent on the threads of the nut. Don't forget to install the plain washer **(see illustration)**.

31 Alternator drive unit and starter drive chain - removal, inspection and installation

Note: *Installing the alternator drive unit is a complicated procedure that requires a dial indicator to adjust its backlash. If backlash is incorrect, the unit will make noise.*

Removal

Refer to illustrations 31.2 and 31.3

1   Remove the alternator rotor and starter clutch (Section 30).

30.10 The springs fit into holes in the starter clutch; the pins fit over the springs and secure the rollers in their holes

30.11 Don't forget the washer when reinstalling the rotor nut

31.2 The sprocket guide plate tab (arrow) is upward when installed; on some models, it's turned downward temporarily during installation

31.3 Pull the drive unit out of the engine; the long bolt goes in the hole with the dowel

2 Remove the sprocket guide plate, then slip the drive chain and sprockets off the alternator drive unit and starter motor **(see illustration)**.

3 Unbolt the drive unit (and the starter chain guide on 1986 and 1987 models). Take the chain guide off and pull the alternator drive unit out of the engine **(see illustration)**.

Inspection

Refer to illustrations 31.5, 31.6 and 31.7

4 Check the both starter sprockets and the chain for wear or damage. Replace the chain and sprockets as a set if problems are found.

5 Inspect the needle roller bearing inside the driven sprocket **(see illustration)**. If it's worn, damaged or corroded, remove its snap-ring and install a new one, using a new snap-ring.

6 Check the gear teeth on the alternator drive unit for wear or damage **(see illustration)**. Spin the alternator drive shaft and check for rough, loose or noisy movement. If problems are found the unit can be disassembled and repaired. However, this requires a press and several special attachments and is a job that even experienced Honda mechanics aren't eager to take on. Repair should be done by a Honda dealer service department or other qualified shop.

7 Check the drive unit's ball bearing in the crankcase **(see illustration)**. If it's rough loose or noisy when rotated, you'll need to remove the crankshaft for access to remove it (see Chapter 2).

Installation and backlash adjustment

Refer to illustration 31.21

8 Clean all old gasket from the drive unit's mating surfaces, then install a new gasket.

9 Make sure the dowel is in place and install the drive unit in the engine.

10 Install the long bolt in the hole with the dowel and tighten it slightly.

31.5 Because the engine must be removed to get to this bearing, it should be replaced if there's any doubt about its condition

31.6 Check the drive unit gear for worn or damaged teeth

31.7 The drive unit's front bearing is mounted inside the crankcase

Chapter 9 Electrical system 9-17

31.21 Correct backlash is necessary to prevent drive unit noise

1984 and 1985 models
11 Install the sprocket guide plate and the other three bolts and tighten them slightly. Rotate the guide plate so its finger faces downward (180-degrees out from its installed position). **Note:** *If you can't rotate the guide plate, the bolt is too tight.*

1986 and 1987 models
12 Install the bolt to the right of the long bolt, but don't install the two bolts that also secure the chain guide. Tighten the bolts slightly, but don't torque them yet.
13 Install the chain guide. Tighten its two lower bolts securely, but don't strip the threads or crack the plastic.
14 Install the remaining two alternator drive unit bolts and tighten them slightly. Don't install the guide plate yet.

All models
15 Lubricate the needle bearing in the starter driven sprocket with Honda Moly 45 grease or equivalent. Lubricate the rollers with the same grease. Install the driven sprocket in the starter clutch, using a rotating motion to push the rollers out of the way **(see illustration 30.9a)**.
16 Place the drive chain on the starter driven sprocket, which is now installed on the back of the alternator rotor/starter clutch assembly. If you're working on a 1984 or 1985 model, install the drive (small) sprocket in the chain.
17 Install the alternator rotor on its shaft, together with the starter clutch, sprocket and chain **(see illustrations 30.6b and 30.7)**.

1984 and 1985 models
18 Engage the drive sprocket with the starter motor.

19 Apply non-permanent locking agent to the threads of the rotor locknut, then install the plain washer and locknut on the alternator rotor **(see illustration 30.11)**. Tighten the nut to the torque listed in this Chapter's Specifications.

1986 and 1987 models
20 Install the plain washer and rotor nut without thread locking agent, then tighten the nut to the torque listed in this Chapter's Specifications. You'll need to remove the nut after adjusting the backlash.

All models
21 Set up a dial indicator contacting one of the holes in the alternator rotor **(see illustration)**. Rotate the rotor back and forth against the dial indicator's plunger and note the reading.
22 If the reading is within the range listed in this Chapter's Specifications, continue with Step 25 below.
23 If the backlash is too little, carefully tap the starter clutch away from the crankshaft with a soft-faced mallet. Don't tap against the rotor itself.
24 If the backlash is too great, tap the starter clutch toward the crankshaft.
25 Recheck the backlash at three evenly spaced points around the rotor. Continue to adjust it until it's with the specified range.

1984 and 1985 models
26 Once backlash is properly set, rotate the finger of the guide plate up into its installed position, then tighten the drive unit bolts.

1986 and 1987 models
27 Remove the alternator rotor and starter clutch (Section 30).
28 Install the guide plate, then tighten the drive unit bolts to the torque listed in this Chapter's Specifications.
29 Reinstall the starter clutch and rotor (Section 30). Install the rotor washer and nut, this time using non-permanent thread locking agent.
30 Place the starter drive sprocket in the chain with its hub offset toward the starter motor. Slip the sprocket into the starter motor shaft.

All models
31 Recheck the backlash of the alternator drive unit.
32 The remainder of installation is the reverse of the removal steps.

32 Radio and speakers - removal, check and installation

Radio
Refer to illustrations 32.1 and 32.2

1 To remove the radio, unlock it with the key and slide it out **(see illustration)**.
2 Installation is the reverse of removal. Engage the radio with the rail inside its opening **(see illustration)**.

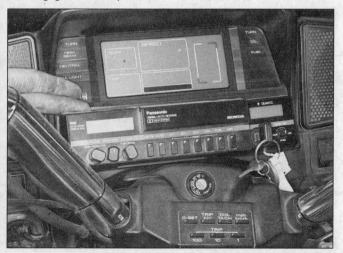

32.1 Unlock the radio with the ignition key . . .

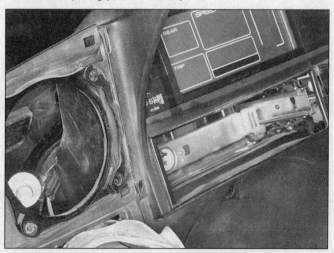

32.2 . . . and pull it out of the opening

Chapter 9 Electrical system

32.3 Pry up the speaker cover trim with a pointed tool, remove the cover screw and take off the cover . . .

32.4 . . . to expose the speaker screws; the drain slots (arrows) go at the top and bottom on installation

Speakers

Removal

Refer to illustrations 32.3 and 32.4

3   Pry the trim piece from the speaker cover screw, undo the screw and remove the cover **(see illustration)**.

4   Undo the speaker mounting screws **(see illustration)**. Pull the speaker out, disconnect its wires and remove it.

Check

5   Select the smallest range on an ohmmeter, then connect it to the speaker wire terminals. The speaker should click instantly when the ohmmeter is connected.

Installation

6   Installation is the reverse of the removal steps. Position the drain slots in the edge of the speaker at top and bottom.

33 Wiring diagrams

Prior to troubleshooting a circuit, check the fuses to make sure they're in good condition. Make sure the battery is fully charged and check the cable connections.

When checking a circuit, make sure all connectors are clean, with no broken or loose terminals or wires. When unplugging a connector, don't pull on the wires - pull only on the connector housings themselves.

Wiring diagrams

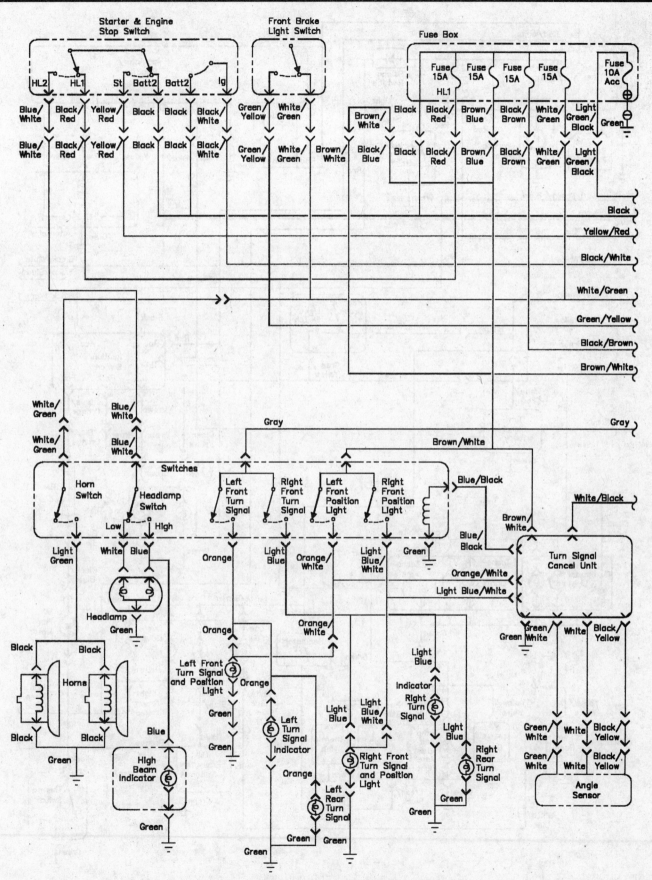

1984 GL1200 Standard wiring diagram - 1 of 3

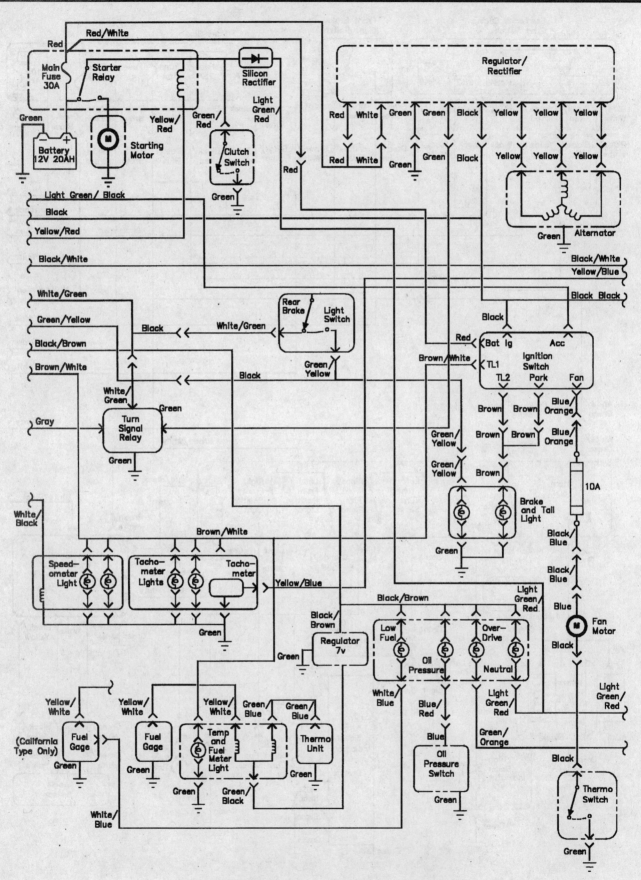

Wiring diagrams

Switch Continuity

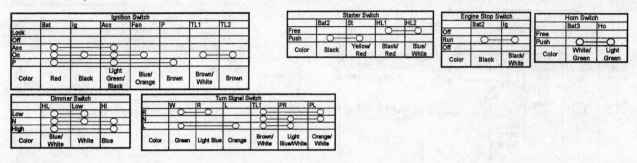

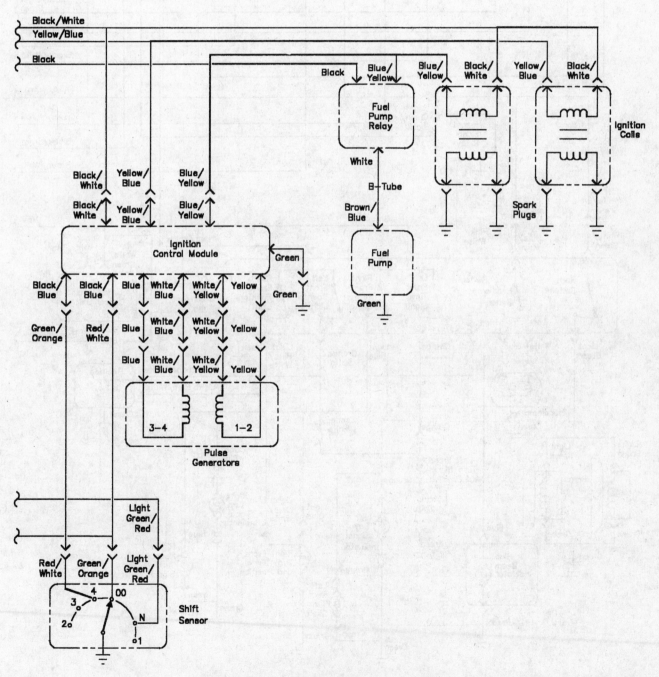

1984 GL1200 Standard wiring diagram - 3 of 3

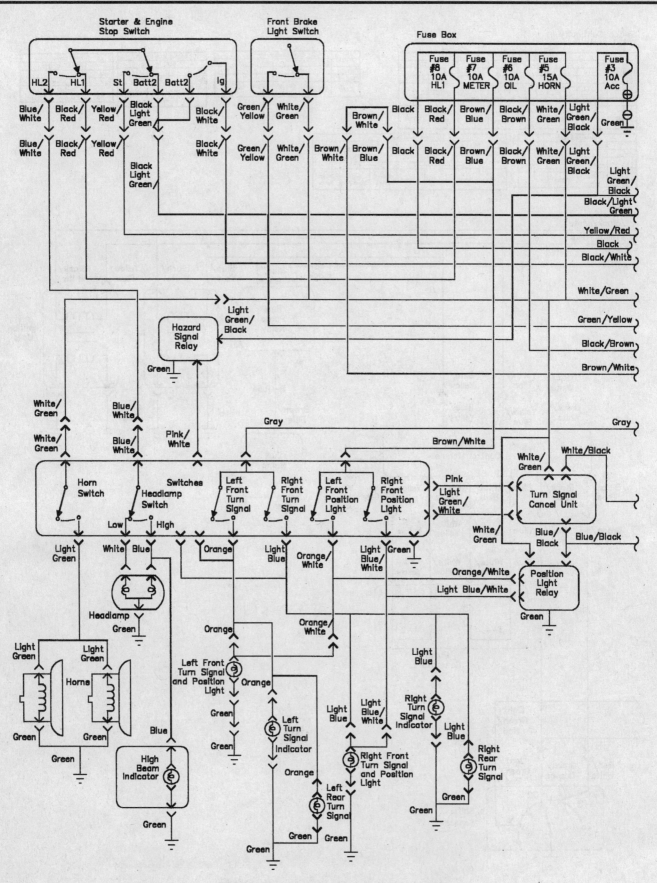

Wiring diagrams

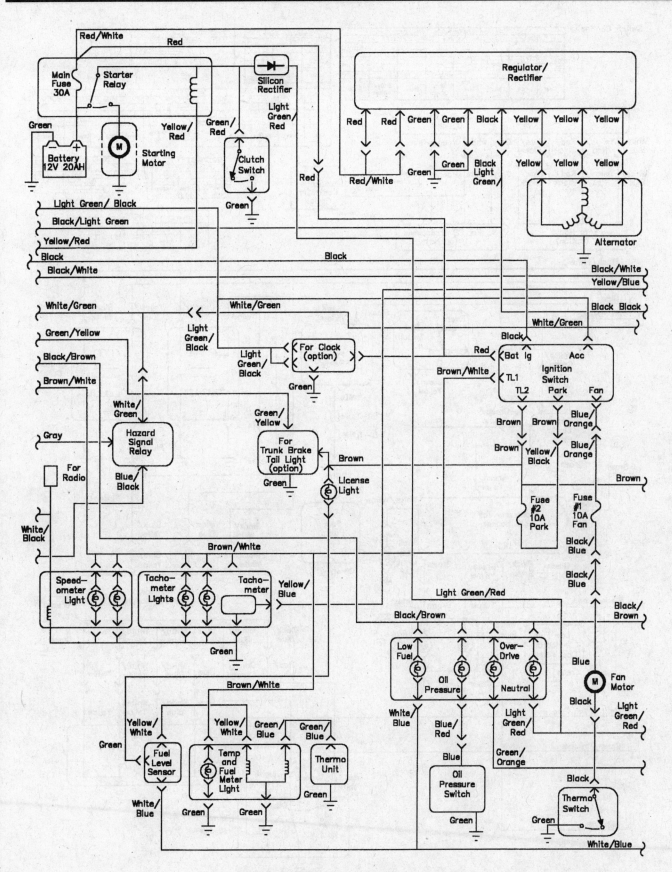

1985 GL1200 Interstate wiring diagram - 2 of 3

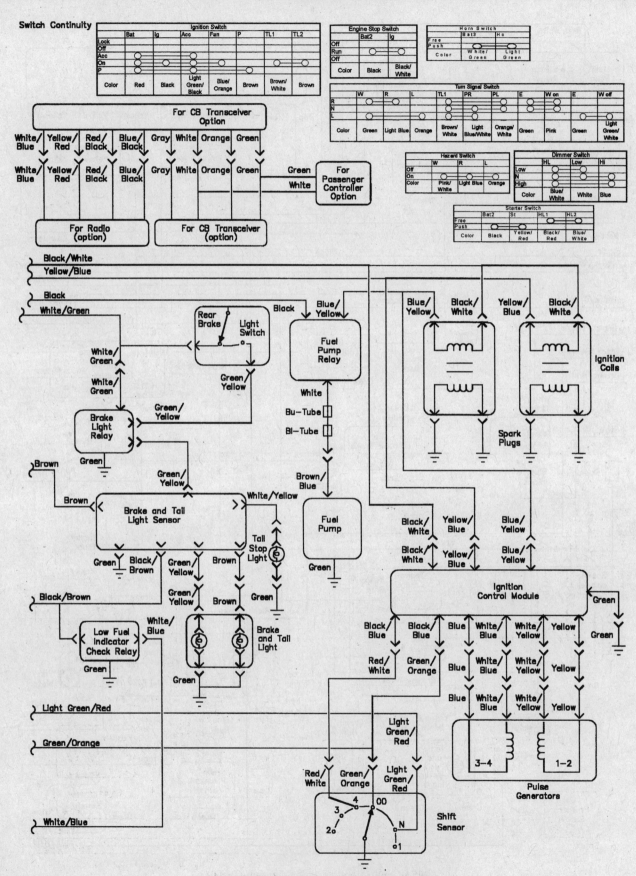

Wiring diagrams

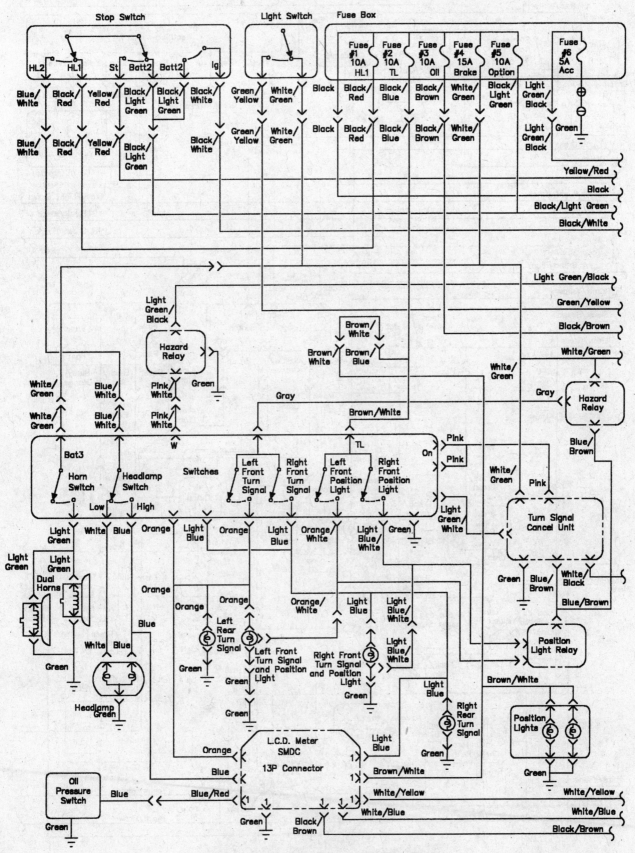

1986 GL1200 Aspencade wiring diagram - 1 of 4

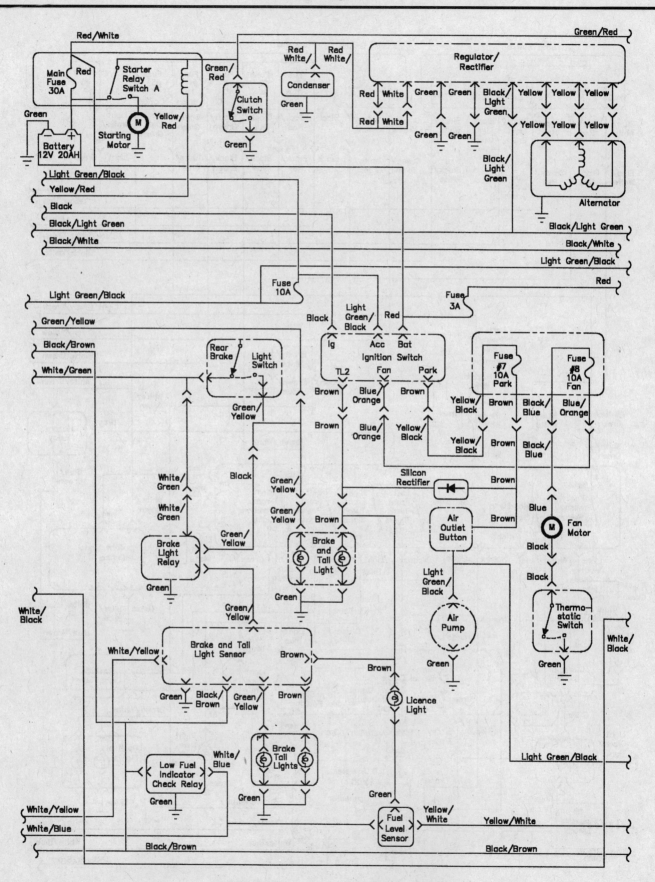

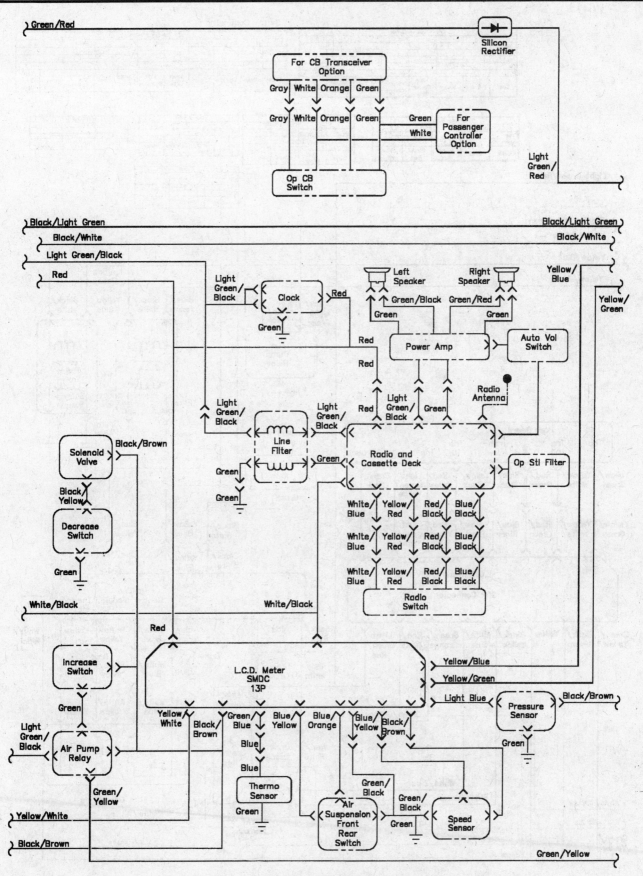

Wiring diagrams

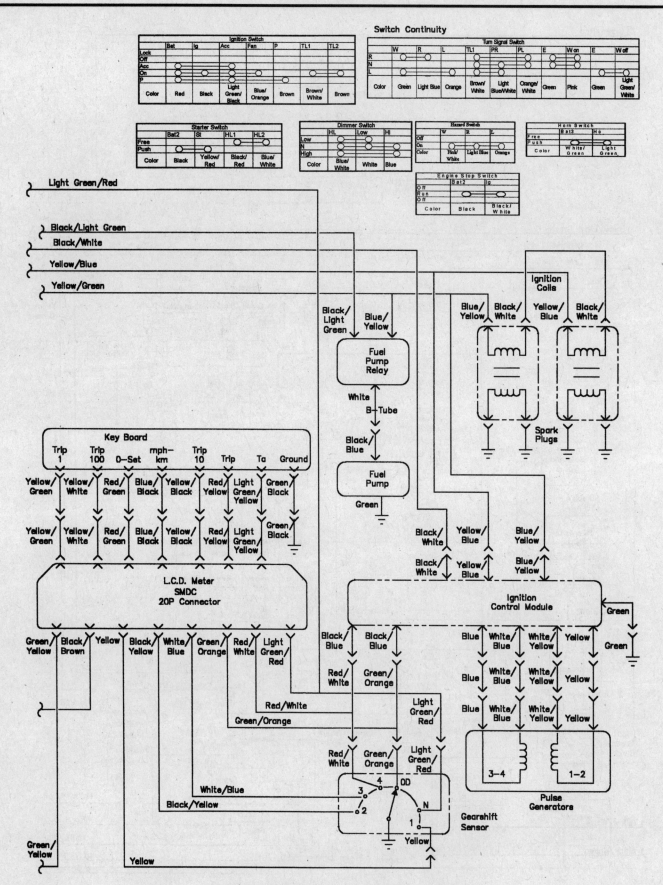

1986 GL1200 Aspencade wiring diagram - 4 of 4

Wiring diagrams

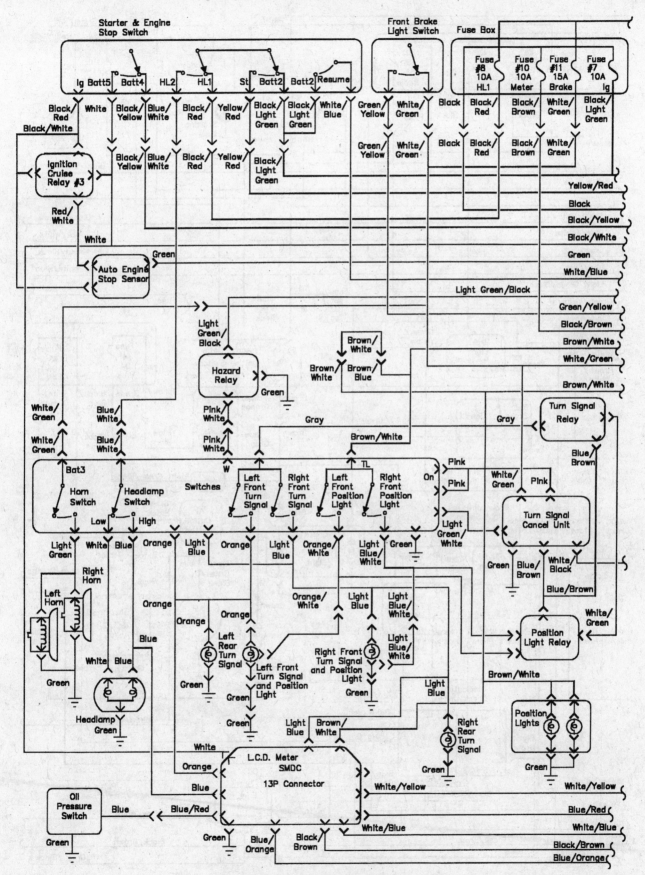

1987 GL1200 Aspencade wiring diagram - 1 of 4

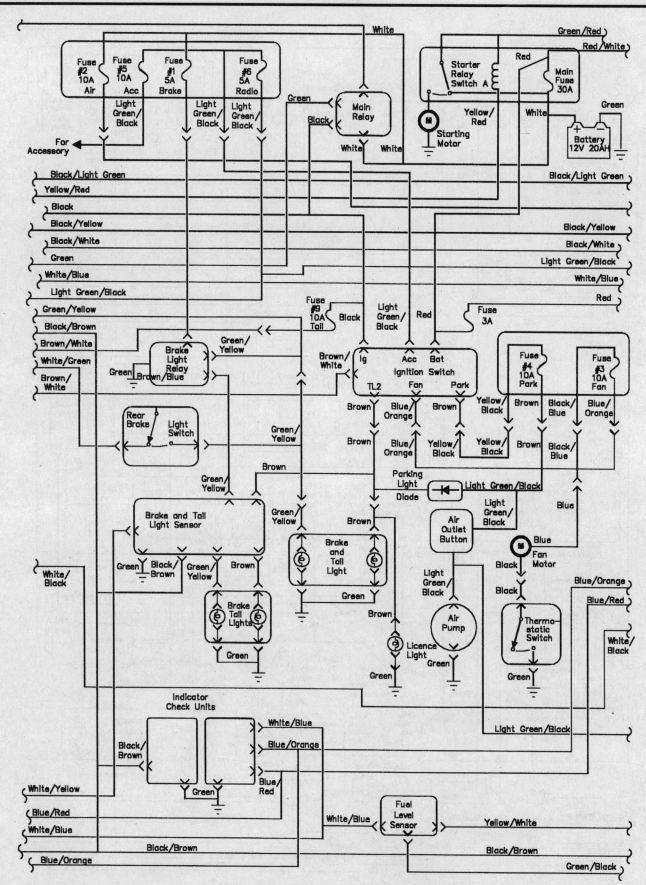

Wiring diagrams

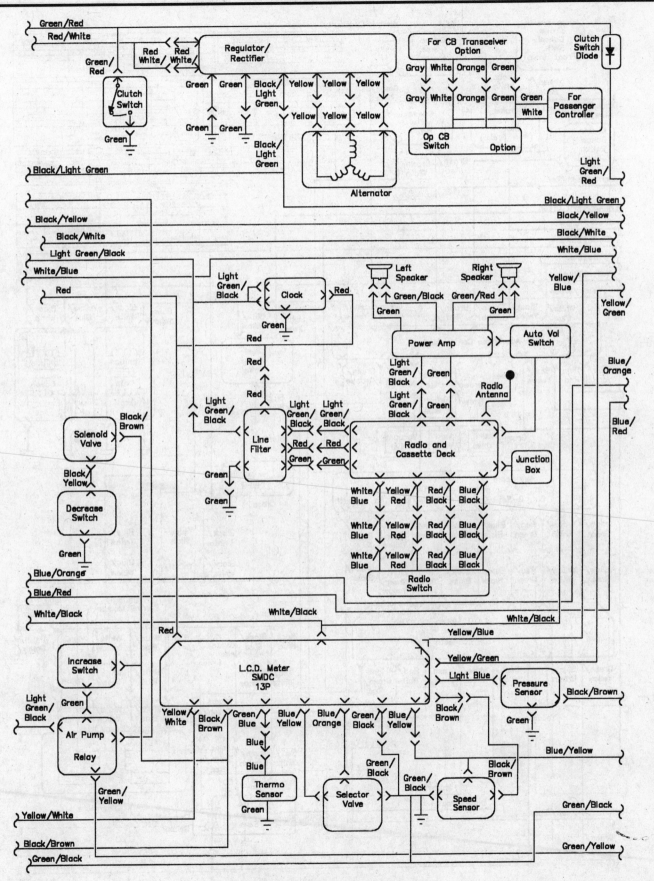

1987 GL1200 Aspencade wiring diagram - 3 of 4

Wiring diagrams

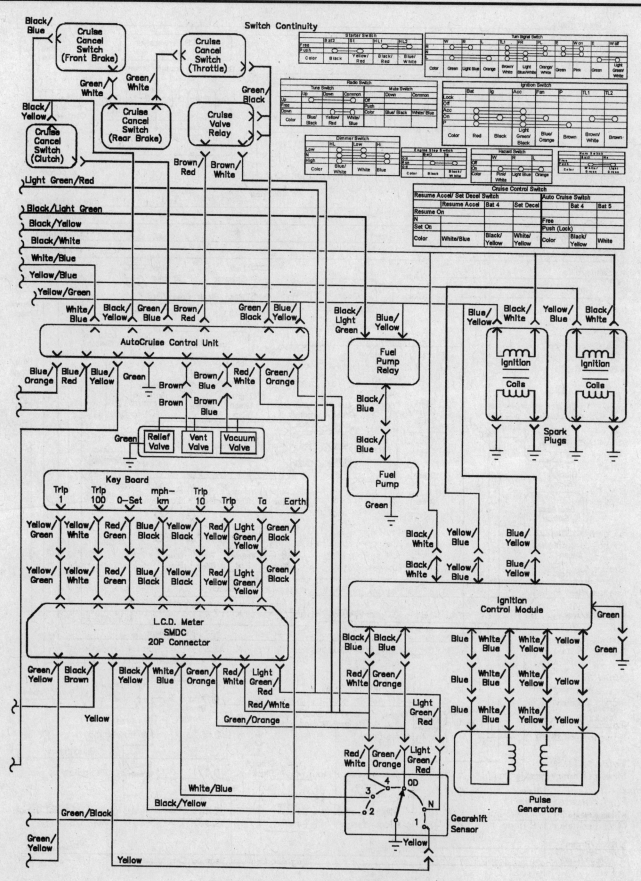

1987 GL1200 Aspencade wiring diagram - 4 of 4

Conversion factors

Length (distance)
Inches (in)	X 25.4	= Millimetres (mm)	X 0.0394	= Inches (in)
Feet (ft)	X 0.305	= Metres (m)	X 3.281	= Feet (ft)
Miles	X 1.609	= Kilometres (km)	X 0.621	= Miles

Volume (capacity)
Cubic inches (cu in; in^3)	X 16.387	= Cubic centimetres (cc; cm^3)	X 0.061	= Cubic inches (cu in; in^3)
Imperial pints (Imp pt)	X 0.568	= Litres (l)	X 1.76	= Imperial pints (Imp pt)
Imperial quarts (Imp qt)	X 1.137	= Litres (l)	X 0.88	= Imperial quarts (Imp qt)
Imperial quarts (Imp qt)	X 1.201	= US quarts (US qt)	X 0.833	= Imperial quarts (Imp qt)
US quarts (US qt)	X 0.946	= Litres (l)	X 1.057	= US quarts (US qt)
Imperial gallons (Imp gal)	X 4.546	= Litres (l)	X 0.22	= Imperial gallons (Imp gal)
Imperial gallons (Imp gal)	X 1.201	= US gallons (US gal)	X 0.833	= Imperial gallons (Imp gal)
US gallons (US gal)	X 3.785	= Litres (l)	X 0.264	= US gallons (US gal)

Mass (weight)
Ounces (oz)	X 28.35	= Grams (g)	X 0.035	= Ounces (oz)
Pounds (lb)	X 0.454	= Kilograms (kg)	X 2.205	= Pounds (lb)

Force
Ounces-force (ozf; oz)	X 0.278	= Newtons (N)	X 3.6	= Ounces-force (ozf; oz)
Pounds-force (lbf; lb)	X 4.448	= Newtons (N)	X 0.225	= Pounds-force (lbf; lb)
Newtons (N)	X 0.1	= Kilograms-force (kgf; kg)	X 9.81	= Newtons (N)

Pressure
Pounds-force per square inch (psi; lbf/in^2; lb/in^2)	X 0.070	= Kilograms-force per square centimetre (kgf/cm^2; kg/cm^2)	X 14.223	= Pounds-force per square inch (psi; lbf/in^2; lb/in^2)
Pounds-force per square inch (psi; lbf/in^2; lb/in^2)	X 0.068	= Atmospheres (atm)	X 14.696	= Pounds-force per square inch (psi; lbf/in^2; lb/in^2)
Pounds-force per square inch (psi; lbf/in^2; lb/in^2)	X 0.069	= Bars	X 14.5	= Pounds-force per square inch (psi; lbf/in^2; lb/in^2)
Pounds-force per square inch (psi; lbf/in^2; lb/in^2)	X 6.895	= Kilopascals (kPa)	X 0.145	= Pounds-force per square inch (psi; lbf/in^2; lb/in^2)
Kilopascals (kPa)	X 0.01	= Kilograms-force per square centimetre (kgf/cm^2; kg/cm^2)	X 98.1	= Kilopascals (kPa)

Torque (moment of force)
Pounds-force inches (lbf in; lb in)	X 1.152	= Kilograms-force centimetre (kgf cm; kg cm)	X 0.868	= Pounds-force inches (lbf in; lb in)
Pounds-force inches (lbf in; lb in)	X 0.113	= Newton metres (Nm)	X 8.85	= Pounds-force inches (lbf in; lb in)
Pounds-force inches (lbf in; lb in)	X 0.083	= Pounds-force feet (lbf ft; lb ft)	X 12	= Pounds-force inches (lbf in; lb in)
Pounds-force feet (lbf ft; lb ft)	X 0.138	= Kilograms-force metres (kgf m; kg m)	X 7.233	= Pounds-force feet (lbf ft; lb ft)
Pounds-force feet (lbf ft; lb ft)	X 1.356	= Newton metres (Nm)	X 0.738	= Pounds-force feet (lbf ft; lb ft)
Newton metres (Nm)	X 0.102	= Kilograms-force metres (kgf m; kg m)	X 9.804	= Newton metres (Nm)

Vacuum
Inches mercury (in. Hg)	X 3.377	= Kilopascals (kPa)	X 0.2961	= Inches mercury
Inches mercury (in. Hg)	X 25.4	= Millimeters mercury (mm Hg)	X 0.0394	= Inches mercury

Power
Horsepower (hp)	X 745.7	= Watts (W)	X 0.0013	= Horsepower (hp)

Velocity (speed)
Miles per hour (miles/hr; mph)	X 1.609	= Kilometres per hour (km/hr; kph)	X 0.621	= Miles per hour (miles/hr; mph)

Fuel consumption*
Miles per gallon, Imperial (mpg)	X 0.354	= Kilometres per litre (km/l)	X 2.825	= Miles per gallon, Imperial (mpg)
Miles per gallon, US (mpg)	X 0.425	= Kilometres per litre (km/l)	X 2.352	= Miles per gallon, US (mpg)

Temperature
Degrees Fahrenheit = (°C x 1.8) + 32   Degrees Celsius (Degrees Centigrade; °C) = (°F - 32) x 0.56

*It is common practice to convert from miles per gallon (mpg) to litres/100 kilometres (l/100km), where mpg (Imperial) x l/100 km = 282 and mpg (US) x l/100 km = 235

Notes

Index

A

About this manual, 0-5
Air compressor (on-board), removal, desiccant replacement and installation, 6-12
Air filter
    element, servicing, 1-11
    housing, removal and installation, 4-4
Alternator
    drive unit and starter drive chain, removal, inspection and installation, 9-15
    rotor and starter clutch, removal and installation, 9-14
    stator, check, 9-14

B

Battery
    electrolyte level/specific gravity, check, 1-7
    inspection and maintenance, 9-2
    removal, charging and installation, 9-3
Brakes
    caliper, removal, overhaul and installation, 7-3
    discs, inspection, removal and installation, 7-5
    fluid, 1-5
    hoses, inspection and replacement, 7-9
    light switches, check and replacement, 9-7
    master cylinder, removal, overhaul and installation
        front, 7-6
        rear, 7-7
    pads
        replacement, 7-2
        wear check, 1-8
    pedal position, check and adjustment, 1-8
    pedal, removal and installation, 7-10
    system
        bleeding, 7-9
        general check, 1-8
Brakes, wheels and tires, 7-1 through 7-16
Buying parts, 0-7

C

Caliper, brake, removal, overhaul and installation, 7-3
Camshafts, rocker arms and lash adjusters, removal, inspection and installation, 2-14
Carburetors
    disassembly, cleaning and inspection, 4-8
    overhaul, general information, 4-5
    reassembly and float level adjustment, 4-9
    removal and installation, 4-5
    separation and reconnection, 4-6
    synchronization, check and adjustment, 1-14
Centerstand and sidestand, maintenance, 8-9
Charging system
    testing, general information and precautions, 9-13
    leakage and output test, 9-13
Choke cables and throttle, removal, installation and adjustment, 4-10
Clutch
    check and adjustment, 1-10
    fluid, 1-5
    release mechanism, bleeding, removal, inspection and installation, 2-26
    removal, inspection and installation, 2-28
    switch, check and replacement, 9-8
Connecting rod bearings, removal, inspection and installation, 2-46
Cooling system, 3-1 through 3-8
    inspection, 1-17
    coolant, 1-6
        reservoir, removal and installation, 3-2
        temperature gauge and sender unit, check and replacement, 3-3
        tubes and thermostat housing, removal and installation, 3-7
    draining, flushing and refilling, 1-18
    fan and thermostatic switch, check and replacement, 3-2
Crankcase
    breather, servicing, 1-12
    components, inspection and servicing, 2-41
    disassembly and reassembly, 2-39

Index

Crankshaft and main bearings, removal, inspection, main bearing selection and installation, 2-47
Cruise valve element (1987 Aspencade), replacement, 1-18
Cylinder compression, check, 1-12
Cylinder head
    covers, removal and installation, 2-13
    removal and installation, 2-20
Cylinder head and valves, disassembly, inspection and reassembly, 2-22
Cylinders, inspection, 2-43

D

Diagnosis, 0-17
Discs, brake, inspection, removal and installation, 7-5

E

Electrical system, 9-1 through 9-18
Electrical troubleshooting, 9-2
Emission control systems, inspection and component replacement, 4-12
Engine, 1-1
    camshafts, rocker arms and lash adjusters, removal, inspection and installation, 2-14
    clutch and transmission, 2-1
    clutch
        release mechanism, bleeding, removal, inspection and installation, 2-26
        removal, inspection and installation, 2-28
    connecting rod bearings, removal, inspection and installation, 2-46
    crankcase
        components, inspection and servicing, 2-41
        disassembly and reassembly, 2-39
    crankshaft and main bearings, removal, inspection, main bearing selection and installation, 2-47
    cylinder head and valves, disassembly, inspection and reassembly, 2-22
    cylinder head
        covers, removal and installation, 2-13
        removal and installation, 2-20
    cylinders, inspection, 2-43
    disassembly and reassembly, general information, 2-9
    external shift mechanism, removal, inspection and installation, 2-37
    front case cover, removal and installation, 2-35
    guards, removal and installation, 8-4
    initial start-up after overhaul, 2-56
    internal shift linkage, removal, inspection and installation, 2-41
    main and connecting rod bearings, general note, 2-46
    main oil pump, removal, inspection and installation, 2-36
    major engine repair, general note, 2-6
    oil type, 1-5
    oil/filter, change, 1-10
    operations
        engine in the frame, 2-6
        engine removal, 2-6
    output shaft, removal, inspection and installation, 2-34
    piston
        inspection, removal and installation, 2-44
        rings, installation, 2-45
    piston/connecting rod assemblies, removal, connecting rod inspection and installation, 2-42
    primary chain and gears, removal, inspection and installation, 2-55
    rear case cover, removal, bearing inspection and installation, 2-32
    recommended break-in procedure, 2-57
    removal and installation, 2-6
    scavenging oil pump, removal, inspection and installation, 2-34
    shift drum and forks, inspection, 2-51
    timing belts, removal, inspection and installation, 2-10
    transmission shafts
        disassembly, inspection and reassembly, 2-52
        shift drum and forks, removal and installation, 2-49
    valves/valve seats/valve guides, servicing, 2-21
Engine/transmission oil, 1-2
Evaporative emission control system (California models), check, 1-16
Exhaust system
    check, 1-16
    removal and installation, 4-11
External shift mechanism, removal, inspection and installation, 2-37

F

Fairing and bodywork, 8-1 through 8-10
Fairing, removal and installation, 8-6
    lower, front and inner covers, 8-4
    pockets and top compartment, 8-2
Fasteners, check, 1-17
Fault finding, 0-17
Fender, removal and installation,
    front, 8-3
    rear, 8-9
Final drive
    oil
        change, 1-18
        type, 1-6
    unit, removal, inspection and installation, 6-14
Fluid levels, check, 1-5
Footrests, removal and installation, 8-3
Forks
    oil change, 6-3
    removal and installation, 6-3
Frame, inspection and repair, 8-9
Front brake master cylinder, removal, overhaul and installation, 7-6
Front case cover, removal and installation, 2-35
Front fender, removal and installation, 8-3
Front wheel, removal, inspection and installation, 7-11
Fuel and exhaust systems, 4-1 through 4-14
Fuel system
    check and filter replacement, 1-15
    pump, testing, removal and installation, 4-3
    tank
        cleaning and repair, 4-3
        removal and installation, 4-2
Fuses, check and replacement, 9-3

G

Gauges and meters, check, 9-11
Gear position switch (gearshift sensor), check, removal and installation, 9-10

H

Handlebar
    removal and installation, 6-2
    switches
        check, 9-8
        removal and installation, 9-8

Index

Headlight
    aim, check and adjust, 1-18, 9-6
    bulb, replacement, 9-4
Honda GL1200 Gold Wing, 0-5
Horn, check and replacement, 9-10
Hoses, brake, inspection and replacement, 7-9

I

Identification numbers, 0-6
Idle fuel/air mixture adjustment, 4-4
Idle speed, check and adjustment, 1-14
Ignition system, 5-1 through 5-4
    check, 5-2
    coils, check, removal and installation, 5-2
    control unit, check, removal and installation, 5-4
    main (key) switch, check and replacement, 9-9
Initial start-up after overhaul, 2-56
Instrument and warning light bulbs, replacement, 9-12
Instrument cluster, removal and installation, 9-11
Internal shift linkage, removal, inspection and installation, 2-41
Introduction to tune-up and routine maintenance, 1-2

L

Lighting system
    check, 9-4
    switches, brakes, check and replacement, 9-7
Lubrication, general, 1-15

M

Main and connecting rod bearings, general note, 2-46
Main oil pump, removal, inspection and installation, 2-36
Maintenance techniques, tools and working facilities, 0-8
Major engine repair, general note, 2-6
Meters and gauges, check, 9-11
Mirrors, removal and installation, 8-5
Motorcycle chemicals and lubricants, 0-16

O

Oil change
    engine, 1-10
    final drive, 1-18
    forks, 6-3
Oil pressure switch, removal, check and installation, 9-9
On-board air compressor, removal, desiccant replacement and installation, 6-12
On-board compressor system check and element cleaning, 1-16
Operations
    engine in the frame, 2-6
    requiring engine removal, 2-6
Output shaft, removal, inspection and installation, 2-34

P

Pedal, brake, removal and installation, 7-10
Piston
    rings, installation, 2-45
    inspection, removal and installation, 2-44

Piston/connecting rod assemblies, removal, connecting rod inspection and installation, 2-42
Primary chain and gears, removal, inspection and installation, 2-55
Pulse air system, inspection, 1-11
Pulse generators, check, removal and installation, 5-3

R

Radiator
    cap, check, 3-2
    removal and installation, 3-4
Radio and speakers, removal, check and installation, 9-17
Rear brake master cylinder, removal, overhaul and installation, 7-7
Rear case cover, removal, bearing inspection and installation, 2-32
Rear fender, removal and installation, 8-9
Rear shock absorbers, removal, inspection and installation, 6-11
Rear wheel, removal, inspection and installation, 7-12
Recommended break-in procedure, 2-57
Recommended lubricants and fluids, 1-2
Regulator/rectifier, check and replacement, 9-13
Routine maintenance intervals, 1-4

S

Saddlebag
    bracket and trunk, removal and installation, 8-8
    removal and installation, 8-7
Safety, 0-14
Scavenging oil pump, removal, inspection and installation, 2-34
Seat, removal and installation, 8-2
Shift drum and forks, inspection, 2-51
Shock absorbers, rear, removal, inspection and installation, 6-11
Side covers, removal and installation, 8-5
Sidestand and centerstand, maintenance, 8-9
Spark plugs
    replacement, 1-13
    type, 1-1
Speakers and radio, removal, check and installation, 9-17
Specifications, general, 0-7
Speed sensor (Aspencade), removal, check and installation, 9-10
Speedometer cable (Standard and Interstate) removal and installation, 9-10
Starter system
    alternator drive unit and starter drive chain, removal, inspection and installation, 9-15
    alternator rotor and starter clutch, removal and installation, 9-14
    motor, removal and installation, 9-12
    relay, check and replacement, 9-12
Steering head bearings
    adjustment and lubrication, 6-8
    check, 1-16
    replacement, 6-9
Steering, suspension and final drive, 6-1 through 6-18
Suspension, check, 1-17
Swingarm
    bearings
        check, 6-16
        replacement, 6-18
    removal and installation, 6-16

T

Taillight bulbs and turn signals, replacement, 9-6
Thermostat, removal, check and installation, 3-4

IND-4 Index

Throttle and choke
    cables, removal, installation and adjustment, 4-10
    operation and freeplay, check and adjustment, 1-9
Timing belts, removal, inspection and installation, 2-10
Tires
    tubeless, general information, 7-16
    wheels, general check, 1-9
Tools, 0-9
Transmission shafts
    disassembly, inspection and reassembly, 2-52
    shift drum and forks, removal and installation, 2-49
Troubleshooting, 0-17
Trunk and saddlebag bracket, removal and installation, 8-8
Trunk, removal and installation, 8-8
Tubeless tires, general information, 7-16
Tune-up and routine maintenance, 1-1 through 1-18
Turn signal circuit, check, 9-7
Turn signals and taillight bulbs, replacement, 9-6

V

Valves/valve seats/valve guides, servicing, 2-21

W

Water pump, check, removal, disassembly, inspection and installation, 3-5
Wheel
    alignment check, 7-10
    bearings, replacement, 7-13
    inspection and repair, 7-10
    removal, inspection and installation
        front, 7-11
        rear, 7-12
Windshield, removal and installation, 8-5
Wiring diagrams, 9-18
Working facilities, 0-13